Lady Nijo's Own Story

Lady Nijo's Own Story

TOWAZU-GATARI: THE CANDID DIARY

OF A THIRTEENTH-CENTURY

JAPANESE IMPERIAL CONCUBINE

translated by

Wilfrid Whitehouse & Eizo Yanagisawa

CHARLES E. TUTTLE COMPANY
Rutland, Vermont & Tokyo, Japan

REPRESENTATIVES

For Continental Europe:
BOXERBOOKS, INC., Zurich

For the British Isles:
PRENTICE-HALL INTERNATIONAL, INC., London

For Australasia:
PAUL FLESCH & CO., PTY. LTD., Melbourne

For Canada:
HURTIG PUBLISHERS, Edmonton

*Published by the Charles E. Tuttle Company, Inc.
of Rutland, Vermont & Tokyo, Japan
with editorial offices at
Suido 1-chome, 2–6, Bunkyo-ku, Tokyo*

© 1974 by Charles E. Tuttle Co., Inc.
*Library of Congress Catalog Card No. 73–93503
International Standard Book No. 0–8048 1117–2*

First printing, 1974

PRINTED IN JAPAN

Table of Contents

Preface

The existence in the Imperial Household Library
of a unique seventeenth-century copy of *Towazu-
gatari* was disclosed by Dr. Yamagishi Tokuhei just
over thirty years ago, the book being first published
by him in 1950. Another edition was published in
April, 1966, by Dr. Tomikura Tokujiro, the present translation being based primarily on his revised
edition of June, 1969, although two separate editions,
one published by Dr. Tsugita Kasumi in November,
1966, and the other by Dr. Nakada Norio in July,
1966, have also been used.[1]

Towazu-gatari is the autobiography from 1271
to 1306 of Lady Nijo, a lady at the Court of an ex-
Emperor. In the first three volumes into which she

[1] Grateful acknowledgement is made to The Libraries and
Mausoleums Division, the Imperial Household Agency, for permission to translate their original edition of *Towazu-gatari*, and
to Dr. Tsugita, Dr. Tomikura, and Dr. Nakada for permission
to use their annotated modernized editions.

7

divided it, she relates the story of her life and loves, in particular her relations with the ex-Emperor, with an influential court-noble who later became Chief Minister, and with an Imperial prince who was a Buddhist prelate, ending with her expulsion from the Court through the jealousy of the ex-Empress. Then in the last two volumes she describes her pilgrimages to holy places in emulation of the famous poet and priest, Saigyo. All this she does with a literary skill which surpasses perhaps even that of the supreme example of Japan's golden age of literature, Lady Murasaki in *The Tale of Genji*.

In Lady Nijo's pages we meet the leading figures of her day during a period when real political, military, and economic power in the country had finally passed into the hands of the Bakufu, the Military Government at Kamakura, which nevertheless still continued to exercise its authority in the name of the Emperor at Kyoto. In *Towazu-gatari* we see through the eyes of a contemporary the unstable conditions which resulted from this and from the never-ending struggle for pre-eminence among the powerful military families. The Bakufu continued to maintain control over the Imperial court by alternating the Imperial succession between two rival lines, a device which, however successful in the short term, was to lead in the next generation to civil war between the northern and southern Courts.

Still, while these literary and historical considerations are obviously of enormous interest and importance to a full understanding of the autobiography, we have thought it preferable to relegate discussion of these and all other background aspects of the work to the end of the volume. With as few editorial footnotes as possible we allow the lady to tell her story in her own way—a very personal document of one woman's life in thirteenth-century Japan.

WILFRID WHITEHOUSE
EIZO YANAGISAWA

Dramatis Personae

Go Fukakusa (1243–1304), the 89th Emperor (from 1247 to 1259), referred to throughout Nijo's autobiography as "the ex-Emperor"; son of Go Saga and elder brother of Kameyama.

Koga no Masatada (1228–1272), Nijo's father.

Go Saga (1220–1272), the 88th Emperor (from 1242 to 1246).

Kameyama (1249–1305), the 90th Emperor (from 1260 to 1274), eighth son of Go Saga and brother of Go Fukakusa.

Shojo (1247–1281), fifth son of Go Saga and half-brother of Go Fukakusa and Kameyama. Chief Priest of the Ninnaji temple, he became Nijo's lover, being referred to in her story as "Wan Morning Moon."

Saionji no Sanekane (1249–1322), a most important statesman of the period especially in liaison between the Imperial Court and the Military Government, rising to the post of Chief Minister. As Nijo's lover, she refers to him as "Snowy Dawn."

Shijo no Takaaki (1243– ?), Nijo's uncle, known as the Zenshoji Dainagon.

11

SHIJO NO TAKACHIKA (? –1283), Nijo's grandfather; a most influential court noble, holding the office of Minister of War.

HIGASHI NIJO (1232–1304), chief consort of Go Fukakusa, referred to in the story as "the ex-Empress." Sanekane's aunt and Omiya's sister, she was throughout hostile to Nijo.

OMIYA (1225–1292), Higashi Nijo's elder sister, mother of Go Fukakusa and Kameyama. As Go Saga's consort, she is referred to as the Empress Dowager Omiya.

TOKIWAI (1195–1302), mother of Higashi Nijo and Omiya, she is referred to as the Titular Empress of Kitayama.

GENKIMON (? –1329), second consort of Go Fukakusa, she is referred to in the story as the Lady of the East Wing.

FUJIWARA NO KANEHIRA (1227–1294), Chief Minister and Imperial Adviser, he is referred to by Nijo as the Great Lord Konoe.

GO UDA (1267–1324), the 91st Emperor (from 1274 to 1287), son of Kameyama, referred to in the story both as Crown Prince and Emperor.

FUSHIMI (1265–1317), the 92nd Emperor (from 1287 to 1298), son of Go Fukakusa and the Lady of the East Wing, he figures in Nijo's autobiography as both Crown Prince and Emperor.

Book One

Lady Nijo enters her fourteenth year on New Year's Day, 1271, and attracts the attentions of the ex-Emperor Go Fukakusa

CHAPTER

I

The morning mists were still lingering when all of the ladies-in-waiting at the Tominokoji palace, in their bright glossy robes, were assembling for the New Year celebrations. Naturally I was there with them. I was wearing, I remember, a dark red set of under-robes with a light green robe over it and a scarlet mantle over that, the linings showing a colour scheme of purple under red. My robe with its pattern of plum-blossoms and vine-tendrils had embroidered on it a design of plum-trees against a fence of bamboo. My father, the Dainagon,[1] was there too; he was to serve the New Year's spiced wine to His Majesty the ex-Emperor.

When the ceremony outside was over, all the court-ladies and maids were also invited to the party, which as time passed became much less formal as everyone was getting more and more mellow. The wine cups had already been exchanged nine times, three-times-

[1] One of the Great State Counsellors, Koga no Masatada.

three, between the Dainagon and the ex-Emperor, and my father had suggested another round of three-times-three, when His Majesty insisted that their next round should be one of nine-times-three. It was then that I noticed the ex-Emperor whispering to my father as he exchanged his last cup with him.

"Perhaps, now, I may be able to have that which I have set my heart on for so long," His Majesty said, and continued in such a low voice that I could hear no more of the conversation. I certainly did not realise how much this whispering concerned me.

When I went to my room after the ceremony, I found there a letter. "From now on I shall not hesitate to write to you," it said. With the letter had been sent a present, eight sheets of tissue paper, a purple unlined gown, a light green robe, a cloak, a skirt, double and treble padded silk gowns and other robes, all folded in a cloth wrapper. The present was quite unexpected and I could think of no reason why this lord should have sent me one. Then as I was wrapping it up to send it back, I found a poem written on thin paper attached to one of the sleeves,

> My hopes appear gone
> Of laying my sleeves on yours,
>   But with faint hope still
> I send to you these dresses
> To wear on that occasion.

A great deal of loving thought had obviously gone into the preparation of this beautiful present, and I was loth to have to return it. But I finally did so, enclosing a message that I was reluctant to promise to wear the dresses on the occasion on which the writer wished me to wear them until I was assured of the sincerity of his affection,

> If I should wear these
> Without being sure of your love,
> The time might come when
> Tears would perhaps rot these sleeves;
> Of your love I must be sure.

"Still," I added, "I would willingly wear them as you wish me to do, if your love for me remains constant."

That night, while I was on night duty, there was a knock on the door in the middle of the night. A maid who happened to be near opened the door and was handed the same parcel by a messenger who then hurried away. The poem with it expressed the hope that I would accept the present,

> If as you promise
> Your love should remain steadfast,
> I would wish you wear,
> As you lie alone at night,
> These robes I now send to you.

I thought it rather presumptuous on my part to return the present to the sender once more and so I kept the dresses.

On the third day of the month, on the occasion of the visit of the Retired Emperor[2] to the ex-Emperor's palace in Tominokoji, my father, upon seeing me wearing these robes, commented on the beautiful colour and gloss. "Are they a present from His Majesty?" he asked.

"No," I answered, in as casual a tone of voice as I could manage although my heart quivered uneasily. "I received them from my great-aunt, the Empress Dowager of Tokiwai."[3]

On the fifteenth of the month, towards evening, I received word to go at once to stay at my father's mansion at Kawasaki. It was most inconvenient having to go at such short notice and for a moment I wanted to refuse but finally thought better of it and went. At the mansion, looking round, I was surprised at the magnificence of the furnishings; the folding screens, the mattings on the floor, the curtains and the hangings, all gave the impression of being more splendid than those in ordinary use. I concluded that the house had been specially furnished for the New Year.

By then it was sunset.

Next morning there was a great deal of excitement

[2] The Retired Emperor (Ho-o) Go Saga (1220–1272), Emperor from 1242 to 1246, was the father of both the ex-Emperor Go Fukakusa, at this time twenty-seven years old, and of the then reigning Emperor, Kameyama.

[3] Also referred to by Lady Nijo as the Titular Empress of Kitayama.

in the mansion. People were asking what meals were to be served, where the horses of the nobles were to be stabled, and where the princes' ox-carriages were to be put. My father's step-mother and other people were bustling about and consulting my father in whispers.

"What is this all about?" I asked my father.

He laughed. "Well," he said, "we have been informed suddenly that His Majesty is going on a state visit and wishes to stay here the night before. I thought you had better come here to wait on him."

"But why should he wish to do that?" I said. "Why should he have to change his direction today? It isn't the Spring Festival yet."[4]

My answer was greeted with a laugh. "Oh, isn't she just too innocent for words!" they said. But in spite of all this I still had not the slightest idea of what it was all about.

Even my own room had been furnished with splendid screens and curtains. I commented on this. "Is my room also being used for His Majesty's visit?" I asked. But all the reply I received from anyone was a laugh, and no one gave me any information at all.

Towards evening I was dressed in triple, unlined white robes and a dark purple skirt. Incense from hidden censers filled the air with perfume, so much so that it seemed to me to be all rather too sumptuous.

[4] The reference is to the custom of commencing a journey from another house when necessary in order to avoid starting in an unlucky direction. At the festival of *Sechibun* it was customary to stay at another house to change one's direction.

After the candles were lighted, my step-mother brought in a dazzlingly bright patterned gown for me to wear. A little later my father came in with robes on hangers for the ex-Emperor to wear.

"Don't go to sleep before His Majesty arrives," he said to me. "And remember, a court lady is always gentle and obedient."

I was not at all pleased at being given instruction on my duties at such a time; it seemed quite out of place. With such thoughts going through my mind, I sat there leaning against the side of the charcoal brazier and at last fell asleep. What followed I naturally do not know exactly, but while I was asleep the ex-Emperor arrived. My father bustled about welcoming him and arranging things. Then, when the meal was ready to be served, it was seen that I was still fast asleep.

"Wake her up," my father cried loudly.

The ex-Emperor heard him. "No, no, let her sleep on," he said, and no one woke me.

I had been reclining against the brazier which was placed just inside the doorway of the room when I had felt sleepy. I had covered myself over and gone to sleep. Now something suddenly awakened me. I found that the lights had been dimmed and the curtains lowered. I was now lying well inside the room away from the doorway, and someone was lying close to me quite at his ease. Wondering what was happening, I jumped to my feet to run away.

"Don't run away," he said to me, holding me down. "I began to love you long ago when you were only a child. For fourteen years I have been waiting for this moment . . .'' So he went on talking to me, saying lots of things I cannot find the words to express and which I was really too upset at the time to listen to properly. I could only weep until his sleeves were drenched with wiping away my tears. He tried to comfort me, but this led only to his becoming distressed himself. Still he continued to act tenderly and used no force against me. ''So,'' he went on, ''as the years passed and you showed no signs that you returned my love, I wanted to take this opportunity to tell you of my affection. Now that everyone will know of our meeting in this way, if you still continue to be so cold-hearted towards me, I do not know what I can do.''

Certainly everyone now knew what was afoot even though there had been no dream-like love meeting. I realised what mental sufferings the morning after would bring to me. As I now recall the events of this night, I am surprised at the calm and collected manner in which I thought and acted at the time. I wondered why he had not given me any inkling beforehand of what he intended to do. If he had done so, I could have talked the matter over with my father. I burst out weeping again. ''I am not going to be able to face people after this,'' I thought to myself. At the same time I was well aware that he must be thinking that I was talking and acting in a very childish manner. I saw too that he was hesitating as to whether he should leave or stay. All this saddened me, and the night ended without my giving one word of reply to his pleas.

Soon people began to stir. "His Majesty is leaving this morning, isn't he?" I heard people saying to one another.

"To everyone else this will have all the appearances of a happy morning return from a love meeting," he murmured to himself as he rose. "Your quite unexpected coldness towards me," he went on, "has shown me how useless our friendship ever since you were a little girl has proved to be. Please do not behave in any way that people will think strange; if you hide yourself away from everyone, they will wonder why." I realised that he was saying this not so much to reprove me as to comfort me in some measure. But still I made no answer. "How helpless I am to do more than I have done!" he murmured to himself as he rose. He put on his robes and left the room. "Bring round my carriage," he ordered.

"Will Your Majesty take breakfast?" I heard my father say to him, and I wished with all my heart that things between us could be as they had been on the day before when I could be in his presence all the time with the old friendly relationship between us.

I heard the carriage leave but I continued to lie in bed with the clothes drawn up over me. Then I learnt to my surprise that a letter had arrived for me from him; naturally everyone took this to be his morning-after letter. My step-mother and my grandmother came in to me.

"Why haven't you got up yet?" they asked me.

"I have felt very miserable since last night," I said sadly, knowing full well that they would attribute my low spirits to our parting after the first night together. They were highly excited about the arrival of the ex-Emperor's letter, but I refused to look at it.

Meanwhile to my further distress the messenger who had brought the letter was becoming impatient, demanding that something be done about the answer and pressing my father to see me about it.

He came in to see me. "Are you feeling so unwell that you cannot answer the letter?" he demanded. "How can you be so indifferent about it when everyone else is so excited about it? Aren't you going to answer it?"

I heard him unfold the letter. He read it aloud. On a thin sheet of purple paper, the ex-Emperor had written a letter bewailing the fact that it was because of the long years of our intimacy and not through any recent closer contact between us that his sleeves were now scented with the perfume of mine,

> We have known each other
> So long a time that your sleeves
> Leave their scent on mine,
> Even though tonight I may have
> Failed to lay my sleeves on yours.[5]

When the people of the house heard the poem, they commented to one another, "She is so different from

[5] In lovers' embraces the long broad sleeves of their *kimono* lie on each other's. The sleeves of each leave on the other's the scent of the incense with which they have been perfumed, reviving the memory of their happy meeting.

girls of the present day, isn't she?" But still I continued to feel hurt and stayed in bed.

"Well, there's nothing else we can do," they decided. "It would never do to get anyone else to write the letter for her." So they gave the messenger a tip and sent him away with the message, "The lady is still lying down in bed and refuses to answer the letter no matter what we say to her. In fact, she has not even read the letter yet."

About noon another letter arrived. It was from the one I was not really expecting to hear from. He wrote that he would die broken-hearted if he found that I was turning away from him in another direction,

> I should die of sorrow
> If now in that direction
>   You should firmly turn
> Like the top of a pillar
> Of smoke, blown thus by the wind.

"Until now," the letter accompanying this poem read, "I have tried to keep my miserable self alive buoyed up with the hope that one day my life might be bound up with yours. But on what can I now fix my hopes?" The letter was written on a thin sheet of pale blue paper on which there was an illustration of the old poem,

> Fly away from sight
> Ye clouds which hide the summit
>   Of Mount Shinobu;

The troubles which cloud my heart
May also disappear.

I tore off that part of the paper with the words "the summit of Mount Shinobu" and on it wrote a poem in answer,

You know not the reason
Which impelled me to refrain
From that step you dread;
If you did, you would know
You were the main cause of it.

I could not really tell why I wrote in such a way.

So the day passed and I did not even drink the infusion which was made for me. The people of the house began to think that I was really ill after all. Then towards evening I learnt that the ex-Emperor had arrived. While I was wondering what would happen next, I heard him push open the sliding door. He came in, looking quite unconcerned.

"They tell me you are feeling ill. What is the trouble?" he said.

I did not dare to answer him, but continued to lie there motionless. He lay down with me and talked to me at length to persuade me of the sincerity of his feelings for me. Realising that the inevitable would happen, I was ready to tell him that I was willing to do as he wished if I could be certain that I could trust myself to him, but remembering the "pillar of smoke" I felt reluctant to make such a definite turn in another direction. I therefore kept silence. This night his behaviour was really quite atrocious and soon my thin robe was ripped at the seams. He did just as he pleased with me. I wished in very truth that the morning moon would never rise so that I would not have to conceal my face from everyone when I met them next day. My thoughts found expression for themselves in the poem,

> Not by my own will
> Was my girdle then untied;
>   This I alone know;
> Those who do not know, I fear,
> Will be slow to believe this.

I feel it strange now that my mind should have been working on those lines at such a time.

"However much the world changes," he said to me, "our intimacy will remain unbroken and our feelings for each other will remain unchanged, even if we cannot meet every night." He went on talking in this strain until the too-short night passed and the dawn bells rang out.

"If I stay till it is light, it will inconvenience people," he said as he rose. "Even though you feel no 'pang of parting,' please come out to see me off," he begged me earnestly. I could not feel it in my heart to be so cruel as to refuse this and went out with him, first putting on a thin unlined robe over my gown, the sleeves of which were drenched with wiping away the tears of the night.

The moon, two days after the full, leaned to the west and a bank of clouds lay across the dawn in the eastern sky. In his yellowish-green robe over red under-robes with a light purple cloak over it and his brocade trousers tied at the ankle, to my eyes he looked a very impressive figure as he stood there. How different he now seemed to me, I thought, and marvelled at the way one learns these things without any instruction.

My uncle, the Zenshoji Dainagon, Shijo no Takaaki, was there dressed in pale blue robes, having had the carriage drawn up to the entrance. Another lord, Nakamikado no Tamekata, was in attendance too with two or three guards. The birds were chirping merrily as if they knew what had happened. The bell of the Kannon temple rang out, each booming clang startling me so that my sleeves waved as I trembled. I could now understand the feelings of the lady in *The Tale of Genji* as she expressed them in her poem,

> Now with floods of tears
> Are my sleeves quite drenched through,
>   The left with sad tears
> Of remorse, the right with tears
> Of a different emotion.

The ex-Emperor still continued to linger at the entrance. "Accompany me on my lonely drive," he said persuasively. But I remained standing there, my mind in a whirl. Was I doing him an injustice in believing him quite insensitive to my feelings of distress?

The bright, unclouded morning moon gradually paled.

Then suddenly, before I had realised what he was doing, he had caught hold of me and pulled me into the carriage which started off at once. It was all just like an episode in an old romantic story to be thus carried off without an opportunity of saying farewell. Wondering what fate had in store for me, I expressed my thoughts in a poem,

> Awake the whole night,
> I had no need of dawn bells
> To awaken me;
> The morning light saddens me
> Bringing dreamlike memories.

On the way, just as if I were someone he was abducting from her home, he continued to reassure me again and again of his sincerity. I could not fail to appreciate the humour of the situation, even though as we drove on and on, it seemed to me that my only comfort was in tears.

So we arrived at last at the Tominokoji palace where we went in through the main gate to a pavilion in a corner of the grounds, where we descended.

"She is like a baby who will not listen to reason," the ex-Emperor then said to my uncle Takaaki, "and so I have brought her here. I want to keep her presence here a secret from everyone for the time being." He then went away to his own apartments.

The palace did not seem to be the same friendly place I had known from childhood. Now I felt very shy of meeting anyone; I felt that for the future I had to be cautious and wary lest my behaviour should bring shame on myself and my family. I wept as I thought of what might happen.

Just then I heard my father's voice. This moved me as I knew how anxious he was about my happiness. I heard my uncle Takaaki tell him what the ex-Emperor had said. "It is not fitting," I heard my father say in reply, "that she should receive any different treatment now. She should take her turn of duty just as before. The more one tries to keep this sort of thing secret, the sooner everyone knows about it."

I thought that what my father had said was quite true and was overwhelmed again by sad forebodings. Just then, however, the ex-Emperor came in and once more consoled me with soothing words as to his continued love so that gradually I became easier in mind and finally, trusting in his promises, I resigned myself to my lot.

Ten days or so passed in this way. Every night without fail the ex-Emperor paid me a visit. But all the time my mind was troubled with jarring conjectures as to what was happening to the one who had feared that like a pillar of smoke in the wind I was turning away from him.

My father continued to protest that no good would come of my staying secretly in the palace in this way and so at last I was allowed to go home. There I stayed indoors the whole of the time on the pretence of being ill; the true reason was that I still found it too painful to be seen by people.

Then I received a letter from the ex-Emperor. "I am now so accustomed to having you with me," he wrote, "that I miss you very much. It seems such a long time since you went home. Come back as quickly as possible." With the letter was a poem,

> You cannot love me
> And miss me as I do you;
>   How true my words are
> You would learn if you saw me
> Weeping now in solitude.

Only a little time before, I had found it extremely distasteful to receive a letter from him, but now I could hardly wait to open this letter. It was with a happy heart that I wrote a poem in answer to it, a poem which was perhaps in the circumstances a little affected in manner,

> Though it may not be
> Because of your love for me
>   You weep so sorely,
> When I hear of you weeping
> I weep too in sympathy.

Some days later I returned to my duties at the palace, but nothing seemed to go right and the other court ladies were very spiteful. "The Dainagon has brought his precious Nijo back with as much ceremony as if she were an official Imperial consort entering the palace," they said. Everyone was engaged in retelling these slanders, and it was soon clear that the ex-Empress[6] was taking something of a dislike to me. I was miserably unhappy. Also, the ex-Emperor was visiting me less and less frequently. This made me very miserable, but there was no one to whom I could complain about it. Nor could I complain as the other ladies of the court did that he passed so lightly from one lady to another. Still, when, in the course of my duties, I had to usher in to him another lady, I found it extremely distasteful to have to conform to the ways of the world.

In the belief, however, that the present would appear a happier time when in the future I looked back on it, I passed my days in resignation to my fate until autumn came.

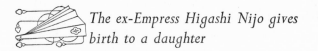 *The ex-Empress Higashi Nijo gives birth to a daughter*

CHAPTER

II

The ex-Empress was expecting to have a child in the eighth month in the Corner Pavilion at the palace. As she was no longer young and as her previous accouchements had all been difficult, everyone was most anxious about the outcome.

---

[6]Lady Higashi Nijo (1232–1304), Go Fukakusa's consort, now thirty-eight years of age, eleven years older than he.

Prayers and incantations with all due rites and ceremonies were offered by Buddhist dignitaries before the images of those Buddhas and saints whose aid was considered to be most efficacious in such cases. My father performed the usual rites to Gundari in Owari province for protection against all misfortune, and at the special wish of the ex-Emperor, he also on this occasion made intercession for protection in childbirth to Kongo Doji at the palace, assisted by the High Priest of the Joju-in temple.

About the twentieth of the month, the ex-Empress's labour pains began and all soon worked themselves into a panic. Everyone was expecting things to happen any minute now, and when nothing happened for two or three days, everyone was nearly hysterical. Then the ex-Emperor, being informed that there was a change in her condition, went to her room. She seemed very weak, and he called the High Priest to the room to offer prayers with only a screen between him and the ex-Empress.

The Erudite Priest, Ajari, Prince Shojo, who was the ex-Emperor's half-brother and chief priest of the Ninnaji temple, was there too.

"What is there that we can do?" the ex-Emperor said to him as he invited him inside the screen. "It looks as though the Lady is beyond our aid."

"The promise of the Buddha is that it is possible for us to avert even our destiny by means of intercession. Do not be anxious, therefore," he answered.

So the prince continued to offer fervent prayers inside the screen, accompanied outside by the High

Priest making intercession before a holy picture of Fudo, the god of fire, counting his beads and chanting from a sutra the promises that one who serves the god of fire will be venerated as a saint and that one who observes his statutes will come to eternal salvation. "From my childhood," he prayed, "I have spent my nights and my days in reciting sutras and in spiritual communion with Fudo and have lived a life of penance. Can the stored-up merits of such a life of self-abnegation be of no avail?" As the critical moment approached, he redoubled his efforts until a cloud of steam from perspiration enveloped him.

All the court ladies passed out unlined under-robes and silk gauze robes from below their screens. The lord on duty took them and handed them to another lord, who passed them to the upper guards, and these passed them to the lower guards, who handed them out as presents to the priests praying outside. At the foot of the steps some courtiers were seated waiting for the birth to take place. In the courtyard the soothsayers had set up a table with eight legs and were repeating a purification prayer a thousand times over paper cut-outs. Courtiers then took these cut-outs from them and the court ladies spread out their sleeves under their screens and received the cut-outs on them. Votive horses were led into the courtyard by guards for the ex-Emperor to accept them with a courteous bow, after which they were led away to be sent to the twenty-one national shrines. How fortunate indeed is the lady who gives birth to her child surrounded by such loving solicitude!

The chief priest of the temple of the Seven Incarnations of Yakushi, the Divine Physician, had been invited to the palace to recite the Sutra of the Divine Physician, assisted by several priests with deep and impressive voices. And now while they were chanting the passage, "All those present rejoiced at the sight of the newborn Buddha," the child was born. All the people inside and outside the palace shouted for joy, offering their congratulations. According to custom, the hub of a wheel was thrown down from the roof of the palace into the north garden. That was the only blemish on the people's happiness, for on the birth of a prince the wheel-hub was thrown into the southern garden. Still, the ceremonies ended with the priests receiving a liberal donation.

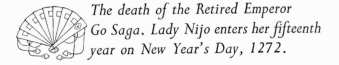 *The death of the Retired Emperor Go Saga. Lady Nijo enters her fifteenth year on New Year's Day, 1272.*

CHAPTER III   For all that, even if it were only a princess and not a prince who was born, the child's grandfather, the Retired Emperor Go Saga, made a great fuss over her and had the Fifth Night and the Seventh Night ceremonies performed in a magnificent manner.

After the Seventh Night celebrations, the Retired Emperor was talking with the ex-Emperor in his apartments at the Tominokoji palace when, about two o'clock in the morning, a great wind began to blow in the orangery with a sound as of waves beating wildly on a rocky shore. I was told to go out to see what it was. I did so, and this is what I saw. Jumping up and down were ten or so brightly shining objects, each about the size of a wine bowl, bluish white in colour, with heads looking rather like jelly-fish and with long slender tails. I shrieked with fright and rushed back inside.

"Why are you making such a din?" the courtiers in the anteroom said. "They are just death-watch fires."

Other people reported seeing something like slimy seaweed scattered about under the great willow tree. As a result of these omens, the ex-Emperor called in the soothsayers and had rituals for long life performed as they are at the temple of Taisan in China.

About the ninth month, the Retired Emperor Go Saga was reported to be very ill. His legs and feet were swollen. He was cauterised with moxa a number of times, but to everyone's great alarm this had little effect and he grew worse every day. The year drew to a close and New Year's Day came, but no one had any heart for celebrations with the Retired Emperor so ill.

His condition was so threatening that about the seventeenth of the first month, the Retired Emperor was taken by palanquin to the palace at Saga. The ex-Emperor followed him in a carriage. I was in the same carriage. The Retired Emperor's consort, the ex-

Empress Omiya, and her sister, the ex-Empress Higashi Nijo, were in another carriage, accompanied by Lady Mikushige, who was at the moment the ex-Emperor's favourite lady-in-waiting.

In the presence of the ex-Emperor, the Retired Emperor's physicians, Wake no Tanenari and Wake no Moronari, had prepared medicine for the patient to drink on the way. This had been poured into jars which were carried by the Gon Chunagon, Yoshida no Tsuneto, and a guard, Nobutomo. When they arrived at Uchino, the site of the ancient Imperial palace, they wished to give the patient some of the medicine to drink, but both the jars were found to be empty—completely dry. It was a mystery where the medicine had disappeared. This incident added to the patient's depression and possibly aggravated his illness.

The ex-Emperor stayed at the Oi mansion within the precincts of the Saga palace and was constantly sending people, men or women, high or low, to enquire how his father was at that moment. One had to go along a roofed connecting passage to the palace, and I well remember how I dreaded this walk alone at dead of night with the roar of the river Oi in my ears.

At the beginning of the second month we were just waiting for the last moments of the Retired Emperor. The two High Commissioners, Hojo no Tokisuke and Hojo no Yoshimune, arrived on the ninth to express the sympathy and concern of the Military Government at Kamakura. The Dainagon Saionji no Sanekane made public announcement of the fact that they had shown grief and expressed their condolences. The reigning Emperor Kameyama arrived on the eleventh, stayed for the twelfth, and returned to the Capital on the thirteenth. Everyone was very busy. There was no sound of music in the palace. The Emperor and his brother, the ex-Emperor, met and wept together, all the bystanders being moved to weep in sympathy.

About six o'clock on the evening of the fifteenth day, a great column of smoke was seen rising in the direction of the Capital. I asked whose house it was and was told that it was the house in Rokuhara of the High Commissioner, Hojo no Tokisuke, which had been suddenly attacked and set on fire.[1] What an ever-changing world this is! On the ninth, Hojo no Tokisuke had been with the party which had come to Saga on a visit of sympathy. Six days later, the dying Emperor was still alive, but Tokisuke was dead. How true it is that death is no respecter of age or youth. This tragedy shocked me deeply. The Retired Emperor was not informed of what had happened, for he had not spoken since the night of the thirteenth.

On the morning of the seventeenth everyone was greatly alarmed by a sudden change for the worse in the patient's condition. The learned prelate, Keikai, of the Enryakuji temple, and the abbess of the Ojo-in temple came and exhorted him to put his trust in the invocation of Amida Buddha.

[1] On orders from Kamakura, Hojo no Yoshimune had attacked and killed his fellow High Commissioner, who was, it was alleged, planning revolt.

"Forasmuch as in your previous existence," they said, "you faithfully observed the Ten Virtues, Your Majesty has in this life enjoyed all the blessings and glories which appertain to an earthly throne and you are well assured of a life of bliss in the next world. Take, therefore, your seat now on the exalted throne of the Lotus Flower so that you may be a guide to Paradise for those who still sojourn in the prison-house of this world."

So they tried, sometimes with gentle persuasion and sometimes with warning exhortations, to convert him to faith in the invocation of the sacred name of Amida, but in vain, for the Retired Emperor refused to sever himself from the ties of earthly relationships and effect a last-minute change of heart.

So at last on the seventeenth day of the second month in the ninth year of the Bun-ei era, he breathed his last at six o'clock in the evening in the fifty-third year of his age. The whole sky was suddenly overcast, and the whole nation overwhelmed with grief. Gay floral dresses were discarded, and black mourning robes were donned.

On the eighteenth, the body was removed to the Yakuso-in temple in the palace. Fujiwara no Sanefuyu, Director of the Imperial Archives, arrived, bearing messages of condolence from the Imperial Court. All the sons of the Retired Emperor who had entered the religious life came from their temples, the Ninnaji, Emman-in, Bodai-in, and Shoren-in temples, to take part in the funeral ceremonies. The grief expressed at the ceremony that night was beyond the power of pen to describe. Everyone was expecting that the Gon Chunagon, Yoshida no Tsuneto, who had been such a special favourite of the deceased and had mourned his passing more deeply than anyone else, would take the opportunity to renounce the world and enter religion. People were therefore much surprised to see him in his formal dress of soft silk crepe carrying the late Emperor's ashes in an urn to the Yakuso-in temple. The ex-Emperor's grief was very deep, his tears flowing without ceasing night and day so that all the people round him were moved to tears. During the period of national mourning, there was no music, and no loud shouting was allowed, not even by forerunners calling out to the people to clear them off the roads as a procession approached. One felt afraid that even the cherry trees when they bloomed that year would put on a mantle as sombre as any monk's habit. My father, the Dainagon, wore deep mourning and suggested that I should do so too.

The ex-Emperor disagreed. "She is still very young," he said. "She need not go into deep mourning. She can wear just the ordinary mourning." And I did as he wished.

My father made several applications to the ex-Emperor and his mother the Dowager Empress Omiya for permission to retire and enter the religious life, but they refused, thinking this step was not warranted by the circumstances. His grief seemed deeper than other people's and he visited the grave every day. He renewed his appeal through his cousin, the Gon Dainagon, Minamoto no Sadazane. "Since the age of nine," the memorial read, "when the Retired Emperor first took notice of me and I became a page in his household, I have received nothing but marks of favour from him. After my father died and my step-mother disinherited me, I still continued to enjoy his favour. For this I was full of gratitude and devoted my whole life to his services. I received very rapid promotion both in office and in Court rank, always being well pleased on the morning of the publication of the list of honours. I have had no cause for complaint, either public or private, and have performed all my duties with the utmost zeal. I have for many years had the joy of attending all the greater festivals, all the banquets and all the performances of sacred dances at the Court and important shrines. I am used to wearing the ceremonial robes at these celebrations with, as the poet says, 'my image reflected in the waters of the river Mitarashi' at the Great Shrine of Kamo. I am now a Dainagon in the senior grade of second court rank, the highest rank that a Dainagon can attain, besides being at the same time officially recognised as the head of the Minamoto family. I was offered the post of Minister, but I declined it on the advice of my elder brother, Koga no Michitada, General of the Bodyguard of the Right, who was of the opinion that one should have seen service in the post of General of the Bodyguard before accepting promotion to the post of Minister. Now that the Retired Emperor has passed away, I have nothing to rely on, no tree in whose shade I can rest. No further rank or post is worth striving for. I am now fifty years of age and am perhaps not very long for this world. I cannot express my gratitude for all these favours received by me in a better way than by renouncing all these honours to enter the religious life to engage in prayer for the happiness of His Majesty's soul in the other world, provided I have your permission to do so."

The ex-Emperor, however, refused to give his consent and was kind enough to reason with my father to persuade him to give up his resolve. So the days passed one by one and it was as if the seed of forgetfulness had been planted in men's hearts. Soon it was the forty-ninth day after the Retired Emperor's death. All the religious ceremonies of that day were duly performed and the people returned to the Capital. From this time the ex-Emperor was kept busy with government affairs such as arranging to send an envoy to the Military Government at Kamakura. So at last the fifth month came.

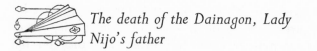 *The death of the Dainagon, Lady Nijo's father*

CHAPTER

IV

In the fifth month when the rains come to drench one's sleeves, my father in his grief for the death of the Retired Emperor drenched his sleeves with tears even more than do the autumn rains. Formerly he had always been one who hated to sleep alone, but now he had ceased to be so inclined. Formerly he had enjoyed drinking parties, but now he had ceased to find any pleasure in them. He was becoming thinner, and people were ready to attribute this to his present life of abstinence.

On the night of the fifteenth of this month, returning from a special service at the temple at Otani cemetery, he was served with food in his carriage. He complained that it all looked yellow to him. People wondered what was wrong and the doctors diagnosed his complaint as yellow jaundice. He was cauterised several times with moxa, but in spite of everything that was done he seemed to be growing worse instead of better. I was very worried over his condition when, from the beginning of the sixth month, I began to be still more worried by suspicions about my own condition. And I could not bring myself to tell him what I suspected to be the case when he was so ill.

"I know that I shall never recover from this illness," my father said. "My sole wish now is to be able to join the late Emperor as quickly as possible." He did not, however, make this hope the subject of any special intercessions. He stayed for some time at his father's house at the Rokkaku Kushige crossing where his step-mother was still living, and then on the evening of the fourteenth day of the seventh month moved to his own mansion at Kawasaki, leaving his younger children behind at the other house so that he might prepare himself peacefully for the end. Considering myself grown up in comparison with the others, I alone of his children went with him to

Kawasaki. Believing it was because of my grief at his illness that I was unwell and had no appetite for food, he at first tried to comfort me, but soon realised from the symptoms that I was pregnant. He then resolved to cling to life a little while longer until after the birth of my child. First, he had prayers solemnly offered for seven days at the Kompon Chudo chapel at the Enryakuji temple before the image of the god of Taisan in China. Next he had seven series of sacred music and dances performed before the seven shrines at Hiye. He had the whole of the sutra of Wisdom recited in one day at the Hachiman shrine at Iwashimizu. Among other things he had a cairn of boulders erected on the dry bed of the river Kamo. All these things he had done, not that he might recover his own health and prolong his own life, but only that he might live to see that nothing untoward should happen to me. It made me feel very guilty that I was responsible for his not being able to prepare himself for the end by severing himself from all earthly relationship.

On the twentieth of the seventh month, as my father's condition remained unchanged, I returned to my duties at the Tominokoji palace. The ex-Emperor was especially kind to me when he learnt of my condition, though I wondered uneasily how long this warmth of feeling would last. Lady Mikushige's death in childbirth in the sixth month came as a warning to me; I was scared that I might go the same way. I feared too that my father would not recover from his illness. It was with such fears and forebodings overwhelming me that the seventh month drew to its close.

On the evening of the twenty-seventh there were fewer people than usual about when the ex-Emperor invited me to his apartments. No one was there as we talked over old times.

"How cheerless it is when one considers the uncertainties of this fleeting world!" he said. "After all, it is to a better world that your father is going. But when he goes, you will have no one to lean on. Who else beside myself will show concern about you?" So he spoke with tears in his eyes, and his sympathy deepened my sorrow the more.

The moon had not risen yet. It was dark inside the room with only one dimly-burning light as we talked in intimate confidence late into the night, when the silence was broken by the sound of someone approaching and calling for me.

"Who is it?" I called out. It was a messenger from Kawasaki to say that my father's condition had worsened.

I had no time to make any preparations, but went just as I was, afraid all the way that I should be too late and that I should find when I got there that my father was already dead. As in a dream I hurried along as quickly as I could, but the road seemed endless. I seemed to be pushing my way through the dense undergrowth of some wilderness in the wild eastern province. With what joy it was that at last I arrived to find my father still alive!

"Like a dew-drop still clinging to the leaf waiting for the wind to dislodge it, I am still hanging on to life,'' my father said, weeping helplessly. ''It grieves me to think that I must now go from this world, leaving you alone and in the delicate condition in which you are.''

Just then when the midnight bell was tolling, we heard that the ex-Emperor's procession was approaching. That threw us all, and my father too, into something of a panic. As I could hear the sound of the carriage coming near, I hurried to the entrance, just as the ex-Emperor was alighting from his carriage, accompanied only by one lord and two guards, as this was intended to be a private visit. He stood there in the bright light of the waning moon just rising above the rim of the mountains. He was dressed in a light-coloured robe with a pattern of simple, darkish-purple flowers. We felt honoured by his coming to visit us thus in informal attire, obviously hurriedly put on.

''I haven't the strength to put on my formal robes,'' my father sent word to the ex-Emperor, ''and so I regret that I cannot have a personal audience with Your Majesty. Nevertheless, I am grateful that you have deigned to make me this informal visit. It has indeed given me a last happy memory of this world.'' He had hardly sent this message, however, when the ex-Emperor pushed aside the screen and came in. My father tried in vain to sit up.

''Lie as you are,'' the ex-Emperor said, seating himself on a cushion. He began to weep, his sleeves not large enough to stem the flood of tears. ''Since my childhood,'' he went on, ''we have always been on familiar terms with each other, and it is with great grief that I have now learnt that the end is near. I felt I had to see you once again in this world.''

"Your Majesty's visiting me in this way gives me more pleasure than I deserve," my father said with a flood of tears. "The one thing which worries me, however, is leaving my daughter with no one to care for her. She was left motherless when she was two years of age with me alone to look after her. And now I have to leave her in the delicate condition in which she is. I have no words with which to express my pity, my sorrow, my misery.''

"My sleeve may not be large enough to dry her tears at your going," the ex-Emperor said, "but I will do my best to comfort her. Do not allow this anxiety to hinder your passage along the path to Paradise.'' He continued to reassure my father for some time in this way, and saying finally, "I will go and rest for a while," he got up and left the room.

By this time day had broken and so the ex-Emperor decided to start back at once to avoid notice. My father gave a lute and a sword as presents to the ex-Emperor as he was leaving; the lute had been bequeathed to him by his father, the Chief Minister, Koga no Michimitsu, while the sword was one presented to the Chief Minister by the Emperor Go Toba when he went into exile on the remote island of Oki. Attached to the string of the sword was a sheet of thin, pale blue paper with a poem in which my father expressed his belief that they would certainly meet again, for the ties of relationship between master and servant did not end with death.

Though we must now part,
We shall surely meet again;
  The ties which bind us
Are not ties which end at death,
But will bind us for ever.

"Seeing you has moved me deeply," the ex-Emperor said in reply to this poem. "Do not worry about anything." He sent my father a number of comforting messages and went back to the palace from where he sent my father a poem written in his own hand. It looked forward to that bright dawn of the rule of Miroku Buddha when they would meet again. I am sad when I recall how moved my father was by the ex-Emperor's evident pleasure at receiving these presents of his.

On the second day of the eighth month, my uncle, the Zenshoji Dainagon, Shijo no Takaaki, brought my maternity girdle. This was rather earlier in the period than was customary. "My instructions are," he said to me, "to carry out the ceremony in a formal manner disregarding any considerations of its being a period of national mourning." So he came in procession wearing his formal robes and with all the appropriate outriders and guards. Obviously the ex-Emperor had arranged to have the ceremony carried out earlier than usual so that my father would be able to witness it. He was indeed highly delighted and ordered wine to be served to everyone. It was most touching to see what happiness had been given to him by this last episode of his life. He gave to my uncle

Takaaki a highly treasured ox named Shiogama which
he had acquired from the Ajari, Prince Shojo, the
chief priest of the Ninnaji temple.

My father's condition seemed to make a slight
improvement during the day, and I began to wonder
whether it was possible that he might recover after
all. When it became very late, I lay down beside his
bed and before I knew I had fallen asleep. I was
startled out of my sleep by my father's voice.

"How sad!" he said. "Forgetting my own sorrow
at the thought of setting off today or tomorrow on my
journey to an unknown country, instead I find my mind
full of anxiety about your future, especially as I looked
at you lying there having fallen fast asleep in spite of
yourself. Ever since you were left motherless when
you were two years old, I have looked after you by
myself. I seem to have been more concerned about
you than I have been about any one of my children. I
seem to have loved you with a greater love than I
could ever have given to anyone else. When I saw you
smile as a child, I thought you utterly charming. When
I saw you in tears, I wept with you. Fifteen springs
and autumns have passed and now the time has come
when we must part. Even though you enjoy the protection of the ex-Emperor and have no cause for
complaint against anyone, you must be on your guard
against duplicity, for this world is a world of intrigue.
And if you find cause for resentment against the ex-
Emperor and against people in general for their treatment of you and lose your position at the court, then
you must renounce the world to enter the Way of

Truth and pray for your own happiness in the next world and for your parents to be rewarded for their loving care of you so that we may all be reunited in paradise on the same lotus leaf. If the ex-Emperor were to discard you, if you were then to accept the protection of some other lord or were to go to live in someone else's house, even after my death I should regard you as an unfilial daughter. The relation between husband and wife[1] is not a relation which can be changed in this world, for it is a relationship which has been established in a former life. It is utterly unpardonable for a woman in such circumstances not to shave her head and enter the religious life. To do otherwise is to leave a reputation for wantonness in the records of the family. How she behaves when once she has renounced the world is her own concern, for then she has severed her relations with the family."

So he spoke, elaborating on such questions in more detail than he had ever done before. The thought that this might be the last time I should listen to my father's admonitions saddened me still further. At last the bell tolled to announce the dawn, and one of my father's retainers, Nakamitsu, the son of my old nurse, brought in newly-boiled herbs to spread under my father's bed in place of the old.

"It's no use changing them," my father said. "I'm too exhausted. Instead, bring the girl some food." I could not have brought myself to eat anything at that time, but my father went on, "Bring her some food so that I can watch her eating. Quickly now." He

[1] As established in this case by the birth of a child.

wished to see me eating as this was the last time he would be able to do so, I thought with sorrow. Nakamitsu brought in some boiled vegetables on an earthenware dish. "That's not the right kind of food for her to eat in her present condition," my father exclaimed, looking displeased. I too thought it was not very suitable and I got rid of it unobtrusively.

When it was daylight, my father asked that the priest be summoned. He had already in the seventh month sent for a senior priest from the Hokanji temple at Yasaka and had had his head shaved, had taken the vows to observe the five Buddhist commandments, and had taken the religious name of Rensho. He regarded this priest as a man of the highest virtue, but now, I do not know why, his step-mother, the nun of Sanjo, insisted on sending for Shokobo, the chief priest of one of the temples at Kawara, but he did not arrive in time although he was told of my father's critical condition.

"My last moment has come. Lift me up," my father said soon afterwards to Nakamitsu who had been in my father's service from childhood. Nakamitsu now supported my father from behind. There was no one else there except a gentlewoman in front of the priest's arm chair.

"Hold my wrist," my father said to me as I stood near him. While I held his wrist, he told me to put on him over his robe the stole given to him by the priest. He then began to repeat the invocation of the name of Amida Buddha, calling on Nakamitsu to recite it with him. This went on for about half an hour.

Then, as the sun rose, he dozed off, still sitting up and leaning over a little to his left. Wishing to rouse him so that he could go on repeating "Namu Amida Butsu," I shook him gently by the knee. Startled, he woke up and opened his eyes.

"How will things go?" he asked, looking me straight in the eyes, and had hardly spoken the words when he breathed his last. It was eight o'clock on the morning of the third day of the eighth month in the ninth year of the Bun-ei era (1272), in the fiftieth year of his age.

If he had died invoking the sacred name of Amida, he would have died with the certainty of happiness in the next world. Instead he had wakened up startled just to make a completely meaningless remark before he expired. I felt that I had acted quite wrongly in rousing him. I did not know what to think. It seemed as if for me the sun and the moon had fallen from the sky; everything had gone dark. I fell to the floor weeping, my tears streaming forth as if to form a river. My mother having died when I was two years old, my memories of the grief I had felt at her death were faint. Fifteen years had passed since my father had taken me on his knee for the first time, forty-one days after my birth. During all this time, when I looked at my face in the mirror every morning, I was joyful to find some likeness there to his features. Every night when I went to bed, I thought with gratitude of his loving care of me. How grateful we must always be to our parents for high birth and physical health! How could I ever repay my father for his tender care of me, higher than the highest mountain, deeper than the deepest sea, ever since my mother's death! I recalled to my mind what he had said on various occasions. These things I would never forget. I could not bear the thought of our being parted for ever. Yet we had to part now. For though I could have wished that I could keep his remains always with me as they were, I had to send his body away on the night of the fourth to the crematory at Kaguraoka. I wished with all my heart that I could go up with the smoke of cremation to join him, but I returned home from there with my only memento of him my tear-drenched sleeves. As I looked round his empty room, I realised then with deep sorrow that it was only in a dream that I should ever see him again. I recollected his deep affection in urging me at the last moment of his life to eat something to keep up my strength. To tell of his deep love was beyond the power of human words, though I did try to express my feelings in the poem,

> Would that I could see
> The face of my dear father
> Mirrored in my tears,
> Flowing down to that river
> He must now struggle to cross.

Towards evening on the fifth, Nakatsuna, my old nurse's husband, came dressed in black monastic habit. I was very much moved by the unexpected sight of him now in changed guise, for if my father had received promotion to the post of Minister, Nakatsuna as his steward would have been raised to the Fourth Court Rank.

"I am going to visit the grave," he said. "Have you any message?" He wept, and all were moved to tears at the sight of his grief.

On the ninth, at the first Seventh Day Memorial, my step-mother, two of her gentlewomen, and two retainers renounced the world and took their vows in the presence of the chief priest of the temple at Yasaka. Their heads were shaved while he recited the text, "All things flow through the three phases of time, past, present, and future." I wished that I could follow their example, but this was manifestly absurd in the condition in which I was.

The ceremonies of the third Seventh Day Memorial were carried out in a most solemn manner, the ex-Emperor sending a special representative every day with gifts and messages of condolence. How happy it would have made my father, I thought sadly, to have lived to see these evidences of His Majesty's great consideration!

About this time also we were shocked on account of her high birth and her youth to hear of the death of the daughter of the Yamashina Minister of the Left, Saionji no Saneo, first consort and greatest favourite of the Emperor Kameyama and mother of the Crown Prince. She had been persecuted for long by an evil spirit and everyone believed that this was what was wrong with her on the present occasion. I felt a deep and sincere sympathy with the Minister and the

Emperor in their sad loss, for I had also suffered as great a bereavement.

On the fifth Seventh Day Memorial the ex-Emperor sent me a rosary of crystal beads and a crystal spray of dew-pearled flowers so that I should have something with which to reward the priests after the ceremony. The poem with it spoke of these flowers, dew-laden as in autumn, as typifying my sleeves wet with tears.

"My father would have been very pleased to have received such a letter from Your Majesty and would have valued highly your present," I wrote in reply. "I have no doubt that beyond the grave he is full of gratitude to you." The poem I sent with this letter referred to the recent death of the Imperial consort as adding to my grief and tears.

Autumn is gloomy at all times with its long nights; and the constant thud of the cloth-beaters' mallets, a thousand times repeated from every direction, deepened my gloom as I lay weeping in my solitary bed, unable to sleep.

"Snowy Dawn" visits Lady Nijo

CHAPTER V On the morning of my father's death, everyone, from the members of the princely families downwards, came themselves or sent representatives to bring words of sympathy and condolence. There was one exception; my father's rival, his cousin, the Dainagon, Koga no Mototomo,[1] did not appear at all.

One of those who did appear,[2] one who had made daily enquiries about my health ever since, came to visit me on the bright moonlit night of the tenth day of the ninth month. As it was still during the period of public mourning, he was in dark robes with no crest. This made him seem to be in mourning for my father. Because I did not feel it right for me to talk to him through an intermediary, I saw him in the parlour on the south side of the main hall. We talked about the sad events of the past year.

"This year has brought us more sadness than ever before; the tears have never dried from our sleeves the whole year through," he said. "How happy we were on that snowy evening when we exchanged wine-cups and your father suggested that we should meet often in the same way. But nothing came of it. Still, at the time he was really sincere in saying this, wasn't he?"

[1] More successful than Lady Nijo's father, he later rose to the rank of Chief Minister.

[2] This was the same person who had on New Year's day of the year before sent Lady Nijo a present of robes which she had at first refused but finally accepted. She had later been most embarrassed when her father had asked her who had given her this present. He was the one too who had feared that she was turning from him in another direction "like a pillar of smoke" when the ex-Emperor Go Fukakusa had made advances to her. He will be seen to be Saionji no Sanekane, aged twenty-three, at the time a Gon Dainagon, who is later referred to by Lady Nijo by the pet name of "Snowy Dawn."

We passed the night in talking, sometimes with tears and sometimes with laughter, until the tolling of the temple bell warned us of the approach of dawn. The nights are long in autumn, but no night can be long enough for those who are so dear to one another. The dawn chorus of birds began, and still so very much remained to be said.

"People who see me going along the streets at this hour will naturally think I am returning from a happy love tryst," he said as he left, "instead of which we have sat up the whole night talking."

I hated to see him go and I wrote a poem which I sent out by a maid to give him as he set off in his carriage, noting how my tears flowed now at our parting as distressingly as they did at my father's death,

> When my father died,
> That parting caused tears to flow
> Quite soaking my sleeves;
> Parting from you this morning
> Has doubly drenched them again.

He at once replied with a poem agreeing that, while it was proper for me to mourn thus for my father, our parting that morning should provide no cause for sorrow,

> Can parting from me
> Have caused you any sorrow?
> I do not think so.

> The parting from your father
> Must surely be your sole grief.

Recollections of our night-long talk, reclining with no other pillow than my own arm, were the more delightful because it was he and no one else who had been my companion. Tenderly I recalled his looks as I lived over again the events of the night. I was still engaged in such reveries when I came across a retainer in dark red robes holding a letter case in his hand near the main door of the hall. It was his messenger bearing a letter from him, a long and affectionate letter. The poem accompanying it spoke of the possibility that he might be taken to task for his restraint in not showing his love more unmistakably during the course of the night,

> Unable to hide my love,
> In secrecy I met you,
>   My arm my pillow,
> Who is he that can blame me
> That thus I caused you sorrow?

Perhaps because I was at that time at a very susceptible age when trivial things seemed to have tremendous significance for me, I was much affected by his letter. I sent a long letter to him in reply telling him of this and that and enclosing a poem excusing my tears on the plea that it was natural in autumn for our sleeves to be wet with dew,

> In Autumn we see
> The trees and plants dew-laden;
>   Can anybody wonder then
> If in that season of gloom
> My sleeves are dew-moistened too?

The ceremonies of the Forty-ninth Day after my father's death were carried out, my half-brother, Koga no Masaaki, Major General of the Bodyguard of the Left, acting as chief mourner. The chief priest of the temple at Kawara, Shokobo, preached an old-fashioned, platitudinous sermon on the conjugal fidelity of mandarin ducks and those legendary one-winged birds which are able to fly only as a couple, male with female, together. When the sermon was over, a requiem was celebrated with the eminent prelate Kenjichi officiating for the recital of the sutra of the Lotus Flower which my father had written out with his own hand as a religious exercise on the backs of old letters. His cousins, the Sanjo-Bomon Dainagon, Minamoto no Michiyori; Minamoto no Morochika, the Madenokoji Dainagon; and the Zenshoji Dainagon, Shijo no Takaaki, attended the requiem and burnt incense before my father's tablet before returning. I was sad to see them go.

As this was the last day of the period of mourning for him and the day when all the family dispersed, I went to stay at the house of Nakatsuna, my old nurse's home, at the Shijo-Omiya crossroads. I felt unutterably lonesome when the ceremonies were over and everyone left and I had said goodbye to all those who had come to share my grief.

Even during the period of mourning for my father, the ex-Emperor had come to meet me in great secrecy. "Everyone is in mourning now," he had said, "and so your being in deep mourning is justifiable. Come back to the palace as soon as the Forty-ninth Day Memorial is over."

The seventh Seventh Day Memorial fell on the twenty-third day of the ninth month. The chirping of insects now grown feeble in autumn filled me with sadness. The ex-Emperor wrote again. "You stay too long with your family. How about coming back?" he wrote. But I was too depressed to answer; I did not feel like returning to court. So at last the tenth month came.

About the tenth day of the tenth month, my lover's messenger brought me another letter. "Every day I have been wanting to write to you," he wrote, "but I was afraid my messenger might encounter His Majesty's messenger at your house, and then you would blame me for lack of discretion. That is why so many days have passed without my having written to you."

The house I was living in was at the corner of Shijo and Omiya streets. Part of the roof of the plastered wall at the corner on Shijo street had crumbled and fallen. Thorny smilax shrubs were growing over the large gap up to the height of the top of the wall. At the base there were just two thick stems. The messenger, seeing this, said, I was told, "You've placed a guard on this spot, I suppose?" He was told that it had not been thought necessary to do so. He had then cut down the stems of the smilax with his sword, saying as he went away, "That will make a nice short-cut for His Lordship." I wondered what was going to happen next, but I was far from suspecting what would be the consequences of his action.

That night, about half an hour after midnight, judging by the height of the moon, there was a furtive knock at the side door. A little girl named Chujo heard it. "Was that the cry of a water-rail I heard?" she said. "It was certainly a very strange sound." I heard her open the door and then come running back at once. "There's someone outside to see you just for a little while," she said to me in a loud voice, obviously alarmed. His visit was so unexpected that I could not say a word to her. While I was still speech-less with surprise, he came in to my room, guided in the dark by the sound of the girl's voice. He was wearing a robe with a raised maple-leaf pattern and a light purple and green skirt. His style of dress showed that he had intended to avoid being recognised on the way.

"If you have any affection at all for me," I said to him firmly, determined to take no risk that night in my delicate condition, "you will wait for another opportunity for us to meet."

"I know that I must be careful to be on my best behaviour tonight," he said in answer. "I just want to tell you quietly about how long I have loved you. I just want to stay the night with you without going any further than that. The Great God of Ise would allow that as being perfectly innocent."

He seemed so sincere in his protestations and my will to oppose him was so weak that I could not say "No" to him and allowed him into my bedroom. All through the night he continued to tell me of his love for me. His words would have reduced even a fierce Korean tiger to tears; I was not a stick or a stone to remain unmoved by his entreaties. In addition, although I realised that it was not a matter of life or death for me, yet I could not help having the dreadful feeling that this unexpected sharing of pillows would somehow be revealed to the ex-Emperor in a dream.

It was still dark when, disturbed by some early-waking birds, he got up and left. I lay down to try to go to sleep again, but it was not so much a sleep as a day-dreaming after a happy love-meeting. I lay in bed, missing his presence not a little when, still before daybreak, a letter arrived from him. The poem with it protested that on his way home tears had blinded his eyes,

> All the long way back,
> As I went home from your house,
> Tears so blurred my eyes,
> Impossible to see was
> The wan morning moon setting.

"It seems to me now," the letter ran, "that I shall never be able to live till evening, so much do I long to be with you and so violent has my love for you

been during all these years. How agonising it is now
for me to have to dissemble my love for fear of what
the world will say!''

In the poem which I sent in answer to this, I asked
if on the way home he had not seen my face reflected
in the morning light on his sleeves wet with tears,

> All the long way home
> Were my features mirrored there
>   On sleeves moist with tears?
> My sleeves reflected your face
> As weeping I missed you.

My efforts to stave off his advances while I was in
my present condition had then proved fruitless. I
could see that my lot was not going to be an easy
one, and I had no one to whom I could turn for advice
and sympathy. I lay and wept and wept till it was noon.
Then a letter arrived; it was from the ex-Emperor.

''What do you propose doing?'' it read. ''Don't
you think you have stayed away too long? At the court
I have at the moment no government business to
attend to and too few people here to divert my mind
in my leisure hours.''

I was horrified when the other man arrived again
that evening, very early, just after sunset. I was as
dumbstruck as if this were his first visit.

Ever since Nakatsuna had entered religion he had
been living at the Sembon temple and usually there
were no men in the house. This evening, however,
he had come home.

"I've come to stay with my family for the night," he had said. "It's not often I can do so these days." All his children had gathered at the house and were making a great deal of noise.

Now although my old nurse, Nakatsuna's wife, had been reared at the palace of the Princess Sen-yomon, daughter of the Emperor Go Shirakawa, where her mother was in service, she was somewhat lacking in tact and discretion, rather reminding one of the stock character of the foster mother in an ancient story. When she came along to tell me all this, I thought it better not to tell her that I had a visitor, and so I left him in the room in the dark with no light burning while I talked to her as I sat by the brazier at the open doors as if I were enjoying the moonlight.

"My husband suggests we should pass the long autumn night by playing marbles. Do come and join us," she said with an appealing look which distressed me greatly. She went on to give me the names of all the children and step-children who had come to visit them and to suggest what games we should play. "We can have wine too," she added as a further inducement.

This put me in a quandary. How was I to cover up the fact that I had a visitor? "I am not feeling well," I said.

"You will never do what I want you to do," she said. "It's always been so with you." And with that she left, obviously offended.

This old nurse of mine considered herself to be a shrewd woman of the world. She believed it was necessary to keep a close watch on a girl to ensure that she did not get into trouble. My rooms had been selected so that they could easily be observed from the garden and were so close to the rest of the house that the noise of their merry-making in their own part of the house was most distracting. It reminded me of the episode in *The Tale of Genji* when the hero on his visit to the Lady Yugao was so harassed by the thunder of a mill grinding away in the house next door.

However, although it seemed as if unfortunately it was going to be very difficult for me to have that heart-to-heart talk with him that I wished until the household had gone to sleep, I went back to bed with him. Then there was a knock on the main door of the house. Who was this, I wondered. It was one of the sons of the house, Nakayori, who was in service at the Imperial Court.

"I was delayed by the preparations for the Emperor's dinner," I heard him tell the family. "By the way, there's a wicker-work carriage standing on the Omiya corner, a nobleman's by the pattern of large, eight-petalled lotus flowers on the roof. When I went up to it, I found it full of retainers lying asleep, with the oxen tethered to the wheel. I wonder where the owner has gone." It was a great shock to me to hear this.

"Go and see whose it is," I heard the mother say.

Then I heard the father's voice. "What is the use of going to see?" he said. "If it's someone else's affair, you will do no good. And if it is someone who has come on a secret visit to the Lady because he knows she is here on home leave from duty at the palace, he will be waiting at the gap in the wall where there is no guard until everyone in the house is fast asleep. It's no use worrying yourself by trying to protect a girl from harm, whether she's high born or low, right from the time when she's a babe in arms."

"Isn't it provoking!" the mother said. "I wonder who it is. If it were the ex-Emperor, he would have no need to come in such secrecy." Hearing this as I lay in bed with him made me more embarrassed than ever. "She should be careful though," she went on. "She'll make herself a laughing stock if she gets involved with someone of low rank, maybe someone only of Sixth Court Rank." That made me feel humiliated.

Then the talk became more general with one of the sons joining in, but the loud conversation still continued to disturb me. Preparations for a drinking party seemed to be under way and the suggestion was made that I should be invited to join them. Someone came to do so, but the maid told them that I was not feeling well. Then someone else came and knocked loudly on the screen. It was my old nurse who had come again. My heart fluttered wildly; I was as disturbed as if it had been some stranger who had come to visit me.

"Are you feeling any better now?" she said, continuing to beat on the bed-screen. "Look! See what I've got here."

"I am feeling very poorly," I said, for I could not remain silent any longer.

"Look! It's something white and nice you like

very much. You are always asking for it when we haven't got it. And whenever we've got it, then you don't want it. As usual, you're being contrary. Well, if you don't want it, it's all right with me," she said as she went off grumbling. Usually I should have been ready with some witty remark, but now I could not say a word in answer to her. I just wanted to die on the spot.

"What is it you like that's white?" he asked jokingly, to change the subject.

If I had been a woman of refined taste, I might have answered that I liked hoar-frost or snow or hail. I felt, however, that he would think that I was being affected if I answered in this way, and so I made an honest confession. "Strange as it may seem," I said, "I like white wine[3] now and then." But I could not help continuing, "My old nurse does make a great fuss about nothing, doesn't she?"

"How fortunate it is that I came tonight!" he said with a smile. "When you come to stay with me, I will scour the whole of China to find the rarest white wine to please you." I shall never forget that sweet smile of his. I thought that I had never had or ever could have such a happy moment as that, coming though it did in the middle of a most embarrassing situation. I had now spent several nights with him and his love for me had penetrated deep into my heart so that I now felt less and less inclined to return to the ex-Emperor's palace.

[3]Shirozake, made from boiled glutinous rice and rice-malt laced with spirits, used at the Doll's Festival in the third month.

About the twentieth day of the tenth month I heard that my mother's mother, Gon Dainagon, was seriously ill. She had been living for several years at the Ayato shrine near the Zenrinji temple at Higashiyama. I did not anticipate that she would pass away soon, and I was much distressed a few days later to learn of her death. It was the more sorrowful to hear this just then, for her death severed the last link with my parents, even though this had withered and become weakened with the years. I expressed my grief at these two tragedies which I had suffered so close together as being like the dew of autumn and the storms of winter doubly drenching my sleeves,

> The sleet of winter
> Has followed the dews of autumn
> With its gloom and tears;
> Thus two seasons of mourning
> Bring bitter tears to my eyes.

I had had no communication with the ex-Emperor for some time and was beginning to fear that in some way he had got to hear of my unfaithfulness, when I received a letter from him enquiring after my health as he had not seen me for such a long time. He was expecting to have me back at the palace by the end of the year. His letter was even more affectionate in tone than usual.

"My old grandmother died the day before yesterday," I wrote in reply. "I should like to delay my return until the period of mourning is over," I enclosed a poem voicing my grief at this new bereavement,

> Bitter tears I shed
> In the season of autumn
> On my father's death,
> Upon me comes new sadness
> Now with this new bereavement.

The ex-Emperor replied at once with a poem expressing his sympathy; he had not heard of the death of my grandmother,

> I had not been told
> Of this latest bereavement
> You have just suffered;
> In deep sympathy with you
> I shed bitter tears with you.

At the beginning of the eleventh month, I returned to the palace. I had a feeling that there had been many changes there, yet everything reminded me of my dead father. The ex-Empress Higashi Nijo did not seem as friendly to me as she had formerly been. Everything at the palace oppressed me with a feeling of gloom. And I felt embarrassed because I seemed to be carrying myself so ungracefully.

"You two must act as her guardians," the ex-Emperor said to my grandfather, the Minister of War, Shijo no Takachika, and my uncle, the Zenshoji Dainagon, his son, Takaaki, "and look after her as assiduously as her father did. See that she has cloth presented to the court supplied to her for her robes.''

I felt the utmost gratitude to him for his thoughtful care of me. All my hopes were now centred on a quick recovery from the strains of childbirth and settling down to a quiet, uneventful life so that I might offer my prayers for the happiness in the next world of my father and mother and for my own speedy delivery from the Six Worlds of Illusion I had to pass through. At the end of the month I went on leave from my duties at the palace.

Shingambo, Abbess of the Shokutei-in nunnery attached to the Shingon temple of Daigoji at Fushimi, was a relative of mine, and I now went into retreat there to hear her give a course of religious instruction. In the sunken hearth in the hall a pile of brushwood was burning, the rising smoke making the place look less gloomy. Outside in the garden the water-pipes were frozen. Preparations for celebrating the New Year were going forward but in a much more casual manner than elsewhere.

Then on the twentieth day, the ex-Emperor paid me a visit just as the moon was rising, coming in great secrecy in a wicker-work carriage with only my uncle Takaaki accompanying him, sitting in the rear seat.

"I am staying at the Fushimi palace," he said to me, "and it suddenly struck me that it would be a good idea to pay you a visit." I wondered how he had learnt that I was there.

He was in no hurry to leave; he talked affectionately to me the whole night and went away when the bell rang out at dawn. The waning moon was in the western sky, and the ridge of mountains in the east was covered with a bank of clouds. Snow flakes were falling like white petals on the partly thawed snow. The ex-Emperor's uncrested dark robes and trousers of the same dark hue with my own sombre dress made a sad picture of mourning, public and private.

As he left, the nuns were on their way to morning prayers, their stoles flung carelessly, just as a formality, over their shabby robes. I looked at them with something of envy. They had not heard of the ex-Emperor's visit and, unconscious of his presence so close to them, were greeting each other by their names in religion as they met one another. "Hurry, sister. I have already said my devotions." Then at the sight of lower retainers in their dark clothes pulling the carriage round to the entrance, they gathered what was happening and shyly evaded the stares of the men.

"I'll come again," the ex-Emperor said to me as he went away, leaving me a fragrant memory on my tear-drenched sleeves on which his perfume still lingered where his sleeves had lain. I felt as if I were in a happy dream as I listened to the hymn of praise for Buddha's mercy which ended the devotions,

> Even the mightiest of kings must take
> The path all mortals must tread.

It was all most impressive and I was sad that the service had to come to an end.

Before day had fully broken, a letter arrived from the ex-Emperor. "I have never before experienced so deep an emotion as I did this morning when parting from you under the wan morning moon," he wrote.

I answered with a poem,

> See how I weep now
> Tears of gratitude to you
>   For your love for me,
> With tears at having to part
> Beneath this wan morning moon.

About three days before the end of the year, I was feeling even more depressed than usual as I sat that evening with Shingambo. "I wonder when we shall have such a quiet, peaceful time together again," she mused. To help me pass the time more cheerfully, she had called together to her room some of the older nuns, and we sat around talking of old times. It was just like the setting of an ancient story. Outside, the water flowing from the pipe into the trough in the garden was frozen. The blows of a woodman's axe could be heard from the opposite hill. Inside the room candles shone here and there. The first of the evening devotions had been said at eight o'clock, and we were thinking of making an early night of it when a furtive knock came at the door.

"That's strange! Who can be visiting us at this time?" we said. It was he.

"This is most embarrassing," I said to him brusquely through the door. "Any behaviour here that is at all immodest will shock people's eyes and ears. My purpose in coming into retreat here will be frustrated if I do not keep myself pure and do not behave as a true disciple of Buddha should. It is different when the ex-Emperor comes here to visit me; we cannot do anything about that. But if you come to visit me like this in shameless intimacy, all my pious resolutions will be brought to naught. Please go away."

"But this is more than one can bear," he said. "At least allow me to shelter here until it stops snowing." It was in fact snowing heavily and a gale was blowing. It was really a blizzard.

The nuns assembled in Shingambo's room must have been able to hear us wrangling in this way. "But this is too cruel, really too heartless," they said to me. "Whoever your visitor is, he must have some good reason for coming to see you, and in the bitter cold of this mountain storm too." With that they opened the door to him and built up a blazing fire on the hearth. And he came in, complaining bitterly of the cold.

The snow continued to fall all night as if to justify his plea for shelter and not only covered the hills all round but drifted even up to the eaves of the house. The terrifying noise of the storm raging outside kept us huddled together in bed even after daybreak. I hated to see the way he made himself at home, but there was nothing I could do about it.

When it was broad daylight, he had two retainers bring in things they had prepared as presents. Up to that moment I had been rather afraid that the situation might well become very awkward and embarrassing, but when the presents were distributed among the nuns, the abbess was delighted. "We shall be able to stand the cold winds of winter more comfortably now," she said.

I felt that his presenting the nuns with stoles and habits was truly an act of charity which would work for his happiness in the next world as being a genuine offering to Buddha. But this did not prevent my having doubts in my heart about the attitude of the nuns when I saw their evident joy at receiving his presents. What wonderful miracles wealth works! Although they should have welcomed the visit of the ex-Emperor to their house as second only to the visit of a saint from Paradise, they had seen his carriage off with barely polite respect. Now instead of condemning the visit of this other as outrageous, sacrilegious, and utterly unpardonable, they were thrilled to receive his presents.

I myself received from him a New Year's set of robes of a sober pale blue with a set of three white wadded-silk gowns. Then, although I still felt considerable concern at the thought that the news of all this might become public knowledge, we spent the whole day drinking together.

The next morning he left; he thought he really ought not to stay any longer. "Please come and see me off," he said. I got up and went with him to the entrance. The snow on the hill-tops was dazzlingly white in the bright sun. It was a striking sight to see him going through the snow attended by two or three retainers in white. I yearned for him the more as I watched him go, but at the same time I realised that my inconstancy was not a very admirable trait of character.

On New Year's Eve my old nurse sent for me. "It is not proper for you to stay in the mountains while you are in your present condition," she said. She urged me so strongly that I agreed to return.

So the old year came to a close.

 The birth of a prince. Lady Nijo enters her sixteenth year on New Year's Day, 1273

CHAPTER VI New Year's Day came, but there were no ceremonies at the court on the first and third days as it was a period of national mourning. It had been a sorrowful year for me with my father's death continually in my mind. I usually went early on New Year's Day to worship at the family shrine, the Hachiman shrine at Iwashimizu, but this year my condition prevented me from going inside the precincts, and I had to worship from outside the gates. I will not speak further here of the subject of my prayers at the shrine at this time nor of the dream I had about my father, but will write fully about them later.

Towards evening on the tenth day of the second

month my labour pains began. The ex-Emperor's time was fully occupied by political problems, and I was lonely and miserable. Everything seemed to go wrong.

My uncle Takaaki busied himself with all the arrangements. The ex-Emperor sent to Omuro to his step-brother, Prince Shojo, who was now high priest of the Shingon temple of Ninnaji, to have incantations performed there for a safe delivery, and to the chief priest of the Bishamon temple to have other incantations performed there too. My own family asked for petitions to be made to Kannon, the goddess of mercy, by Shingen, the high priest of the Tendai school. My uncle, the high priest Docho of the Ishiyama temple, had just then come back to the Capital from the mountains of Omine where he had been living an ascetic life. "I am still mindful of your father's request to me to look after you," he said and offered up prayers for me.

About midnight on that day, the pains became unbearable. Some commotion in the house was now caused by the arrival of my aunt, Lady Kyogoku, with messages from the ex-Emperor. My grandfather, the Minister of War, also arrived. Weeping at the thought, I wished that my father could have lived long enough to be there too. Leaning on the shoulder of a maid, I dozed off and dreamed that my father was standing there, looking just as he did when he was alive, with a worried expression on his face. He seemed to be about to go round behind me when the announcement was made that a prince was born. I was overjoyed that things had gone so easily. But I was conscious as always of the fear of the consequences of the fault I had committed just as strongly as if I had only at that moment committed the fault.

My uncle Takaaki managed to obtain, though unofficially, a Sword of Protection for the young prince and made all the other arrangements such as giving the priests their presents. He did everything just as my father would have done at his Kawasaki home if he had lived, things like giving presents of clothes to the wet-nurses and arranging for the Twanging of the Bowstring ceremony to ward off evil spirits.

. . . So this whole year seemed to have passed in vain dreams, bright dreams, unhappy dreams, and dreams that had left scars; there had been a time when I had had to show myself off to crowds of visitors. It certainly seemed as if the gods' mercy had not been enough to make up for the shame I had had to hear this year.

 Lady Nijo enters her seventeenth year on New Year's Day, 1274. Relations with "Snowy Dawn," Lord Sanekane, result in a second pregnancy

CHAPTER

VII

During the twelfth month the ex-Emperor was fully occupied with the usual religious ceremonies of that season and had little leisure time. I myself was thinking of spend-

ing the year-end in pious devotions, but my lover,
taking advantage of the fact that the twelfth month
was not a time for visits and social gatherings, came
to spend the whole night with me, and it was almost
broad daylight when we were awakened by a widowed
crow's foolish croaking for her mate. It would have
looked too absurd, he thought, to try to steal away
unobserved at that time of day, and so to my alarm he
decided to stay with me for the whole of the day.

In the course of the day a letter arrived from the
ex-Emperor couched in even more affectionate terms
than usual and accompanied by a poem,

> A dream came to me
> In the darkness of the night;
> In the dream I saw
> Someone to me quite unknown
> Lying, his sleeves spread on yours.

"I wonder whether the dream has any foundation of
truth," he added.

This made me feel very miserable indeed. I wondered exactly what it was that he had seen in his
dream. I felt that I should have to make some reference to his dream in my reply and reassure him,
and so my answering poem read,

> In my bed at night
> Do I lie in solitude,
> No companion
> But the moon which alone spreads
> Its bright beams over my sleeves.

Even as I recollect it now, this evasion of the truth appears to me wholly inexcusable.

Seeing us sitting there together all the day at our ease, the people of the house, especially the women, must have realised what our relationship was. In view of this, it seemed ridiculous for me to say anything to them about my visitor and so I remained silent, choked with uneasiness.

That night I had a strange dream. In my dream he presented me with a hair-oil vessel, offering it to me on a fan with gold-lacquer ribs and a pattern of pine trees. I accepted it from him and concealed it in the bosom of my robes. And just then I was awakened by the bells tolling for dawn. Strange as this dream was, it was even more marvellous to learn from the one by my side that he too had dreamt a similar dream.

The New Year came. In his Rokujo palace the ex-Emperor had twelve calligraphers engaged in making copies of the Lotus Flower sutra. This he was doing, providing all expenses from his own private sources, as a religious exercise with the object of helping to find a solution to the problem which had arisen during the last year with regard to the Imperial succession. He had begun the copying with his own hand on New Year's Day with blood taken from his own thumb, and from then till the seventeenth day of the second month, the third anniversary of the death of the Emperor Go Saga, he devoted himself to this work, observing it as a period of strict abstinence.

Towards the end of the second month, I began to suspect that I was again in a delicate condition. I lost my appetite and for a while thought that I had just got a cold, but gradually I realised that the cause of it all was what had happened on the night on which I had dreamt of being given the silver vessel. How was I going to hide the fact that I was pregnant? What suffering my grave sin was likely to bring on me! The misery I felt was quite insupportable, and there was no one to whom I could go for help. As owing to the national mourning I was often back home, he often came to visit me and even before I told him of my condition, he said, "That is what is the matter with you." After this he was even kinder and more affectionate than ever and came to see me more often.

"How are we going to prevent the ex-Emperor getting to know about this?" he said. We had no idea how we could do this; we offered up fervent prayers continually, but we could blame no one but ourselves for our plight.

At the end of the second month, I returned to my duties at the palace, and in the fifth month I hinted to the ex-Emperor that I was four months pregnant. Actually, of course, it was six months, and I was very worried about how I was going to fill this gap.

On the seventh day of the sixth month, I returned home. My lover had sent word to me pressing me to do this as soon as possible. I wondered why he was so urgent about this, but understood the reason when he presented me with a maternity belt he had had prepared.

"I had thought of having the ceremony performed at the regular time, in the fourth month," he said, "but I postponed it till now in case people became suspicious. Hearing that His Majesty proposed to present you with a maternity belt on the twelfth, I decided that now was the proper time for me to present it." His love for me was so obviously sincere, but I still remained miserable at heart, wondering what fate had in store for me.

For three days, I kept myself secluded indoors, having him staying with me in secret,. On the tenth day of the month I was to have gone back to the palace, but on that day I felt too ill to do so. On the evening of the twelfth my uncle Takaaki brought the maternity belt from the ex-Emperor just as he had done on the last occasion. It moved me to tears as it reminded me vividly of that time and of my father's wonder and delight when the ex-Emperor had visited him at his house.

I was still puzzling over how I was going to account for the discrepancy of at least one month in my time, but still not to the extent of considering whether to drown myself. Instead I was content to let matters drift even though the problem continued to exercise my mind until the ninth month. By this time I was beginning to get rather worried and on the second day of the month I went home on some pretext or other. That night he came to visit me.

"Have you got any suggestion?" I asked him when we began to discuss the matter.

"Tell everyone that you are seriously ill," he said, "and that the soothsayers have declared that it is an infectious disease."

I did as he suggested and stayed in bed all day, allowing no one but members of the household to come near me. I told the two maids in my service to inform everyone that I was refusing to drink even plain warm water. I felt very lonely now that I had no one to cheer me up. I sent a message to the ex-Emperor asking him not to send anyone to enquire as the disease was infectious, and so it was only at long intervals that he wrote to me. All the time I was worried about what I should do if my secret was revealed. But one day after another passed, and for the present everyone seemed quite satisfied that I was really ill.

My uncle Takaaki, however, often came to see me. "Are you sure you will be all right if you let things go on like this?" he asked. "What do the physicians advise?"

"The physicians have told me that the disease is infectious," I said. "I am doing as they suggest and am not seeing anyone."

So I excused myself from seeing anyone, even my uncle. And when he seemed too anxious about me to remain outside the screens, I had the room darkened and hid myself under the bedclothes and would not say a word to him. He went away quite convinced that I was really ill, but it made me very miserable to see him go away and leave me. As I had no other visitor who was so near to me as my uncle, my beloved was now able to stay with me, lying beside me in bed. He had announced that he was going into retreat at the Kasuga shrine. He had sent someone else there in his place and had told his household not to accept any letters addressed to him. We were certainly in a difficult spot!

So the days passed and on the twentieth at dawn, I began to feel the pains. The people of the house could not be told the true facts of the case; only the one or two maids who were in the secret bustled about making preparations. What a scandal I should leave behind me if I died in childbirth, I thought as I watched them doing me all kinds of services.

Night fell without anything happening, but about the time when the candles were lit, the time seemed to be getting near. On this occasion there would be no twanging of the bowstrings to ward off the evil spirits. I lay beneath the bedclothes, feeling very miserable as the late-night bell tolled. Then as the pains grew worse, I sat up.

"I understand that a woman has to be held from the back in someone's arms," he said to me. "Perhaps that is what needs to be done now. How do I have to hold you?" With that he embraced me in the proper way. I held on to his sleeves and the baby was born safely.

"Bring the Lady some thin rice-gruel. Quickly now!" he shouted happily. The maids were touched that he should know exactly what to do to help at such a time.

The candles were lighted and I looked at the baby. Its eyes were opened wide and its baby hair was thick and black. A glance at its eyes drew him to it with a father's love, but he took up a white robe lying near at hand, wrapped the child in it and, taking the dagger from his sword lying beside the pillow, cut the navel string. Then, holding it gently in his arms, he hurried out of the room without saying a word, and I saw it no more. Watching him do this, how I wished I had asked him to let me have just one more look at the child. But what would have been the good of that? I did not say a word but continued to weep bitterly.

When he came back, seeing how bitterly I was weeping, he tried to comfort me. "Everything is all right," he said. "It's all for the best. In the course of time, if you remain alive, you'll see each other again."

The image of my baby's face as I saw her on that occasion would never pass from my mind. For I had seen that it was a girl. I did not know where they had taken her. I knew that it was no use my saying that I wanted to bring her up myself. I knew that this was impossible. All I could do was to stifle my sobs with my sleeves so that the people in the other part of the house could not hear.

When day broke, I wrote to the ex-Emperor. "This morning at dawn," the letter read, "I was very ill and had a miscarriage. The child was far enough developed to tell it was a girl."

He replied at once. "The doctors say that a high temperature may induce a miscarriage," his letter read. "Take good care of yourself." With the letter he sent medicines and other presents. This made me the more ashamed of my conduct.

Several days passed and no complications developed. The one who had been staying with me returned to

his own home. I began to worry about having to
return to my duties at the palace a hundred days
after the birth. But meanwhile I had a more pressing
problem. I remained secluded in my home, and every
night without fail my lover came to spend the night
with me. And he and I were both confronted by the
constant fear of what would happen to us if people
got to know of our relationship.

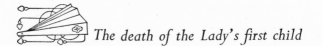 *The death of the Lady's first child*

CHAPTER
VIII
    The little prince to whom I had given
birth the year before had been brought
up by my uncle Takaaki. About this time
I learnt that the child was ill. I felt certain that this
had come as a punishment for the sin I had committed,
and I feared that it would end tragically. Then on the
eighth day of the tenth month I heard that he had died;
he had passed away as the dew or as the rain-drops of
an autumnal shower. My grief was more than I could
bear, though I had been ready for the worst. It seemed
to me that I was singled out to suffer the pangs of
parting from loved ones, the loss of my mother in
my infancy and of my father in the prime of my youth,
culminating in the two more recent bereavements
which had caused me such grief because those snatched
out of my hands were much younger than I.

Besides these, there were the worries and anxieties

arising from my relations with my lover. When I came back to bed after seeing him off in the mornings, I shed tears of longing for him. While I was waiting for him to arrive in the evenings, I sobbed in tune with the tolling of the late-night bell. When he came to visit me, at every moment I was consumed with fears about what people would say if we were found out. On the other hand, when I was away from court, I longed for the ex-Emperor's presence. But when I was with him, I complained that his love was growing cold and I reproached him for spending the nights with others he loved more than me. We all suffer from distracting thoughts; in one day, we are told by the philosophers, each one of us has 840 million distractions of mind. For myself I felt that I alone had been singled out as the target of all misfortunes. Nothing could be better than my becoming a disciple of Buddha, freeing myself from worldly bonds of love and duty.

It was perhaps when I was eight years old that I first read an illustrated biography of Saigyo.[1] In one illustration Saigyo is shown standing in a shower of falling cherry blossoms with a mountain behind and a stream in the foreground. The poem it illustrates describes the happy scene, the beauty of which halts him in his journey and stops him crossing the stream,

> Scattered by breezes,
> The blossoms fall in the stream;

[1] The famous priest, traveller and poet, Sato no Norikiyo, 1118–1190.

> Halted by the scene,
> The wayfarers stop and look,
> Unwilling to ford the stream.

The picture gave me the desire to follow Saigyo's itinerant way of life. The austerities he practised might be too strenuous for a woman but still I had the ambition to follow his example. I wanted to renounce the world and wander through the countryside, composing poems on dew drops under cherry trees in b'ossom in the spring and under the falling red leaves of autumn. I cherished the ambition to leave behind for posterity a travel book such as his. Now that I had found that I could not escape that sad destiny which is the lot of each woman, of obedience to parents when young, to her husband in marriage and to her children when old, I desired all the more to remove myself from the din and bustle of the world, realising as I did that obedience to my father and my lord and master was not a virtue which had always been in harmony with the wishes of my inmost heart.

 The son of the ex-Emperor Go Fukakusa becomes Crown Prince

CHAPTER
IX

It was perhaps in the autumn of the same year that the ex-Emperor became disgruntled at the course of events after the abdication of the Emperor Kameyama and the accession of his son, Go Uda. This had resulted in the ex-Emperor being displaced from his position of pre-eminent political influence in favour of his younger brother, the new ex-Emperor Kameyama.

Upset at this loss of prestige, the ex-Emperor dismissed and paid off all the members of his household except Hisanori, thanking them for their services. All of them parted from him with tears. He then announced his intention of retiring from the world to enter religion. The Imperial consort, Lady Genkimon, known as the Lady of the East Wing, and I were to be the only ladies of the court to accompany him. This may have been bad news to many, but I was highly delighted at the prospect of leaving the court.

The Military Government at Kamakura, however, took steps to placate the ex-Emperor by nominating his son by the Lady of the East Wing, Prince Hirohito, as Crown Prince. The ex-Emperor joyfully selected the Sumi palace as his residence, first removing from it the portrait of the former Emperor Go Saga to the Ogimachi palace.

Lady Kyogoku, who had held a very high position at the ex-Emperor's court, was appointed to the Crown Prince's household. We had not been particularly intimate, but as she was my mother's sister, I had a great deal of respect for her. Now that she had been given my mother's name, "Dainagon no Suke," the world seemed an even more cheerless place, and I had thoughts only of leaving it for a place of religious retreat, but still perhaps the sins I had committed in a former existence kept me bound to the things of this wor'd.

So I sighed away the days as the year was drawing to a close, and at the urgent pleas of the ex-Emperor I went back to the palace, still unable to renounce the world.

 The affair of the former Vestal Virgin. The ex-Empress complains about the Lady's conduct

CHAPTER X   My grandfather, the Minister of War, was very helpful to me at this time in making my life at the court more comfortable, though in devious ways, when I was not provided with robes as a matter of course. The death of my little child still depressed me a great deal as I ascribed his death to that one's crime and to my own lapse from virtue. I remembered how pleased the ex-Emperor had been to look at his own face in a mirror and see how much the child resembled him. Such sad memories filled my mind night and day and I could find no consolation anywhere.

I had also been humiliated by the ex-Empress Higashi Nijo striking my name off the list of ladies who were allowed entrance to her apartments, although I had not been accused of any sin or crime. The ex-Emperor had indeed told me that it would make no difference in his regard for me whatever she did. Although this new twist in circumstances made me very miserable and caused me to be even more retiring in manner, I was determined to serve him as best I could in return for all the kindness and sympathy he had shown me.

The princess, daughter of the former Emperor Go Saga, who had served at the Ise shrine as Vestal Virgin,[1] had had to return from her post after three years of service for the period of mourning for her father and was residing this autumn at Kinugasa near the Ninnaji temple. She was related to my father, who had been in her service for a time and had helped her to make preparations for her journey to Ise when she had taken up her post. For these reasons I was quite friendly with her and, as her residence with its few visitors charmed and attracted me, I often went there to help her while away her time until she returned to her duties at Ise.

About the tenth day of the eleventh month, the princess was to go to Saga on a visit to her step-mother, the Empress Dowager Omiya,[2] who had also invited the ex-Emperor to come to help her entertain the princess.

---

[1] The Vestal Virgin was appointed at the beginning of each reign to serve at the Grand Shrine of Ise. This princess was the daughter of the Emperor Go Saga by the daughter of Koga no Michimitsu, Lady Nijo's grandfather. She was then the ex-Emperor Go Fukakusa's half-sister.

[2] Daughter of Saionji no Saneuji, her mother being the Titular Empress of Kitayama. Consort of Go Saga, she was the mother of the emperors Go Fukakusa and Kameyama and the sister of Higashi Nijo, Go Fukakusa's consort.

The ex-Emperor accepted the invitation. There had been a certain coolness on the part of the Empress Dowager while the problem of the Imperial succession was in debate as she supported the claims of the new ex-Emperor Kameyama, but now that this was settled with the appointment of Prince Hirohito as Crown Prince, her attitude had become more friendly, and he also was anxious to better their relations.

The ex-Emperor took me with him on this visit, riding alone in the rear seat of his carriage, as he knew that I was friendly with his mother, the Empress Dowager, and also with the princess. I was dressed in a set of three royal robes of yellow over light blue with a thin over-robe of scarlet over purple. Over all I wore a red cloak, as all the ladies of his court had been allowed to wear one since the appointment of Prince Hirohito as Crown Prince. No other lady was taken on the visit.

When we had been received by the Empress Dowager, the ex-Emperor in the course of conversation with her began to speak to her about me.

"Agako[3] has been in my care since she was a child," he said, "and she is quite familiar with all the customs and usages of the court. Entertaining unjust suspicions, Lady Higashi Nijo has, however, struck her name off her list. I should not like to have to give her up. Her mother as well as her father did me great service, and for that alone I should wish to keep her, out of regard for their services."

---

[3] *Agako,* literally "My child." It will be seen later that the lady did not like the name *Nijo.*

"You should not give her up," his mother said. "If you had no one in your household who knew how things should be done, you would find things difficult." Then, turning to me, she went on, "Tell me about things quite frankly." Her kindness made me hopeful that she would prove to be a good friend always, though I had some doubts about its being permanent.

The ex-Emperor and his mother spent the evening in conversation and dined together. When it grew late, he retired to the room facing the football ground, accompanied by Lord Sanekane, Lord Takaaki, and other lords. I was his only female companion.

Next morning ox-carriage drivers and ushers and retainers were sent to accompany the Vestal Virgin Princess to the Empress Dowager's residence. The ex-Emperor devoted special care to his dress for her audience with him. He wore an ex-Emperor's formal robes of yellow over pale blue with a pale purple cloak with a pattern of gentians and light purple trousers, all highly perfumed with incense.

About nightfall the princess arrived. The room on the south front of the hall had been cleared and a dark-coloured screen with smaller screens erected. As the Empress Dowager was going out to meet the princess, she sent word to the ex-Emperor to come and help her entertain the guest. He therefore went; as usual I accompanied him, bearing his sword.

The Empress Dowager wore a dark grey silk gauze monastic habit with a grey cloak over it; she sat with small screens of the same colour behind her.

The princess was dressed in a set of three red robes over dark red with a blue, unlined robe under them, a style which, I thought, did not become her at all. Her lady-in-waiting, a relative of hers, wore a set of five purple robes with no mantle or skirt.

The Vestal Virgin was a little over twenty years of age, looking so mature that it seemed natural that she should have been called back to resume duty at the Ise shrine after the end of the period of mourning for her father. Her complexion was like the petal of a cherry flower seen, unfortunately, as if through a haze, for she was shading her face with her sleeves from too ardent an inspection. I began to feel sorry for her, for I could see that some plan was even then germinating in the ex-Emperor's too susceptible mind. A general conversation went on among the three, with the princess making only rather disjointed remarks about Ise, until it was time for bed.

"It is now late and time for bed," the ex-Emperor said. "Tomorrow before returning you should go to see the bare leafless trees on lonely Arashiyama."

So, accompanied by me, he returned to his apartments. "What am I going to do? What am I going to do?" he said. I was amused that I had so accurately judged the direction of his thoughts. "You have been in my service since childhood," he went on. "Help me to satisfy my yearning for her, and I shall know that you are really loyal to me."

I went at once. The open message I carried read, "I was very happy to have this opportunity of meeting you. Don't you feel it rather disagreeable sleeping in a strange bed?'' But with it was a secret message in the form of a poem written on thick white layered paper which told how her face still before him in his mind's eye was preventing him sleeping.

> You know not perhaps
> That the face I saw just now
> Still haunts my mind's eye
> And drives far away from me
> All thought of going to sleep.

It was so late that everyone in her apartments was fast asleep. The princess herself was asleep, protected by a small screen. Going near, I awakened her and gave her the poem. She blushed but said nothing and made no attempt to read it.

"What answer shall I give?" I asked her.

"What answer can I make in reply to such an unexpected message?" she said, lying down again.

This was all most unsatisfactory. I went back and told him what had happened.

"Show me where she is sleeping," he said to me.

I did not know what to do, but deciding that the easiest course to take was just to show him the way and do nothing more, I led the way back to her room in silence. He was wearing just an ordinary robe and a pair of wide-bottomed trousers.

I went in front and opened the screens. She was lying asleep just as she had been when I had come the first time. There was no sound or movement. He squeezed himself between the screens and went in.

That was all I saw. I thought it would be wrong of me to leave him there and go back to our own part of the house, and so I lay down outside the screens by the side of the lady on duty.

"Who is that?" she whispered, waking up in some alarm.

"I am sorry there are so few people on duty and so I have come to help," I answered.

She appeared to be quite satisfied with this answer and tried to start a conversation with me.

"It's very late and I feel sleepy," I said, annoyed that her ladies had not foreseen things like this happening and that she apparently suspected nothing.

I pretended to be asleep but listened attentively. I was lying not far from the screens, and it seemed to me from what I could hear that the princess was making little resistance even to his first tentative approaches. She would have shown more sophistication if she had continued to put up some show of resistance all through the night.

Before dawn he returned to his room. "The cherry blossom is beautiful," he commented, "but the bough is easy to break and the blossom easy to pluck." That was just what I had suspected had been the case.

He lay in bed till the sun was high in the sky, not getting up till nearly noon, surprised to find it so late. "What a thing to do! I've certainly overslept," he said. He wrote a letter to her, the answer to which simply said, I believe, that she had not yet recovered from the pleasant surprise of his unexpected visit.

"Have you prepared any entertainment for our

honoured guest?'' the ex-Emperor asked his mother when he saw her.

''No, we haven't prepared anything special,'' she answered.

The ex-Emperor therefore asked Lord Takaaki to have a banquet prepared and when it was ready, towards evening, the Empress Dowager and the princess were invited in.

As I knew them both, I served the first drinks to each of them. For the first three exchanges they only made a pretence of drinking with empty wine cups. This did not meet with the approval of the ex-Emperor and, at the suggestion of his mother, the princess exchanged drinks with him. I was then told to take the cup to Lord Sanekane and my uncle Takaaki who were seated below the dais, separated from it by screens. I did so, handing the cup to Lord Sanekane.

''I am not in charge of the banquet,'' he said, indicating that I should offer the cup to Lord Takaaki.

''It's you she's chosen,'' he replied.[4] Sanekane took the cup and after drinking passed it to my uncle.

''I've not had a party since my husband passed away,'' said the Empress Dowager. ''Let's amuse ourselves at our ease this evening.''

Her ladies played the Japanese harp. The ex-Emperor played the lute. Sanekane played the lute too. Then Kaneyuki played the flageolet. As the night wore on, the party became very enjoyable. Sanekane and

[4] This is the first clue given by Lady Nijo to the identity of her lover. Her uncle Takaaki hints that he is well aware that Sanekane is involved with her.

Kaneyuki both sang traditional shrine songs. Takaaki sang the song of his Seryo home.

The princess resolutely continued to refuse to drink, however much I urged her. The ex-Emperor was about to fill her cup when his mother said, "Sing us a drinking song to go with the wine." He therefore sang the ballad,

> What a miserable life
> Is the lot of these
> Old charcoal-burners!
> Thinly clad they go out
> To cut wood for the winter fuel,
> But sadly enough
> Not to warm themselves but others.

It sounded most amusing.

"Give me the cup," said the Empress Dowager. She had it filled three times and after drinking passed the cup to the princess who drank and passed the cup to the ex-Emperor. He then returned to his seat.

"An emperor, the Chinese histories tell us, has no father or mother," the Empress Dowager mused aloud. "Still, it is owing to me, though unworthy, that you ascended the throne. Sing me then another drinking song."

"Ever since I was born," the ex-Emperor said to his mother, "I have owed everything to you; my nomination as Emperor and the grant of the title of ex-Emperor were both due to you. How then could I treat your command lightly?" At her wish he sang,

Flocks of cranes fly over Kameoka;
Like them our Lord will have long life,
And all under heaven will be at peace.

He sang this through three times, filling his mother's cup three times. He then asked her for the cup, had it filled three times and drank. He then handed the cup to Lord Takaaki.

"How jealous you must have been when the girl handed the cup first to Sanekane!" he said.[5] Then he passed the cup to the other lords in turn, and the drinking party came to an end.

I had expected that the ex-Emperor would be visiting the princess again that night, but instead he said to me, "I've drunk too much tonight. I don't feel at all well. Massage my back," and stayed in his room all night.

Next day the Vestal Virgin left. The ex-Emperor then went to Imabashi to enquire after the health of the Titular ex-Empress of Kitayama who was suffering from a cold. He stayed there for the night and then returned to the Tominokoji palace.

During the evening of the day of his return, Lady Chunagon came with a message from the ex-Empress Higashi Nijo. "Because of Lady Nijo's inexplicable behaviour," her letter read, "I forbade her entrance to my apartments. Your Majesty has ignored this ban. On this last visit you have made to your mother, you allowed her to ride in your carriage in the robes of

[5] The ex-Emperor also appears to know of Sanekane's liaison with Lady Nijo.

a princess so that people were under the impression that you were being accompanied by an empress. This is to be deplored as it leads to my good name being defamed. For this reason, I desire to be released from your service that I may renounce the world and retire to Fushimi or some such place."

"I have received your message," the ex-Emperor replied. "It is not necessary for you to have to tell me about Nijo. Her mother was a court lady of the highest rank, and when she was Nijo's age, I valued her constant services more highly than anyone else's and should have liked to have retained her in my service. On her death-bed she begged me to look after her child, and I promised to do so. Before he died, her father also begged me to give my protection to his daughter, and I promised to carry out these last wishes of his. It is loyalty on the part of a subject that makes a lord behave as a lord, and it is the favour granted by the lord which causes a subject to behave as a subject. Her father was able to die in peace because I had given my word to give his daughter my protection. An emperor's word is final, and I cannot go back on the promises I made then. Her parents are watching me from beneath the turf to see that I do not do so. How could I drive the innocent girl away from my palace to some unknown place?

"Wearing princely robes is not something she has just begun to do," he went on. "When her father brought her to see me for the first time, he asked that she should receive the treatment to which she would have been entitled if she had been the daughter instead of the granddaughter of the Koga Chief Minister, as he himself was of lower rank. She was therefore given permission to use an ox-carriage with five blinds and to wear princely robes. Her mother also was a step-daughter of the Kitayama Chief Minister. It was because of this that the titular ex-Empress of Kitayama officiated at the ceremony of Putting on the Skirt for her. In the course of that ceremony it was officially announced that she was granted permission to wear thin silk robes and a white skirt. She has always been given the privilege of alighting from her carriage at the main entrance. Now all these things were decided long ago. Why have you waited till now to express your disagreement with them? You speak of rumours that certain low-ranking retainers have accused her of giving herself the airs of an empress. If enquiries were to show that she had done this, even then I could not drive her away from the court, but I would certainly reduce her in rank to the status of a serving maid.

"It is well known that her father objected to her being called Nijo, and I have instructed my house not to do so. Although her father's own rank as Dainagon was low, she entered the service of the court as a daughter of the Koga Chief Minister and her father was of the opinion that she should not be given the name of a street and wished her to be called Agako for the time being. He knew that all men were not fortunate enough to realise their ambition, but he hoped that if he should be promoted to the post of Minister a more fitting name might be given her.

"The daughter of a Chief Minister is officially permitted to wear princely robes. In addition, every family founded by a prince insists on its right to do the same, the Kazan family as being descended from Prince Tankai, and her own family, the Koga family, from Prince Tomohira, the seventh son of the Emperor Murakami and the younger brother of the Emperor Reizei and En-yu. This is a family which has been established at a much more recent date than the others, and daughters of the family are not as a general rule inclined to enter the service of the court, but her mother did so and afterwards left her daughter to my protection, and so she has been in my service since she was a child. I had thought that you knew all this, and your present words of disapproval have come as an unpleasant surprise. As for your wish to enter the religious life, the decision to do this depends on the merits acquired in a former life, and outside circumstances cannot influence this."

This letter, however, did little to improve relations between the ex-Empress and myself. My only consolation was in the ex-Emperor's continued high favour.

The ex-Emperor did not visit the former Vestal Virgin again after the one short meeting at Saga. I felt sorry that my efforts on her behalf had not been more successful.

"Well, are you going to let the year-end pass without a visit to her?" I asked him, and in response to a suggestion from me, he sent me with a letter to invite her to visit him when she could.

Her foster-mother was distressed when I told her of the invitation. "I had hoped," she said to me with tears, "that she would not get involved with anyone but would devote herself solely to the service of the Ise shrine, but His Majesty's passing whim has brought her much sorrow."

I was rather annoyed by her continual lamentation. "I have come just to invite her to visit him sometime when she has the leisure," I explained with a friendly smile.

"We shall do nothing," she answered, "to prevent her going when she has the time."

I returned to tell the ex-Emperor the result of my visit. "It heightens one's love," he said, "when one has to cross mountains to visit someone. But with her I always have the feeling that there are no more mountains to cross."

Nevertheless, in the twelfth month, he sent a carriage to bring her secretly to the palace. The way was long and it was already late when the carriage drew up at an entrance on the corridor to the Oyanagi house, for the Kyogoku front had been handed over for the use of the Crown Prince. He led her into the Four-Pillar room. As usual, I remained outside the screens to serve them. Everything seemed to be happening just as one would have expected it to happen, I thought, as I listened to her complain of his having neglected her for so long since that night at Saga. So, also, were her tears predictable as she came out with him to say goodbye as the dawn bell rang out.

As the year drew to its close, my misery grew

deeper. I could find no contentment in the palace, and yet I could not bring myself to go home. One evening when the Lady of the East Wing was expected to visit the ex-Emperor, I returned to my room on the pretext of having a pain in the stomach. Late that night my beloved came to my door. Horrified at the thought of what people would say, I did not know what to do. But everything seemed to be happening just as one would expect it to happen as I listened to his complaint of my long neglect of him. So, careful to make no noise, I let him in. The sadness with which I saw him go away at dawn was infinitely deeper than that which I felt at the passing of the old year that day. But this was perhaps only to be expected, for I always did attach too great an importance to my own private feelings. Even today when I think of these things, I am still moved to tears.

Book Two

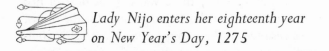 *Lady Nijo enters her eighteenth year on New Year's Day, 1275*

CHAPTER The years galloped past, flowing onward
I like the waters of a river, disappearing
never to return, and on this New Year's
Day I entered my eighteenth year. But the beauty of
the bright spring sunshine, gay with blossoms and the
song of birds, brought no happiness to my spirit, no
peace to my restless heart.

This year the Kazan-in Chief Minister, Fujiwara no
Michimasa, was in charge of the New Year's Day
celebrations at the Tominokoji palace and served
the New Year spiced wine to the ex-Emperor. The
year before, the Chief Minister had been appointed
Lord Steward to the new ex-Emperor Kameyama, an
appointment which had angered the ex-Emperor as it
marked a decrease in his own political influence.
This, however, had now been restored by the nomination of his son, Prince Hirohito, as Crown Prince,
and friendly relations had been established once again
between the Chief Minister and the ex-Emperor, who
had therefore graciously consented to his taking charge

of the New Year celebrations at his palace. The ladies and the maids were all present, dressed in their best, but the happiness of the occasion could not check my tears as I remembered past years when my father had served the wine at these celebrations.

It had been decided that there should be a game of Sides on the fifteenth of the month at the Crown Prince's palace. First, there was a great deal of fuss and commotion over the drawing of lots for the teams, as this resulted in the ex-Emperor's team being composed mainly of men and that of the Crown Prince mostly of women. Then lots had to be drawn for opponents. My opponent was the Nijo Minister of the Left, Fujiwara no Morotada, the Crown Prince's tutor, who was captain of his team.

"Get ready to give your opponent a good present," said the ex-Emperor. "Do them well." The presents we women got were things we thought we should not be called upon to endure. We did not like it either that we were beaten with a stick not only by the ex-Emperor but also by the courtiers.[1]

Afterwards I had a talk about it with the Lady of the East Wing, Lady Genkimon, and we decided to have our revenge on the ex-Emperor on the eighteenth. That morning all the ladies assembled in the domestic quarters: Shin Dainagon and Gon Dainagon at the door of the kettle room, Betto and Kyugo at the front, Chunagon in the ex-Emperor's room, and Mashimizu and Saburo in the outside corridor. In an

[1] The custom originates from a fertility rite. The women thus beaten bore sons.

adjoining room I waited with the Lady of the East Wing, passing the time talking.

"He's sure to come through this way," we said. Just as we thought, he did come that way, dressed in his wide-bottomed trousers only.

"Why isn't there anyone on duty in my apartments?" he was saying as he came in, all unaware of what was about to happen. "Here, somebody, come here." The Lady of the East Wing caught hold of him in her arms. "What's all this about? Come to me, someone," he shouted. But no one came to his help. It was some time before the Madenokoji Dainagon, Minamoto no Morochika, tried to come in from the anteroom but was stopped in the corridor by Mashimizu with a stick in her hand.

"You cannot cross this corridor," she said. "It isn't allowed."

Meanwhile I had beaten the ex-Emperor soundly until he promised he would not in future allow his courtiers to beat us. We were all highly delighted with our success.

That night when the lords assembled in the hall for dinner, the ex-Emperor addressed them. "I am now thirty-three years of age. That is an age which is generally considered a dangerous age. That is perhaps why such an outrageous thing has happened to me today. It is certainly an indignity completely without precedent that an emperor, the acme of virtue and the lord of all might and power, should be beaten with a stick. I regard it as a most serious matter that not one of you came to my assistance. Were you also in this foul conspiracy with the women?" He continued to make one accusation after another while the lords present tried to defend themselves with one excuse after another.

"Court ladies who beat their master in this way must certainly be severely punished," said one.

"Even those who in ancient times rebelled against the emperor never committed such a terrible deed," said another.

"How could people dare to take a stick to the emperor when it is forbidden even to step on his shadow!" said a third.

Such were the opinions expressed by all the lords present: the Nijo Minister of the Left, Fujiwara no Morotada; the Sanjo Dainagon, Minamoto no Michiyori; the Zenshoji Dainagon, Shijo no Takaaki; the recently appointed Dainagon, Saionji no Sanekane; and the Dainagon, Madenokoji no Morochika.

My uncle Takaaki had as usual very definite ideas on the subject and expressed them forcibly. "What are the names of these women who are guilty of this outrage?" he asked. "Tell us their names at once so that all the lords present may pass judgment on them."

"Should they alone be punished?" said the ex-Emperor. "Should not their families also suffer?"

"It goes without saying," said Takaaki. "All their families, parents, brothers and sisters, sons and daughters, should be punished also." All present agreed that this was only right.

"Well," said the ex-Emperor, "the one who beat

me was the daughter of the late Chuin Dainagon, Koga no Masatada, grand-daughter of the Minister of War Shijo no Takachika and niece of the Zenshoji Dainagon, Takaaki, or, we might well say, his adopted daughter, his most beloved daughter. So you see it was all the work of Lady Nijo, and so it is you who are going to be the first to be punished."

At this, all the lords burst out laughing. "It is going to cause a lot of complications," they said, "if we banish a court lady just at New Year. Worse still if we have to banish the whole family too. Instead, the lady and her family will have to expiate their fault by offering presents. There are precedents for this being done."

I would have none of this. "I do not accept the judgment," I said. "On the fifteenth not only did His Majesty beat us unmercifully, but also he allowed lords and courtiers to do the same. We did not like it, but we just had to suffer it. There was nothing a woman of my insignificance could do about it. Later, the Lady of the East Wing asked for my help in getting revenge, and I agreed to help her. I should not be the only one to be punished."

"That may be so but you are the one who struck the blows and should be punished." So it was agreed that compensation would have to be made by my family alone.

Lord Takaaki therefore sent a message to his father, the Minister of War, Shijo no Takachika, telling him of the incident and informing him of the decision that had been made.

"This is impious conduct," the Minister commented. "We must certainly atone for this at once. The longer we leave it, the worse it will be for us. Hurry things along."

Compensation was therefore given in grand style by the Minister on the twentieth and splendid presents made to all concerned. Robes and a sword were presented to the ex-Emperor. Each of the six lords was given a sword and each of the ladies a hundred quires of fine crepe paper.

On the twenty-first, Lord Takaaki, extravagant in ideas as ever, gave a banquet in lavish style and presented the ex-Emperor with a model Japanese harp and a lute in purple brocade and a blue glass wine-cup with a silver cover round it in the form of basket-work.

The High Priest Ryuben, my uncle Takaaki's younger brother, happened to arrive at the court just as the banquet was beginning and was invited in. A carp having been brought in to serve with the wine, the ex-Emperor told the priest to carve it up. "Show us your culinary skill," he said. "Your family is said to be famous for it, as the High Priest of Uji temple has shown." The High Priest declined to do this, and the ex-Emperor repeated his order. Lord Takaaki placed a chopping-board before the priest with a carving-knife and chopsticks.

"Now everything is ready for you," the ex-Emperor said as the wine-cup was set before him ready for him to drink. The High Priest reluctantly began carefully to cut up the fish. It was a rare sight to see him in his dark orange-red robe doing this.

"I can't cut off the head," he said, laying down the knife when he had cut a small portion.

"You can't stop there," said the ex-Emperor. Finally, the High Priest cut off the head in expert style and hurried out of the hall. The ex-Emperor was so struck that he sent out the blue glass wine-cup with the silver basket-work as a present to the priest, who by this time had already reached the main gate.

Now Lord Takaaki had another suggestion to make. "My father and I," he said, "as being her grandfather and her uncle have now made due reparation for Lady Nijo's fault. We are her relatives on her mother's side. But on her father's side, she has a grandmother and an aunt. Why has it not been suggested that they should make compensation too?"

"That is reasonable," the ex-Emperor said. "But they are not blood relations. We mustn't go to extremes in this matter. Your proposal is too inflexible and oppressive."

Lord Takaaki demurred, but had a further suggestion. "Then send Lady Nijo as your messenger to the ex-Empress of Kitayama. She looked after her as a child, and her mother was a frequent visitor to her place."

Without replying to this suggestion, the ex-Emperor turned to the Dainagon, Saionji no Sanekane. "In any case," he said, "aren't you more responsible for her behaviour than the ex-Empress of Kitayama?"[2]

"We are not such close relations," Lord Sanekane

[2] The ex-Emperor again shows that he is aware of Sanekane's close relations with Lady Nijo.

said. But his repeated pleas sounded extremely weak and were summarily rejected; finally he too had to make compensation. As the others had done, he gave presents, to the ex-Emperor robes and a model boat of aloe wood with three boatmen modelled out of musk, to Lord Morotada an ox and a sword, to each of the other lords an ox, and to each of the ladies a hundred quires of crepe paper diapered with gold or silver or dusted with gold or silver, or reddish purple in colour.

My uncle Takaaki thought that my grandmother should certainly be informed. He told her what had happened and how all concerned had indemnified themselves.

"Lady Nijo's father," she wrote in reply, "took a great deal of trouble looking after her when she was a child after the death of her mother. She was still in diapers when she was taken over by the court where she was brought up. At the time I thought this was a great blessing for the child, far better for her than my adopting her. I never dreamt that under His Majesty's tender care she would grow up to be so mischievous. He must, I feel, realise that it is all the fault of her upbringing. Is it perhaps because she has not been taught to distinguish differences of social position? Or is it because His Majesty has spoilt her? I really couldn't say. For my own part, if His Majesty were to send his own representative to demand indemnity, I should do what I could. Until he does so, however, I do not wish to become involved in this matter. If her father were alive, I have no doubt that he would show his love for her by offering adequate compensation. But for my own part I feel no such affection for her and if His Majesty were to order me to disinherit her, I would do so quite willingly.''

When this letter was read publicly before the ex-Emperor, the lords present were of the unanimous opinion that my grandmother had right on her side. She had, they thought, shown conclusively that as Lady Nijo had been brought up at the court, the fault obviously lay there. Also, they added, a woman's first lover had most responsibility for her good behaviour; he it was that would carry her after death across the Three-Way river into the world to come.

"What do you mean?" protested the ex-Emperor. "Do I have to compensate you all for my fault when you have all just compensated me? Hasn't it all happened because I made a claim for damages done to me?"

"When those who are above acknowledge their fault, then those who are below should receive compensation," they answered. The ex-Emperor could not but agree that this was only just, and Yoshida no Tsuneto was instructed to arrange for each lord to be given a sword and each lady a robe.

So ended this most amusing incident.

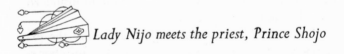 *Lady Nijo meets the priest, Prince Shojo*

CHAPTER In the third month a requiem for the repose of the soul of the Emperor Go **II** Shirakawa with a recital of the Lotus Flower sutra was held for four days in the hall of the Ogimachi palace, the hall at the Rokujo palace having been destroyed by fire just over a year before. On the thirteenth day, the last day of the celebration, while the ex-Emperor was attending the service, someone[1] came to see him.

"I will wait until His Majesty returns," he said, when he learnt that the ex-Emperor had left the palace.

When he was shown into a room off the gallery, I went in to greet him. "His Majesty will be coming back soon," I said to him. I was getting up to go to my room, when he urged me to stay with him a little while. I could not think of anything in particular he

[1]He is identified later as Prince Shojo, third son of the late Emperor Go Saga, and younger brother of the Emperors Go Fukakusa and Kameyama. He had entered religion in early life, as so many of the younger sons of an emperor did, and had the title of Ajari, Erudite Priest, of the esoteric school of Buddhism, the Shingon sect. His name has been mentioned in the narrative several times already; when his relationship with Lady Nijo becomes closer, she refers to him by the pet name of "Wan Morning Moon."

might want to discuss with me, but at the same time there did not seem to be any reason for me to avoid him out of shyness or fear, and so I stayed. We talked together of this and that, of old times. He spoke of things which my father used to say which he would never forget. This all put me into a sympathetic frame of mind as I sat peacefully opposite to him.

Then he began to talk to me in a way I had not expected at all. "Buddha would not approve of what I am going to say," he said, "and would reject the devotions I offer to him as foul, unacceptable, despicable." At this, I excused myself, stood up and tried to leave, but he held me back by the sleeve.

"Promise to meet me some time," he said, "for however short a time." He wept and I felt that the tears he was shedding genuinely showed the depth of his feelings. I was hesitating over what to do when I heard a cry go up that the ex-Emperor was returning, and I took advantage of the opportunity to pull my sleeve from his grasp. Whenever I looked back on this unexpected meeting, it seemed like some unreal mysterious dream.

The ex-Emperor came in to meet his brother. "It's a long time since we met," he said. They dined together, and as I served the wine, I smiled at my secret thoughts.

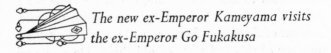

*The new ex-Emperor Kameyama visits
the ex-Emperor Go Fukakusa*

CHAPTER Since the Military Government at Kamakura
was receiving reports that relations between
III the two ex-Emperors were not good, the
new ex-Emperor, with a view to improving these, came
on a visit to see the ball-court and enjoy seeing a ball game.

"What has to be done?" the ex-Emperor asked
the Great Lord Konoe. "What preparations do we
have to make?"

"Refreshments should be served early in the game,"
said Lord Konoe. "Dried persimmons soaked in wine
should be served by a lady-in-waiting while the players
are changing their clothes."

On being asked to suggest the name of a lady for
this service, Lord Konoe thought that from the points
of view of age and rank I should be the most suitable
for this duty. I decided to wear a set of seven robes of
dark red lined with violet pink, a scarlet robe over
it with a cloak of yellow lined with deeper yellow and
a blue mantle and a skirt of raw silk. Underneath I
wore gowns of red shading off to pink.

When the new ex-Emperor arrived, he found his
seat placed opposite his host's. "This is not as it
should be," he said. "When the late Emperor was
alive, he decided how we should sit." He then had his
own seat moved down to a lower place.

"In *The Tale of Genji* the Emperor has his host's seat moved up to face his," the ex-Emperor said when he came in and saw how the seats had been placed. "It is strange that today you should have moved your seat to a lower level than your host's." People thought his allusion to the change of seats both graceful and cordial.

The banquet proceeded uneventfully, the wine-cups being offered formally three-times-three. The Crown Prince arrived and the ball game began. Then, at half time, the new ex-Emperor went through the eastern door to the pavilion. Betto went with me carrying a wine-cup in a basket-work cover and a kettle containing the wine with the persimmons soaking in it. She wore a set of five robes of light green lined with purple, a scarlet over-robe, a white cloak lined with blue, and a yellow mantle lined with light green.

I offered the wine to the new ex-Emperor. "You taste first," he said, kindly offering the cup to me. He sat watching the ball game till twilight and left for his own palace with torches burning.

Next day he sent his retainer, Nakayori, the son of my old nurse, with a letter to me written on thin red paper attached to a willow twig with the poem,

> How can I believe
> It was in reality
> That I saw your face?
> Rather was it in a dream,
> A dream that will never end.

I could not be so impolite as not to reply. My poem in answer reminded him that the cherry blossom, however beautiful, begins to fall as soon as it blooms, so fleeting are the things of this world. This I wrote on a sheet of pale blue paper attached to a spray of cherry blossom,

> What does it matter
> If it was in reality
>   Or a passing dream?
> Rather think how the cherry blossom
> No sooner blooms than it falls.

From this time he often wrote to me, but I discouraged his approaches, and finally had my carriage made ready and left the palace for the home of my cousin the Dainagon Minamoto no Morochika.

 The illness of the ex-Emperor. The Ajari, Prince Shojo, continues his efforts

CHAPTER IV   The hall of the Rokujo palace having been rebuilt, the Emperor moved there in the fourth month. The service of dedication took place before a picture of the Mandala symbol hung on the wall with the Tendai High Priest Kogo presiding and twenty priests assisting. Later another service was held in the Jocho chapel at the palace with the priest Kenjichi officiating.

The removal had been made just before. There were five carriages of ladies in the procession. I rode in the place of honour in the first carriage, with Lady Kyogoku in the second place on the right. I wore a set of seven robes of scarlet with a purple lining and a blue cloak lined with light red, Lady Kyogoku a set of five light purple robes with a blue lining.

For three days after the removal, we remained indoors wearing white with dark scarlet mantles and skirts. A competition of garden-plot flower arrangements was organised to mark the occasion. The courtyard was divided into plots and allotted to each of the lords and ladies of the middle and upper ranks. I was assigned two small plots on the eastern side of the main building near the Jocho chapel. In my plot I placed a beautiful little arched bridge, but to everyone's amusement my uncle Takaaki stole it in the night and placed it in his own plot.

In the eighth month the ex-Emperor fell ill. At first it did not appear to be anything very serious, although his appetite was poor and he perspired a good deal. Still, the symptoms continued for a long time and we began to get rather worried. Doctors were called in and he was cauterised at as many as ten points. Nevertheless, his condition showed no signs of improvement. Services of intercession for long life were held for seven days from the eighth day of the month, but at the end of the period his condition remained unchanged.

The Erudite Priest who now came to visit his brother was the same priest who had come to visit him in the spring and who had declared his attachment to me with his words and his tears. He had reminded me of this on every occasion whenever I had been sent with a message to him by the ex-Emperor, but I had so far evaded any further intimacy on one pretext or another. On one occasion I had received an affectionate letter from him urging me to make the response to his pleas which he desired. The letter had embarrassed me so much that I had torn off a piece of hair-tying paper, had written on it the one word "Dream" and left it near him as if I had accidentally dropped it. On another occasion when I had gone to the temple with a message for him, he had thrown towards me a spray of star anise. I had picked it up unobserved and found written on the leaves the poem,

> Rising up betimes
> To pick this spray of anise,
>   I find wet with dew
> These sleeves long since drenched with tears
> That my dreams have not come true.

I thought the poem very cleverly contrived, and after this I found myself more inclined to think tenderly of him, and rather looked forward to having the opportunity to see him whenever I was sent to the temple with a message for him. When I was there, I found too that I could sit and talk to him and answer him without any feeling of embarrassment.

When he came to visit the ex-Emperor at this time, he was grieved to find that the ex-Emperor's health was not improving, and asked that some article of clothing that had been in contact with the ex-Emperor's body should be taken into the chapel before the service began.

I was therefore told to take a robe which the ex-Emperor had been wearing[1] into the chapel before the service began at eight o'clock in the evening. I did so and found that not one of the priests was there, perhaps because they were all in their own rooms putting on their vestments. There was no one at all there except the prince who was still in his ordinary habit.

"Where shall I put His Majesty's robe?" I asked him.

"Place it in the reading room next door," he said. I went into the room and found it lighted up. Then to my surprise he followed me in.

"'Buddha leads us even when we go along dark paths,'" he quoted, weeping, as he took me in his arms. I was shocked at his action, but he was not someone whom I could push away or tell to take his hands off me. Resisting the impulse to cry out, I could only whisper a reminder of the warnings of Buddha, but no plea of mine was of any avail. Our dream of love was, however, of very short duration and

[1] So that by the power of prayer this robe might absorb the impurities which were the cause of his illness and could then be thrown into the river. Paper cut-out images were often used for this purpose.

the memory of it now too faint to recall, for it was interrupted almost immediately by the priests calling out that the service was about to begin.

At this he fled out by the other door. "See me again after the service at dawn," he said as he left.

The service proceeded uneventfully, but it was horrifying for me to think how unworthy he was to be there taking part in this solemn service. The shadowless bright light of the candles contrasted so startlingly with my thoughts of the darkness of the world to come that I was still further saddened.

I was not exactly burning with love for him, but after the midnight service I went to his room unobserved. The service was over and we could meet with less apprehension. I was sorry to see him weep so pathetically.

When the noise of people moving about at dawn disturbed us, he pressed me to exchange with him the gowns we had worn next to our bodies so that we might have something to remind us of this meeting. The sadness of parting when we got up and left did, however, seem to be somewhat one-sided. It was true that I could have wished that he had been able to stay longer with me, but it was with a look of despair on his face that he went away. I could never forget that look.

When I went back to my room, I found a poem on a torn-off scrap of paper attached to the hem of the gown which he had given me in exchange for my own,

> In sorrow gazing
> At the autumn moon at night,

> I wonder whether
> It was in reality
> Or in a dream that we met.

I wondered when he had found the time to write it.
I could no longer doubt the strength of his affection,
and taking advantage of every opportunity while he
was at the palace, I visited him in his room every other
night.

The priest must have carried out this series of
services with a lack of devotional purpose which must
have been most displeasing to Buddha, but in spite
of this, at the end of the twice-seven days of continual intercession, the ex-Emperor showed definite
signs of improvement in health, and after the third
period of seven days the prince went back to his
temple.

"When shall we have another opportunity of
meeting?" he had said to me the night before he
left. "I am afraid that the dust is going to collect on
the floor of the chapel of the invocation of the Sacred
Name of Amida and the fire on the altar will become
dim. If you feel about me as I do about you, you will
put on a habit of the same dark hue as mine and
retire with me into the depths of the mountains
where we may spend in peace our remaining years
in this transient world."

This proposal showed a sad lack of worldly wisdom
on the part of the prince and was really too shocking
even to consider. Yet I could not help being moved
by his words, wondering how long he had been turn-

ing over this scheme in his mind. It was sad indeed
to watch him getting up on this last morning as the
bell for dawn rang out and see him trying to hide his
tears which, I was much afraid, might reveal to all our
secret. So with the last day of the prayers for the ex-
Emperor's well-being, I was left alone with new worries added to a heart already overflowing with griefs
and anxieties.

In the ninth month the Ceremony of Offering
Flowers to Buddha was held, the shining newness of
the Rokujo palace adding beauty to the scene. As the
new ex-Emperor had asked that a lady might be
selected for his service, all the ladies were vying with
each other in attracting notice, but I remained gloomy
and unapproachable. After the ceremony the two
ex-Emperors went to the new palace at Fushimi to
plant pine tree seedlings. Lord Konoe was to have
accompanied them but instead he sent a poem expressing the hope that the newly-planted pine trees
might flourish for thousands of years to come,

> May the young pine trees
> Planted now at Fushimi
> Live a thousand years
> And flourish, together with
> the palace of Fushimi.

The ex-Emperor replied with a poem also praying
for the prosperity of the Fushimi palace,

> For a thousand years

> May the Fushimi palace
> Flourish and prosper
> As do the ancient pine trees
> Standing upon the mountain.

The two ex-Emperors stayed two days at Fushimi, held a drinking party together happily, then returned.

The story of the fan-maker's daughter

CHAPTER
V
Two years before, during the time when I was home for a little while in the seventh month, I had sent to be made up into a fan with camphor wood ribs a drawing on gold-dusted paper of a stream of water in pale blue with the words in white across the pale blue band, "Smoke of smouldering fires." The fan-maker's daughter, who was herself a clever artist, admired this fan and made a drawing of an autumn moon with the title, "The autumn moon seen from the other shore on that unforgettable night." I gave her my own fan in exchange for this.

When the ex-Emperor looked at this fan, he could see that it had been painted by someone else. "What man gave you that?" he asked.

To avoid any trouble from any suspicions he might have, I told him the whole story. The beauty of the drawing stirred his curiosity about the girl who had drawn it, and this excited his wandering fancies. For over two years he had pressed me to arrange a meeting with her. Somehow or other I managed this, and it was settled that the girl should visit him on the tenth day of the tenth month.

Restless with anticipation, he was ready, carefully dressed, when the Yamashina Chujo, Fujiwara no Sukeyuki, came to report that she had arrived.

"Let her wait in the carriage," he was told, "at the Fishing Pavilion at the south end of the Kyogoku front."

When the bell tolled at eight o'clock in the evening, the girl for whom the ex-Emperor had been waiting for over three years was ushered in to him. I was wearing a set of two robes with diagonal blue stripes and a pattern of ivy in purple, a light brown over-robe lined with dark red and a red mantle. Having been told to bring her into the eight-mat room adjoining the ex-Emperor's apartments, I went to the entrance where she was to alight. She made a great deal of noise getting out of the carriage; even the rustling of her garments seemed over-loud.

The room into which I showed her had been specially prepared, furnished and perfumed with incense. Her robe was embroidered with a pattern of large fans, fully one foot long, with cypress ribs. Over this she wore a cape of white, lined with blue, and a scarlet skirt. All her robes looked too ungainly and stiff, and her collar stuck up so high and wide as to hide her face completely from the back. She was really lovely with well-shaped eyes and nose and a fair skin. Perhaps she was not exactly of the princess type, but she was plump and tall and well-built so that I felt she would look splendid as a court lady with hair done in formal style, bearing the sword at a court function on one of the greater State occasions in the Daigokuden hall of the palace.

"She has entered the room," I reported to the ex-Emperor, and he went in to her, dressed in a formal light-coloured robe with a chrysanthemum pattern and wide-bottomed trousers, all so lavishly perfumed with incense that it could be smelt past the screens a hundred paces away. I listened to them talking and noted that she had much more to say than he had. That would not be to his liking, I thought to myself with a smile. They lay down, and I lay down outside the screens to keep night watch. Lord Sanekane was on night watch too, lying behind the screens in the next room. Everything was quiet. It seemed to me such a great pity that it should be so quiet so early in the night.

It was not very long before the ex-Emperor came out of the room and called me to him. " 'The village of Tamagawa,' " he quoted.[1] From this I understood that the girl had not come up to his expectations. I was sorry to hear this and told the girl to go back to her carriage before the midnight bell tolled. The ex-Emperor was so disappointed that after changing his clothes he refused to have anything to eat but asked me to massage him until he finally went to sleep.

It rained heavily during the night, and it was not

[1] The poem continues, "I was very miserable there."

until much later that I suddenly remembered the girl who had been sent away. Her sleeves would be drenched but not by the sorrow of a morning parting.

"What about the girl whom Sukeyuki brought?" I said to him.

"Oh, I'd completely forgotten about her," he said. "Go and see about her."

I went out to find that it was nearly dawn. Her carriage, which had been standing in front of the Fishing Pavilion, was in a dreadful condition through standing in the rain all the night.

"How awful!" I thought and called to the attendants to bring the carriage to the entrance. The men who had been sheltering under the roof of the gate came out and brought the carriage to the door. The girl was wet through, for the roof had leaked, and the design of the flowers painted on her robe could be seen through the upper robe, and all looked bedraggled. Her sleeves were doubly drenched with the tears she had shed the whole night through; her hair was as wet as if she had just washed it.

She would not get out of the carriage. "I'm not fit to be seen in these clothes," she said.

"I've a new robe I haven't worn yet," I said, rather curtly perhaps, for I was not too pleased with the way things had gone. "Come and put it on so that you can go and take leave of His Majesty. I am sorry you were kept waiting all this time. His Majesty had some important business to attend to."

She continued to weep bitterly and would not alight from the carriage. It was pathetic to see her rubbing her hands together as she pleaded to be allowed to go away. It was now nearly daylight, and there was nothing I could do but let her go.

"How cruel I have been to her!" the ex-Emperor said when I told him what had happened. He sent her a letter, but she did not answer it. Instead she sent a present, an inkstone lid of lacquer on which were engraved the words, "Like spiders in the confused maze of the reeds during a raging storm," no doubt symbolising thus the harassed state of her mind. Inside there was a pale blue sheet of paper with the words, "You led me astray," and wrapped up in this was a lock of hair and the poem,

> What story will be told
> Of this so humble woman
>   Who as by a dream
> Was deceived and led astray
> While trusting in your kindness?

That was all she wrote.

Wondering if she had entered the religious life, the ex-Emperor tried in vain to trace her. No one knew where she had gone. It was not till many years later that I learnt that she was at the Hashi temple in Kawachi province, where she was held in high respect by the nuns for the asceticism of her life. Her trying experience at the palace may have set her feet on the True Way of Buddha, and for that reason she may have come finally to regard it as a happy accident which was the occasion of her conversion.

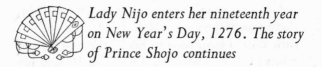

Lady Nijo enters her nineteenth year on New Year's Day, 1276. The story of Prince Shojo continues

CHAPTER About this time I received an unexpected letter from "Wan Morning Moon"[1] by **VI** the hand of an acolyte in his service. The very affectionate tone of the letter rather surprised me as, although he had written to me several times, he had made no further effort to meet me. I was not entirely free from longing for his presence, but at the same time I was quite content that he should be so far away.

So the New Year came. The two ex-Emperors arranged a cherry-blossom party, and as we were kept busy searching in the remote recesses of the mountains for beautiful sprays of flowers for the competition, I had no leisure this spring for secret meetings with my lover. For this reason I only sent him letters expressing my sorrow at my loneliness.

This year I remained in service at the palace until the autumn. Then, about the middle of the ninth month, I received a long letter from my uncle, Lord Takaaki, in which he said, "I have something I wish to say to you. I am at the Izumoji temple. There is a lady here who wishes to see you. Be certain to come here to see me. I will do all I can for you."

[1] Here for the first time the Ajari, Prince Shojo, is referred to by this pet name.

My uncle had taken it for granted that I was just as eager for this meeting as the other party was. My uncle had known him since he was a child, and the prince had asked my uncle for help as he was a relative of mine. I could not but excuse my uncle's tricking me in this way as it showed his love for me.

When we met, however, I was so disgusted, repelled, and finally horrified by his ardour that I could not say a word. "I could do nothing but just sit upright in the middle of the bed."[2] Still, even then, I could appreciate the humour of the situation.

All through the night, with floods of tears, he pleaded and promised, but I remained indifferent, determined never to agree to meet him again. "This night marks the end," I decided.

At last the crowing of the cocks told us that it was time to get up. This brought fresh outpourings from his sad heart, but to me the coming of day brought the promise of a release from this most embarrassing situation. Outside the screens Lord Takaaki coughed to call him out and he left. But just before they were about to leave the house, the prince came back and, after saying this and that, begged me at least to see them off at the door.

"I don't feel well enough," I answered, still lying in bed. It was pitiable to see him go out leaving his heart behind. I felt I was doing him a great wrong.

[2] Referring to the poem (anon.) in *Kokinshu,* the tenth-century anthology, / Assailed by love / From the bottom of the bed / As well as the head, / I could do nothing but just / sit upright in the middle.

Feeling that my uncle's conduct was far from praise-worthy, I excused myself by saying that I had work to do at the palace and hurried back to my duties before it was really daylight without seeing him. Lying in bed then in my own room, I recalled with horror all the events of the night, all the prince's pleas and pledges.

His letter arrived about noon, filled with pro-testations of his love. With it was the poem,

> My great misery
> Or sadness I cannot tell;
> I long to see you,
> For vividly your image
> Is impressed on my mind's eye.

Now that his passion neither saddened nor horrified me, I felt I had nothing to say to him who was so consumed with love. I made no answer to his letter except by this poem,

> I cannot tell if
> My mind is changed or not;
> I care not whether
> Your love for me has grown cold
> Or whether steadfast remains.

After that he continued to write to me occasional-ly, but I did not answer his letters, much less arrange to meet him, and evaded any approach which he made. Then, possibly because it was nearing the end of the year, he wrote again. His letter was in a sealed envelope enclosed in a letter from my uncle.

"I am enclosing a letter," my uncle wrote. "It is a pity things have turned out as they have. You must not let yourself become obsessed with dislike of his manner. It is perhaps by the force of destiny that he is attracted to you. You repulsed him in a very abrupt way. I regret everything went wrong. It will make me most unhappy if you reply as unkindly this time as you did before."

The prince's letter was wrapped in a piece of stout paper and securely sealed at both ends with rice paste. Inside it were a number of amulets and charms issued by the ancient Kumano shrine and all the great shrines and temples of Japan with the names of countless gods and Buddhas written on the backs of the amulets.

"Since I became a follower of Buddha, when I was seven years of age," the prince wrote, "I have lived a life of perfect asceticism. Weaving spells with my hands over the fires of invocation on the altar, I have prayed on the one hand for long life for all the members of the Imperial house and on the other for the forgiveness of sins and the happy rebirth in the next world of all the nation committed to its charge. I was hoping, with the assistance of all the gods, the saints and Buddhas, to continue this work all my life, but by some evil destiny during these last two years my mind has to my great grief been obsessed by thoughts of you. When I opened the volume of a much-loved sutra to read before the image of Buddha, it was the words that you had spoken that came into my mind. I kept your letters on the altar as if they were the words of the sacred writings. I read them first to comfort myself when I lighted the candles on the altar. When my longing for you became unbearable, I consulted your uncle, Lord Takaaki, to find some way of meeting you. I thought that you could not but have the same longing for me as I had for you. I found I was wrong in this. I have now to abandon all hope of writing to you and talking with you. Yet as I find it completely impossible to drive all thoughts of you away from my mind, I am destined to suffer all the torments of purgatory. Penances can be of no avail to me either in this world or the next. I can only pray that the austerities I have undergone in this world may aid me in making my life here futile and help me in the next world in purgatory to which I must pass as a soul with a curse laid on it. I have no memory at all of my life before my head was shaved and I put on a black monastic habit when I took my vows at seven years of age. Since that time, though, I can swear that I have never even dreamt of sleeping with a woman or even for a moment entertained the thought of falling in love with one. You have been the only woman in my life. And now I must give you up. I regret that, thinking that he always speaks the truth, I trusted Lord Takaaki in my last effort to renew our relationship."

I realised how deep the prince's grief was, and it saddened me. But there was nothing I could do about it. The sight of all the sacred names of gods including that of the Sun Goddess herself filled me with horror.

I collected together all the amulets, wrapped them in a sheet of paper, on which I wrote,

> I shed bitter tears,
> As I ponder over this,
> This sorrowful fact,
> That this is the last letter
> I shall ever have from you,

and sent the parcel to the prince. I heard nothing further from him at this time.

Lady Nijo enters her twentieth year on New Year's Day, 1277. The ladies of the court play ball

CHAPTER
VII

Nothing else worth recording took place before New Year's Day when Prince Shojo came early to pay a New Year visit to the ex-Emperor and was entertained to wine. No one else was present, and everything was extremely quiet. I could not avoid waiting on them.

"Serve him with wine," the ex-Emperor ordered. I stood up to do so, and everything went black. I felt dizzy, and my nose began to bleed. I had to leave the room, and for the next ten days I was seriously ill. I was terrified, thinking that this might be due to the curses the prince had called down on me.

In the second month the new ex-Emperor Kame-yama paid a visit to the ex-Emperor. They enjoyed an archery contest together, using the short bow.

"If you lose," said the new ex-Emperor, "you must show me all your ladies-in-waiting, high and low. If I lose, I will do the same." This was agreed.

The ex-Emperor lost the match. "I will let you know about the parade of the ladies," he said afterwards to the new ex-Emperor.

After the new ex-Emperor had left, the ex-Emperor consulted the Nyudo[1] Dainagon Fujiwara no Sukesue and other lords as to how the parade should be arranged. "Have you any original ideas?" he asked.

"It would not do," the lords agreed when they were consulted, "to have them all sitting side by side as they do in the ladies' apartment on New Year's Day. And it would certainly not be a happy idea to have them come in one by one for an interview; that would be too much as if they were coming in to consult a fortune-teller or a palmist."

"Wouldn't it be a good idea," the ex-Emperor said, "to have two ceremonial barges built? Then the ladies could stand in them carrying vases, as the ladies did in *The Tale of Genji*."

The lords did not agree; it would cost too much to have two barges built.

"I suggest," said Lord Sukesue, "that eight of the high-ranking ladies, eight of the middle rank and eight of the lower rank should play ball, dressed as boys, on the Mandarin Orange courtyard."

[1]The title given to a noble who had entered religion.

All the lords agreed to this and so it was decided. Each of the ladies was to have a man of corresponding rank as her adviser. All the ladies were to wear ordinary male robes with trousers, shoes and socks.

The ladies did not favour the idea. "How perfectly awful!" they said. "All the more so as the game is to take place in the daytime." They all felt terribly miserable about it, but there was nothing they could do about it, and so they began to make their preparations for the game.

Lord Sanekane was my gallant. He had prepared for me a boy's robe and trousers of pale blue with an under-robe of scarlet. On my left sleeve was a design of a miniature waterfall in white thread over rocks of aloe wood, and on my right sleeve a spray of cherry blossom with fallen blossoms scattered below it. On my trousers also there were designs of rocks and weirs with scattered cherry blossoms. This was all to call to mind the words of the poem in *The Tale of Genji,*

> Thus was I moved to tears by
> The sound of the waterfall.

Lady Gon Dainagon, who had the Nyudo Lord Sukesue as her gallant, wore a robe and trousers of pale green lining. On her left sleeve was a design of a miniature castle tower and on her right cherry blossoms, with a bamboo branch on the left leg of her trousers and a lighthouse on the right. Her under-robes were scarlet. The main hall was divided off into sections by screens, and the sight of the ladies all dressed in similar style but differing in details was a most interesting one.

We ladies were all of the opinion that it would be enough if each of us in turn took the gaily decorated ball and placed it in front of the ex-Emperors, but it was decided that according to the rules the ball must be kicked and that each of us must catch the ball in our outstretched sleeves, take off our shoes, and present the ball to the new ex-Emperor. As the ladies begged with tears to be excused from kicking the balls, it was agreed that Lady Shin-emon, in the service of the ex-Empress Higashi Nijo, should do the kicking on behalf of the ladies of higher rank. She had the reputation of being extremely skilful at this game, not that I consider this a particularly enviable accomplishment. I felt rather elated, for at the head of the eight ladies of higher rank, I was to catch the ball and place it in front of the new ex-Emperor.

The two ex-Emperors and the ex-Emperor Go Fukakusa's son, the recently appointed Crown Prince, were to sit at the southern front of the main hall with the bamboo blinds raised, princes and lords being seated on both sides of the steps with courtiers standing about here and there in the courtyard to see the ladies cross the southern courtyard, each accompanied by her gallant, all in robes of different colours.

The new ex-Emperor arrived just after noon, and the banquet started soon afterwards.

"Quickly now," said the master of the ceremonies,

Nakamikado no Tamekata, "Start the ball game at once."

"We are going to begin right away," we answered. But we did not actually start until it was so dark that torches had to be used.

The new ex-Emperor had asked that all the ladies should be announced by name, and so when each of the ladies came before our guest, with sleeves folded over in front of her, her gallant, torch in hand, announced her name and rank as she passed in front of him. Too shy to say a word, first the ladies of lower rank passed by, then those of middle rank, and finally those of higher rank. All then stood in order among the newly planted trees, making a perfectly beautiful sight. For myself, when I had placed my ball before the new ex-Emperor, I tried to hasten away, but I was told to stay awhile and serve the wine. Still in my boy's costume, I felt very shy doing this.

For two or three days previous to the game, each lady's gallant had been constantly in and out of his ward's apartment, seeing after her hair styling, the fitting of her boy's costume and her shoes. One can easily imagine that all sorts of pleasant happenings were enjoyed in each one of the apartments.

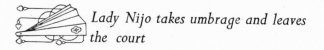 *Lady Nijo takes umbrage and leaves the court*

CHAPTER The ex-Emperor having won the return
match, the new ex-Emperor invited him
VIII to the Saga palace[1] where his thirteen-
year-old daughter, Princess Togosho, so named because she had been brought up in secret by Lady
Azechi, was to perform the Dance of the Five Maidens.
She would be supported by ladies of the highest rank
dressed as attendants and servants; by lords, their
cloaks wadded at the bottoms; and by courtiers,
their shoulders bared, all parading on the roofless
stage erected between the main halls from the northern
guardroom. Everyone enjoyed the dancing and the
music on various instruments.

When this entertainment came to an end, however,
the ex-Emperor wished for more. He issued another
challenge to an archery contest and, being defeated
in this, had to arrange to have a concert given by his
ladies at the Fushimi palace in exact reproduction of
that given at the Rokujo palace as described in *The
Tale of Genji.*

The Lady of the East Wing was to play the part of

---

[1] Literally, "Out-of-the-way palace." She was generally believed
to have been the daughter of the ex-Emperor Kameyama by his
half-sister, Princess Gojo, this being the reason for her residence
being called by this name.

Lady Murasaki, Genji's much loved second wife. The role of the Third Princess, intended by her father, the Emperor Suzaku, to be Prince Genji's wife, was to be taken by the young daughter of my grandfather, Takachika, the Minister of War, who had just entered service at court. She was, however, to play a thirteen-stringed harp instead of a seven-stringed one. I was annoyed, rather unreasonably perhaps, at this arrangement which had been made at my grandfather's insistence, and would have liked to have been excused from appearing in the concert altogether. The ex-Emperor insisted that I should be present, however, to play the lute in the role of Lady Akashi, Prince Genji's lover while he was in exile at Akashi. The new ex-Emperor knew me, having had some conversation with me on the occasion of the ladies' ball game.

With regard to playing the lute, I had studied under my uncle, Koga no Masamitsu, when I was seven years old, and had learnt two or three pieces. I am afraid, however, that I was not a particularly diligent student at that time. Later, when I was nine years of age, I took up the lute again with the ex-Emperor as my teacher. I could play a few simple pieces but was not good enough to tackle the three classical compositions for the lute. When I was ten, I did take part in a recital of court dance and music at the Shirakawa palace at the celebration of the fiftieth birthday of the Retired Emperor Go Saga. On this occasion he made me a present of a lute of Chinese quince wood with four rosewood tuning pegs in a red brocade bag. Still, although I had practised on the lute from time to time, it was never with any great enthusiasm, and I was rather embarrassed at the ex-Emperor's insistence, but I went on with preparations for the concert.

I was instructed to wear just what Lady Akashi reportedly wore, a white under-robe with blue lining, a scarlet robe with an over-robe of light green, and a cloak of pinkish yellow lined with light green.

I wondered why it was that I had been given the part of Lady Akashi, who was not one of the principal characters in the story, while one of the main roles went to the Lady of the East Wing, who was actually not much better than a beginner in playing the six-stringed harp, for she had never made it a rule to practise every day. Obviously everything had been arranged by the War Minister so that his young daughter would have the opportunity of playing the thirteen-stringed harp.

The part of the Princess of Akashi, Lady Akashi's daughter, was to be played by the Lady of the West Wing, a daughter of the Kazan-in Chief Minister, Fujiwara no Michimasa, who was therefore entitled to sit side by side with Lady Murasaki. I was told to sit in the highest position on the opposite side, actually in the same place in which I had sat at the ball game. I did not agree with this decision, for it appeared to me that the newcomer, the Minister of War's daughter, should have had a higher seat than mine, as she was playing the part of the Third Princess. There was, however, nothing that I could do about it as this was the ex-Emperor's decision.

I went to Fushimi in the carriage with the ex-Emperor, while the newcomer drove there in her own basket-work carriage, adorned with her family crest and attended by her father's retainers. Recalling happier days, I was most unhappy to see her arrive in such a stately fashion.

The new ex-Emperor arrived and the banquet began in another room while the ladies took their places for the concert, each with her own instrument in front of her, just as in the scene described in the chapter "Young Herbs," of *The Tale of Genji*. The ex-Emperor was to take the part of Prince Genji, the hero of the story, while the new ex-Emperor had the role of General Yugiri, his son. Lord Kanetada and the Toin Chujo were to play the flute and flageolet below the steps. The ladies' seats had all been checked again and all was ready for the ex-Emperors to come in from the banquet, when my grandfather, the War Minister, came in and looked over to where the ladies were sitting.

"This is all wrong," he shouted. "My daughter is playing the part of a princess. The girl's part is that of a mere gentlewoman; she should not be sitting in a higher position than my daughter. My daughter is actually that girl's aunt; a niece should never take precedence over her aunt. And I hold a higher rank than her father ever did. They will have to change seats."

Lord Takaaki and Lord Sanekane tried to intervene. "The ex-Emperor suggested this arrangement," they said.

The Minister would not listen. "In any case, there's

no sense or reason in this arrangement,'' he said. No one else would venture to express any further opinion. The ex-Emperor was away in another room where no one could disturb him in the middle of the banquet. I was therefore obliged to move down to a lower position. I was utterly downcast as I thought of the grand style in which the newcomer had arrived in her own carriage with her father's retainers attending her, and now she was supplanting me. I could see no reason why the order of seating should depend on who was whose aunt. Some aunts have mothers of low birth. I could see that there was nothing to be gained by staying at an entertainment which would bring disgrace upon me. I got up and went out of the hall.

When I reached my room, I wrote a letter for the maid to give to the ex-Emperor if he came to look for me with a message that I had returned to the Capital. In the letter I enclosed the first string of my lute cut into two pieces and a poem on thin white paper,

> Now I have been shown
> How worthless I am indeed;
> And in this knowledge
> I vow that henceforth never
> Will I play the lute again.

From Fushimi I went to Kobayashi nearby to the home of my old nurse's mother, Lady Iyo, who had been in the service of Princess Sen-yomon and who on the death of her mistress had taken vows and settled down near her tomb at the Sokujoin temple.

I was told later that, when the ex-Emperors left the banquet to come to the hall and found no one there to play the lute in the part of Lady Akashi, they inquired the reason and the Lady of the East Wing explained just what had happened.

"It is natural that Agako would take offence at that," the ex-Emperor said. He went to my room, where he received my message. Much displeased to hear that I had left the palace, he showed my message to his guest.

"A very pathetic message," commented the new ex-Emperor. "Well, this has spoiled the evening's entertainment. Still, there's nothing we can do about that. May I keep this poem?" He was given the poem and returned to his own palace.

And the outcome of it all was that the newcomer completely lost her chance of playing the harp to the distinguished company. People's reactions were generally sympathetic to me. "The War Minister was crazy to act like that," people agreed when they discussed the incident. "Or can we say that it was due to an old man's silly prejudices? In any case, Agako did the right thing."

Early the next morning the ex-Emperor sent his men to the house of my old nurse at Shijo-Omiya and to the house of my father's step-mother at Rokkaku Kushige, but they had to report that the people there had no knowledge of my whereabouts. He then sent his men to other likely places, but no one could tell him where I had gone.

For myself, it was in my mind all this time to take

this opportunity to renounce the world, but already in the twelfth month, feeling unwell, I had realised that I was pregnant again. I had therefore to postpone once more taking this step. I did, however, make a vow not to play the lute again, and presented the lute given me by the late Emperor Go Saga to the Hachiman shrine at Iwashimizu. With it I presented a copy of the Lotus Flower sutra which I had copied on the backs of my father's letters to me. A poem on the sutra explained the reason for this gift,

> As now I have vowed
> Never to play it again,
> I present my lute,
> Together with the sutra
> I have copied, to the shrine.

I reflected that it was just two years before this time that Prince Shojo had first confessed his love for me, and that it was a year and a half later, in the twelfth month, that he had sent me that terrible letter laying all those curses upon me. Soon after that, on the twelfth day of the third month, I had left the palace where I had lived so long, and had also given up the lute I so much enjoyed playing. I had also lost at the same time the affection of my grandfather whom I had regarded as my guardian after my father's death. "She left the concert because she disagreed with my instructions," he would explain to all. "Consequently she will never come back as long as I live." It frightened me to death to think that there was now no way in which I could restore the old friendly relations between us.

The ex-Emperor went on searching for me, and Snowy Dawn[2] sought for me in vain in every shrine and temple. But I remained concealed in the house at Kobayashi till I moved to the nunnery of the Abbess Shingambo at Daigo.

 Lady Nijo discloses her whereabouts to her uncle, Lord Takaaki

CHAPTER IX Soon afterwards I learnt that the War Minister was having a stand erected for a party including the two ex-Emperors whom he was inviting to view the Aoi festival procession. In the same month initiation ceremonies were to be held for the Emperor Go Uda and the Crown Prince, Prince Hirohito, on their attaining manhood. A noble of mature age of the rank of Dainagon was required to preside over the rites, and the War Minister, in his anxiety to demonstrate his loyalty to the throne, arranged that his son the Zenshoji Dainagon Takaaki should temporarily relinquish his title in his own favour so that he could take this lower rank in order to preside at the ceremony, an action which called forth high praise from everyone. When

[2] Here for the first time Lady Nijo uses this pet name for her lover, Lord Sanekane.

the Minister relinquished the post, however, instead of it being restored to Lord Takaaki, it was given to Yoshida no Tsuneto.

Lord Takaaki was understandably very bitter about this transaction, ascribing this loss of the office to his father's underhand tricks. It appeared to him that his parent was working for the eventual promotion to the post of his son by his second wife, Takayoshi. Feeling that it was impossible for him to continue living in his father's house any longer, he went to live in his wife's family home, that of the Kujo Chunagon, Fujiwara no Tadataka, and confined himself to the house there.

When I heard it, the news came as a great shock to me. I thought at first of going to see him, but, realising that the news of my reappearance would soon get abroad, I sent him a letter telling him where I was and asking him to come to visit me.

"Ever since I heard the news that you had disappeared so completely," he wrote in answer, "I have been very depressed. How happy I am now to learn that you are safe and well. I will come to you this evening to talk over the unhappy events that have occurred to us recently."

My uncle came as soon as it was dark. It was the end of the fourth month. The cherry trees were green with leaves. Only the last of the blossoms gleamed white in the moonlight. In the dark shade of the trees, deer could be seen, some lying down, others wandering slowly about. It was a picture I should love to have painted. And over this peaceful scene, from the neighbouring temples the evening bells rang out.

We were in the anteroom of the chapel from where we could hear the constant repetition of the invocation of the sacred name of Amida Buddha. The sight of the nuns in their hempen habits coming out of the chapel in solemn procession affected my uncle deeply. A big burly man, he was not easily moved by such things, but now he wiped away his tears with his silk sleeve.

"I am resolved," he said, "to cut myself free from all the ties of human affection and, renouncing all the things of this world, enter upon the True Path. The only consideration which has delayed me thus far has been your father's fervent request to me on his deathbed that I should not be negligent in my duty as your guardian. He would be right to reproach me if I failed him in this." Though weeping at the thought of parting from him for good, I could not but approve of his resolution to renounce the world. My thin sleeves were damp with my tears.

"When my time is over," I said, "I too will retire into the depths of the mountains. Then I will put on the same sombre habit as you." Thus we talked on, expressing to each other the sad thoughts of our hearts.

"Prince Shojo's last letter," my uncle went on, "was really horrible, wasn't it? Even though I knew that I was not to blame for my part in the affair, my hair stood on end as I read it. I cannot help feeling that all the misfortunes which have come upon us

recently are all due to his curse. While I was searching for you, I came across him one day as he was
coming back from the palace. He asked me whether
it was true that you had disappeared completely. I
answered that at the moment your whereabouts were
unknown. I do not know what kind of impression this
made on him, but he stood for a moment at the main
gate, hiding with his fan the tears streaming down his
face, and then recited the words of the sutra in a low
voice: "In the raging fire of this world there is no
peace." I feel a deep compassion for anyone who so
yearns, who is so sad, wretched, and woebegone.
How much more does it grieve me to see him suffer
thus! One can hardly imagine the frame of mind in
which he returns to his temple to offer up his worship
to Buddha."

While I listened to my uncle, I recalled that night
when the prince and I had met amicably for the last
time. In his poem he had expressed his doubt, as he
looked up at the autumn moon, as to whether it was
in dream or in reality that we had met. I wondered
why it was that at our last meeting I had resisted him
so stubbornly. Filled with vain regrets, I wept bitterly.

At last day broke. "What will people think?" my
uncle said as he left. "They will be sure that I am
returning from a love tryst." Then, changing his tone,
he added, "As a motive for taking your vows, you
must never forget the emotions we have shared this
night and those with which we part this morning."
He expressed in a poem his feelings about the uncer-
tainty of life and his grief at his own misfortune,

How easy it is
To forget life's uncertainties,
    And forgetting this,
How bitter the tears we weep
When forced to encounter this!

"We all know we must expect to suffer in this life," I said. "And yet we grieve when misfortunes overwhelm us. I am sadder still when I realise that this is so." This thought, that the bitterest thing in life is the difficulty of persuading ourselves that life is really uncertain, I expressed in a poem,

All men are agreed
That this life is uncertain;
    Surely sad it is
How difficult we find it
To force ourselves to believe it!

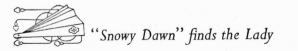 *"Snowy Dawn" finds the Lady*

CHAPTER
X
Worried because he could find no trace of me, Snowy Dawn had gone into retreat at the Kasuga shrine for two periods of seven days to pray for my safe return. On the eleventh night of his vigil, he dreamt that he saw me standing in front of the Second shrine there, looking just as I used to look before I went away. He immediately went to the

Second shrine as quickly as he could, and at Fujinomori he met a servant of my uncle's carrying a long narrow letter case. Wondering why the servant was there, he surmised that he was returning from delivering a letter to me from my uncle. Feeling quite sure that this was the case, he spoke to the servant before he could utter a word.

"You are on your way back from the Shokutei temple, aren't you?" he said. "Have you heard when Lady Nijo is taking her vows?"

It seemed to the servant that this lord was well informed about my whereabouts. "Last night Lord Takaaki came from Kujo to visit her," he said. "He went home this morning and I am just coming back from taking a letter to her. I have not heard when she is entering religion, but it seems certain that she will be doing so sooner or later."

Overjoyed at getting news of me, he took the horse his servant was riding and presented it to the Kasuga shrine as a token of his gratitude. Then, fearing that to visit me in the daytime might cause some scandal at the temple, he went, as I learnt later, to the house of a priest at Upper Daigo to wait for dark.

Meanwhile, knowing nothing of this, I was nearby at Lower Daigo, enjoying the view of the summer foliage in the garden and listening to the Abbess Shingambo speaking on the teachings of the Great Teacher of Jodo Buddhism, Zendo. Towards evening, without any warning, there was the sound of someone stepping up on to the verandah. At first I took no notice of this, thinking that it must be one of the nuns. Then I heard the rustle of silk robes. I turned and saw Snowy Dawn closing the sliding door.

"You have shown your spirit of independence by hiding yourself away here," he said to me, "but the god of the Kasuga shrine has guided me to you."

My heart fluttered in my alarm. But there was no way for me to escape. I was caught. "I felt bitter against everyone," I said, "and so I left the court. I felt I could make no distinction between one person and another." I went on talking at random in this way, saying what was in my inmost heart, things I would really have preferred to have remained unspoken. Realisation of this made me all the more sad and confused. Still, I thought, I had now taken the decisive step of leaving the court, and I had no intention of returning there. Yet, on the other hand, I could not help wondering who would take tender care of me in my delicate condition.

"His Majesty's affection for you," he said, "was not something you could discard as being half-hearted. It was not very clever of you to run away just because the War Minister acted in a senile fashion. Just for this once, trust His Majesty to see that justice is done to you and return to the palace." So he continued to urge me, staying with me for the night and all the next day.

During the day he sent a letter to my uncle. "By chance," he wrote, "I discovered that the Lady was here, and so I came to see her. I should like to see you too."

In response to this request, my uncle came to see

me again that evening. Just to kill time, as they said, they drank together the whole of the night.

As he was leaving early next morning, my uncle stopped for one last word with Snowy Dawn. "You had better tell His Majesty that in the course of your search for her, you found her here," said Snowy Dawn.

So they talked things over, and Snowy Dawn decided to go home too this morning, leaving me alone and feeling very miserable.

I went out to the entrance to see them off. My uncle left while it was still dark. "I don't want to be seen on the way back," he said. He was wearing a robe of figured silk crepe with a pattern of gourd vines climbing over a basket-work fence. Snowy Dawn, dressed in a light orange robe, left towards daybreak just as the bright full moon was setting over the hill top.

While his carriage was being brought round, he walked along the verandah to talk to the abbess. "I am glad I have had the unexpected pleasure of meeting you again," he said.

"It is our faith," she replied, "that through our constant invocation of the sacred name of Amida, the Buddha will appear attended by two saints to lead us to Paradise. We live in a remote spot here, and it is because of the Lady's chance stay that nobles such as you, still wearing the dress of the people of the world outside, bring a certain brightness to our lives."

"In spite of a diligent search everywhere in every corner of the countryside," he said, "we could find no trace of the Lady, but by the guidance in a dream of the god of the Kasuga shrine at Mikasa, we found her at last with you.'' The whole incident was, I felt, just like the story in *The Tale of Sumiyoshi*[1] where the hero finds the lady who has disappeared.

The tolling of the dawn bell was urging his departure, and, as he hurried out, I heard him murmuring to himself. I asked him to speak up and he repeated the poem,

> Now I have found you,
> My worries for you are gone,
>   Yet sad is the bell
> Warning me to part from you
> Under the wan moon of dawn.

I was also sad to see him go, and whispered to myself the poem,

> The sound of the bell
> Reminds me of the sorrows
>   And troubles of life,
> And the moon makes me all the more
> Unwilling to have you depart.

All the resolutions I had been making during this long period were that day utterly destroyed. The

1 *Sumiyoshi Monogatari* as now extant is an adaptation probably made in the Kamakura era of the original, now lost, mentioned in *Genji Monogatari*. Like *Ochikubo Monogatari*, it is the tale of a cruel step-mother, with a happy ending.

abbess agreed with me that I must go back to the court. "The advice which the two lords have given you is reasonable," she said. "When messengers from the ex-Emperor came and asked for you, I was able to say quite truthfully that you were not here. Now that they will report that they have found you here, it will make things easier for us if you return to the house at Kobayashi."

This appeared to be the best course to take, and so I went there in the carriage I had asked my uncle to lend me. "This is certainly a very pleasant surprise," my old nurse's mother Iyo said to me that evening as we talked after an uneventful day with her. "Since you left we have had several visits from messengers of the ex-Emperor. Lord Sugawara no Kiyonaga often came."

Listening to her, I was sadly reminded of my troubles, so aptly expressed by the words quoted by Wan Morning Moon, "There is no rest in the raging fire of this world." Hearing amid the showers of the fourth month the first call of the cuckoo from the greenery of the Otowa hills, I composed the poem,

> Ask me, dear cuckoo,
> Why I weep so bitterly,
>   And I shall reply,
> "Because the sky is gloomy
> Though the moon is shining above."

It was still dark when the nuns arose to sing their matins. The bells of the Sokujo-in temple wakened me with a start, and I got up to recite a sutra.

Later that morning I received a letter from Snowy Dawn, enclosing a letter from his retainer who had cut down the thorny smilax bushes.[2] He told me how lonely and forlorn he had felt when he had left me. "Your memories of our child," he went on, "must be as indistinct as a face seen in a dream, for you have never seen her since she was taken away from you so soon after her birth. To this you may well have become resigned as being something that could not be helped. Since spring, however, the child has been rather unwell, and as it seemed that it might be something serious, the soothsayers have been consulted. They are of the opinion that the illness is caused by the child's mother's anxiety about her. It is natural that a child should know of her mother's love for her. Next time you come to the Capital, I will arrange to let you see her."

I wondered what to do. My love for the child and my desire to see her again were not unbearably strong, but still the memory of her had not entirely gone from my mind. Sometimes, indeed, I could recall clearly what she looked like, and I wondered how she was growing. I considered that it was quite possible that her illness was caused by our separation, and decided I ought to go and see her soon.

"Your news alarms me," I wrote in reply. "Please let me see her as soon as it is convenient." The child was on my mind all the day; I dreaded to think that I might soon be hearing bad news about her.

[2] Why should such a letter be enclosed? It must be that this retainer had been entrusted with the care of Nijo's daughter by Snowy Dawn.

That evening the early evening service was being held, and I was in the chapel where an ancient nun was reciting from a sutra something about "an opportunity of salvation," when, the folding doors being open, there was a sound of people entering the courtyard. I had no curiosity as to who it was, nor did I particularly care; I was not expecting a visitor. Then the sliding doors of the chapel were opened, and I saw a palanquin escorted by warriors and officers. It was the ex-Emperor who had arrived. His visit was so unexpected that I just stood there feeling like a fool. Our eyes met. We gazed at each other. It was no longer possible for me to run away and hide. I could only stand there motionless while the palanquin halted before me, and the ex-Emperor got out.

"I have had much trouble getting here," he said to me. I could make no answer. Then turning to the officers, he went on, "Have the palanquin sent away and get the carriage ready." He turned to me, and while we waited for the carriage, he said, "I came to fetch you because you seemed determined to renounce the world. You may have good reason for feeling offended with the War Minister, but you have no cause for complaint against me."

This was true enough, and I could not but agree. I explained, however, that feeling this world to be full of miseries, my grandfather's spiteful action was only the occasion and not the cause of my resolution to renounce the world.

"I was on a visit to Saga palace," he went on, "when I learnt that you were here. Thinking that there was sure to be some slip-up if I left it to someone else, I decided to come here myself, telling them I was going to Fushimi palace. Whatever you feel about the depressing things that have occurred, let us talk them over quietly together in the carriage.'' So, listening to him justifying himself in this way, I found myself getting into the carriage with him, just as weak-willed as I had always been.

Sitting in the carriage throughout the whole of that night, he protested his innocence of any complicity in the War Minister's action, and swore by the Sacred Mirror[3] and the war god, Hachiman, that he would always think as much of me as he did of anyone else. Much moved by this, I felt more inclined to go back to the court, although I still had the uneasy feeling that I was letting slip a good opportunity of freeing myself from the troubles of this world. As it came up to dawn, I agreed to go with him, realising that in any case this was inevitable now.

At the palace, all things in my own apartments had been sent home, and I went to the house of my aunt, Lady Kyogoku. On my return to court, I found that life there rather jarred on me, but about the last day of the fourth month my maternity belt was presented to me by the ex-Emperor, an episode which brings back several memories.

---

[3] One of the divine symbols which comprise the Imperial regalia. The others are the sword of Kusanagi and the curved jewels of Yasakani.

 *Lady Nijo sees her child*

CHAPTER At last I was able to see the baby girl who
up to this time I had seen only in my
XI dreams. I saw her in a strange house, as it
was not convenient to do so in the place where she
usually lived. I had suggested that I see her on my
way to visit my mother's tomb on the anniversary
of her death, the fifth day of the fifth month. But
this date was inconvenient, and it was also pointed out
that it would in any case be most unlucky to see her on
my way to visit a tomb. So on the thirtieth day of the
fourth month, I went to the appointed place. The
child wore a white silk robe with a raised pattern, lined
with dark red. Her hair had been allowed to grow
for the last three months; I was much moved to note
that it looked just as I remembered it to have been on
the day she was born.

Just about the time that my child was born, Snowy
Dawn's wife had given birth to a child which had died
soon after birth. My child had therefore been taken into
his family, and no one but those directly concerned
knew of the circumstances. They were thinking of
allowing her to enter the service of the court and were
obviously bringing her up with the greatest of care. In
these circumstances it would have been perverse for
me to feel anything but happiness that the child was so
fortunate in her life simply because she was now

regarded as someone else's child. The ex-Emperor still knew nothing of this rather discreditable episode and firmly believed that I was dependent solely on his protection. For myself, I could not feel otherwise than shocked at my duplicity.

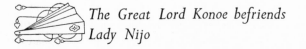 *The Great Lord Konoe befriends Lady Nijo*

CHAPTER   About the eighth month the Great Lord
  XII   Konoe visited the ex-Emperor. The late
          Emperor Go Saga had on his death bed
begged him to give the ex-Emperor the same support as he had always given him, and consequently he often visited the ex-Emperor, who invariably showed him great hospitality. That day he was entertained informally to drinks in the usual hall.

"In what remote mountain then did you hide yourself?" he asked when he saw me. "I was told that you couldn't be found anywhere."

"Even a miracle-working mountain hermit would have had difficulty in finding her," said the ex-Emperor. "I found her on the mountain-island of Eternal Youth."

"Certainly," said the Great Lord to the ex-Emperor, "the War Minister's exhibition of senile jealousy was really inexcusable. Also, Lord Takaaki's enforced retirement was quite absurd. It appears to me to show faults in the court administration." Then he turned to me. "By the way, have you entirely given up playing the lute?" he said. I remained silent.

"She has sworn a solemn oath to the guardian-god of her family, Hachiman, on behalf of herself and all her descendants, to give up playing the lute in perpetuity," said the ex-Emperor.

"Well," the Great Lord said to me, "in spite of your extreme youth, you have succeeded in causing a great scandal by what you have done. The members of your family, the Koga family, have on the whole had a high regard for the reputation of their family. They can claim to have had an unblemished record since the foundation of the family by the Emperor Murakami. The family of your old nurse's husband, Nakatsuna, has furnished loyal retainers for the Koga family for generations. I recall that my elder brother, the Imperial Adviser, Konoe no Kanetsune, at one time wished to have Nakatsuna in his own service, but when he was asked, Nakatsuna replied that he could not do so as he was a retainer of Koga no Masatada. In answer to this, it is said, the Imperial Adviser replied in a letter in his own handwriting that the Koga family was an exceptional one and that there could be no objection to his being at the same time in the service of the Imperial Adviser. It was really quite absurd also for your grandfather, Lord Takachika, to argue that, as his daughter was your aunt, she should therefore take precedence over you. When my son, the former Imperial Adviser, Tadatsukasa no Mototada, visited the new ex-Emperor, in the course of conversation the new ex-Emperor expressed the opinion that the writing of poetry was the best accomplishment for a lady to cultivate and that he had been much impressed by your poem composed in the difficult circumstances brought about by your grandfather's actions. While it was true, he admitted, that the study of poetry had been traditional in the Koga family for eight generations, it was indeed remarkable that a lady as young as you are should have mastered the art so completely. The conversation having now turned to the question of your disappearance, the new ex-Emperor informed him that at that moment your old nurse's son, Nakayori, was out searching for you at every shrine and temple throughout the country and that he himself was greatly distressed because no trace of you could be found." Then, changing the subject, he went on, "By the way, my son, the Chunagon Chujo, is very talented in singing Imayo popular songs. Would Your Majesty please initiate him into the mysteries of this accomplishment?"

The ex-Emperor agreed to do this. "The Capital is not a suitable place for this, however," he said. "Perhaps Fushimi palace would be better."

The ex-Emperor therefore gave orders to move there in two days' time. It was not an official visit and few people would be accompanying him to Fushimi. Only picnic meals would be served and only one cook taken. I had been travelling a good deal from place to place recently, and my clothes, I felt, were very shabby. I could not now depend on my grandfather, the War Minister, for help in this, and I was therefore more highly delighted than usual when Snowy Dawn made me a present of a set of two yellow under-robes, lined with blue, a red mantle with a pattern of dewy autumn flowers on the sleeves, together with a skirt and a tight-sleeved gown of raw silk.

At Fushimi palace, the ex-Emperor, Lord Sanekane and two of my cousins, Gon Chunagon Minamoto no Michiyori and Gon Chunagon Madenokoji no Morochika, met the Great Lord Konoe and his son, Chunagon Chujo, Takatsukasa no Kanetada, and his brother, the former Imperial Adviser, Takatsukasa no Mototada. No one else was there.

At Kujo nearby, Lord Takaaki was staying at his father-in-law's house. The ex-Emperor sent to him several times, asking him to join the party as no one was present whom he would wish to avoid meeting, but he refused on the plea that he was now living in retirement. At last Sugawara no Kiyonaga was sent and he persuaded him to come. He brought with him two Shirabyoshi dancers but told no one of this, leaving them in his carriage where he had left it outside the Upper House during the ceremony of initiation into the secret of Imayo singing.

After the ceremony Lord Takaaki called the girls in for the drinking party in the Lower House. The ex-Emperor took a great deal of interest in the girls and made them sit near him. They were sisters, the elder, named Harugiku, just over twenty years of age, wearing a set of two purplish-red robes and skirt. The younger, Wakagiku, wore a blue-striped boy's robe lined with bluish green and wide-bottomed trousers with a bush-clover pattern. After they had sung a few Shirabyoshi songs, the ex-Emperor wished to see them dance, but they had brought no hand-drum player. They searched round and found a hand drum, which Lord Takaaki played and Wakagiku danced. Then the ex-Emperor wanted to see the elder girl dance, but she refused at first as she was out of practise. Eventually after further pressing she agreed. She first put on her sister's boy's-robe over her own clothes. This looked rather singular but quite attractive. At the ex-Emperor's wish, she danced several long dances suitable for a wedding celebration. All this time the ex-Emperor continued to drink heavily and the girls were not allowed to leave the party till quite late. All were told that they should stay the night and go back to the Capital together the next day.

While the ex-Emperor was asleep, I had occasion to slip over to the Tsutsui annex on some little business or other of my own.[1] The sound of the wind among the pines was awesome, and the chirping of insects whose sole object seemingly is the enjoyment of the listener sounded extremely pathetic. The waning moon just rising in its cold splendour added a further touch of pathos to the broad landscape. I was hurrying back to the ex-Emperor's apartment, dressed only in a nightgown, for it was a country house and all the people seemed to be asleep, when from under the bamboo blind hanging at the front of the Tsutsui house, an arm came out and

[1] We may conjecture that she was paying a visit to the room of Snowy Dawn, Lord Sanekane.

caught me by the sleeve. I screamed, for I thought an ogre had got me.

"If you scream like that at night," my captor said in a low voice, "the monster who lives in the tree will come and get you. It's very unlucky to scream like that."

I knew who he was by his voice,[2] and this made me more scared than ever. I made no answer and struggled to get away, but I could not; my sleeve was almost torn off at the shoulder seam. No one came in answer to my scream, and I was pulled inside the room. There was no one there except him.

"What are you doing?" I cried.

"I have been waiting for a long time to get more friendly with you," he said. His method of approach was such a hackneyed one that I did not feel constrained to listen to what else he had to say in pledging his undying love. I just kept on trying to pull away.

"The nights are long at this season of the year," I said. "His Majesty will be waking up and looking for me."

"Promise to come back to me when you can," he said, and in order to get away from him, I promised to do this, swearing it by the names of all the gods of the shrines in all the four quarters of the land, though, as I swore the oath, I shivered with horror at the thought of having to break it. So I escaped.

Then, when I got back to the ex-Emperor's apartment, he woke up and had everyone get up to start

[2] It will be apparent later that this was the Great Lord Konoe, then forty-nine years of age.

drinking again. This they did with a great deal of noise. Wakagiku had gone home and there could be no more dancing. The ex-Emperor therefore decided we should all stay another day and have another party that night. When he had got everyone to understand that, he felt free to concentrate his mind on the drinking until he fell fast asleep. For my own part, however, I could not get to sleep for thoughts of what had happened at the Tsutsui house. I knew it must really have happened; I couldn't have slept and dreamed it all; the memory was too vivid. It was daybreak before I finally fell asleep.

As the ex-Emperor was to be the host at next day's party, Fujiwara no Suketaka was put in charge of the arrangements, which were on an elaborate scale. The two dancers came, and everyone was merry. Many dances were performed, the elder sister being rewarded for her performances with a metal wine cup and three lumps of musk on a wooden tray, and the younger one being given a blue glass vessel and a lump of musk on a metal tray. The party lasted till the dawn bells rang out.

While Wakagiku was dancing, the ex-Emperor had sung, "When the priest So-o offered his worship before Fudo, the god of fire, the god's image split down the middle," and when he had come to the lines, "So even after his death, the infatuation of Shinsai,[3] the priest of the Kakinomoto temple, for the

[3] Shinsai (800–860) was the disciple of Kukai, founder of Shingon Buddhism. The Empress Somedono (829–900) was the consort of the Emperor Montoku (827–858).

Empress Somedono still had its evil influence in the world,'' my uncle Takaaki looked up at me suddenly. Our eyes met, and I was so horrified at recalling Prince Shojo's vindictive feelings towards me that I sat there petrified with fright, until at last with the dawn bells ringing the party came to an end in a tumult of talking and dancing.

When the ex-Emperor had retired to his room and I was massaging his hips, the person who had confronted me the night before came to the room.

"I've something to say to you," he called out to me. I could not get up and leave, and I made no attempt to do so. "At least come while His Majesty is asleep," he said, urging me to go to him.

"Get up and go quickly," the ex-Emperor whispered to me. "I don't mind your going." I was ready to die with shame at his thoughtfulness for me. He put out his hand to help me to get up from where I was sitting behind him, and I did get up, but most unwillingly.

"We had better stay just outside the room in case you're wanted," said the man outside the room. I was ashamed, for I knew that the ex-Emperor was not asleep, as the man thought, but was listening to all this conversation. Sad at heart, I continued to weep. He was very drunk, but he did not free me finally till daybreak. Though I could not blame myself in any way for what had happened, I continued to weep bitterly. Then, when completely exhausted, still sobbing, I lay down beside the ex-Emperor, he was as kind as ever and completely unruffled.

The ex-Emperor was to have returned from Fushimi that day, but Lord Konoe persuaded him not to do so. "The two girls are still here. They don't want to leave yet," he said. "We should all like to stay another day. I will be the host."

The ex-Emperor agreed to stay and, fearful of what might be said to me, I thought it expedient to stay in my room to rest, though it was not in any way the sort of apartment I was accustomed to. The usual letter came to me in the course of the morning,

> Your face that I saw
> In last night's short dream of love
>   Lives in my mind's eye,
> And your scent still on my sleeves
> Rouses me to greater love.

To this he added the note, "I did not write to you earlier in case the one sleeping near you should be awakened."

My answering poem read,

> Sad of heart am I,
> I cannot think our meeting
>   Aught else but a dream;
> In proof of this see my sleeves,
> All drenched with tears of sorrow.

During the day I went to the ex-Emperor's room only when he called for me. He seemed to want to show his sympathy for me in my wretchedness by being as cheerful as possible, but these signs of his affection only grieved me the more.

In the evening the party started up again. Today we went before it was quite dark to the Fushimi Lower House to have the boats prepared. Later, when it was dark, the cormorant fishermen were called and their boats tied up to ours. They then started to catch fish. Afterwards the three cormorant fishermen were each presented with under-robes that I had worn. When we got back to the hall, the drinking party began. The ex-Emperor was drunker than usual that night, and late at night the same person came again to where we were in bed.

"It's very trying being away from home for several nights," he said. "Fushimi is always spoken of by the poets as a place where people find it difficult to sleep. Light a torch to keep away these troublesome insects." His importunity made me feel utterly miserable especially as the ex-Emperor had suggested the night before that I should consent. "Forgive the selfishness of an old man," he went on, now lying down beside us. "Won't you consent to my pleas? You must, if I am to be your guardian. Whatever you may think of it, there have been many similar cases from olden times." I need not say how wretched, how grieved, how horrified I felt.

"I shan't be happy sleeping by myself," the ex-Emperor said. "Still I shan't mind if you are not far away."

So it was that I spent the rest of the night in the same place as I had the night before.

The next morning, preparations for our departure began while it was still dark. We two got up and parted at once as if nothing but remorse was left. I rode in the rear seat of the ex-Emperor's carriage with Lord Sanekane by my side. All the carriages went together in procession as far as the Kiyomizu bridge. From there the ex-Emperor's carriage went north along Kyogoku street. Seeing Lord Konoe's carriage turn west here, I felt I was left forlorn and longed to see him again. As I watched him go from me, I marvelled how amazingly my thoughts about him had changed in so short a time.

Book Three

Lady Nijo resumes the story of her life in 1281[1] when she is in her twenty-third year. Prince Shojo comes into the story again and Lady Nijo again becomes pregnant

CHAPTER

I

My relations with other people had become increasingly difficult for me with the same kind of vexing situation continually recurring. This all made me wish that I could abandon this kind of life to live in peace in a cottage beyond the mountains. But this yearning was in vain. It was proving very difficult for me to give up my life at court, and I could blame no one but myself for everything that had happened to me. I had an uneasy feeling too that a break with the ex-Emperor was imminent. I had been striving my utmost to avoid this, but it seemed as if all my efforts were to be in vain.

It was about the middle of the second month. The trees were beginning to come into flower, and the scent of the plum blossom was brought on the

[1] As Book Two ends with the events of the eighth month of 1277, we have no record of the events of 1278, 1279 and 1280. There are grounds for supposing that one whole book of the autobiography has disappeared.

breezes. Yet all this gave me no pleasure. More than ever before, I felt depressed, dispirited, sorrowful, troubled.

Hearing the ex-Emperor call for me, I hurried to his apartment, wondering what he wanted. He was standing in the kettle room, alone.

"Most of the ladies have gone on leave," he said. "I am being left alone. And you stay cooped up in your room the whole of the time. What is the attraction there?" This was his usual attitude towards me at the time and I could make no answer.

Just then the arrival of Wan Morning Moon was announced, and soon afterwards he was shown into the room. I sat there, taking no notice of him, apparently unconcerned. I did not see what else I could do.

At this time the ex-Emperor was very worried about the state of health of his daughter, the one later to become the Empress Yugimon, who was then about twelve years of age. She had been suffering from a painful disease for some time, and prayers had been offered for her recovery at the palace and for the ex-Emperor's well-being at the Narutaki temple.

The two brothers conversed together for some time in an even more unhurried fashion than usual, though I was a little disturbed, having an uneasy feeling as to what was going on in the prince's mind. Then a message came that the princess appeared to be worse. The ex-Emperor got up immediately to go to see her.

"Stay here till His Majesty returns," I said.

There was no one else there at the time, and the prince began to talk of all the sad times he had had to live through, beginning with his unhappy boyhood right up to the present time. He tried in vain to hide his tears with his sleeve. There was nothing I could say; I just listened in silence. What I did not realise was that the ex-Emperor had come back and was listening outside the door to his brother's complaints. Unaware of this too, the prince continued to plead for my love. Unusually quick to grasp any situation, the ex-Emperor could have been in no doubt about the intimacy of our relations. When the ex-Emperor came back into the room, the prince put an innocent face on our conversation, but I was worried that his damp sleeves would reveal our secret.

When the candles were lighted that evening, the prince left the palace. No one was with us, and the ex-Emperor seemed even more friendly than usual as I massaged his legs.

"I heard something this afternoon that I was not expecting to hear," he said to me, friendlily enough. "How did all this happen? How did you two get into this situation? He and I have been very close to one another ever since we were boys together. I did not think he was the sort of man to get involved in any kind of scandalous behaviour."

As it was obviously no use my telling him that there were no grounds for his suspicions, I made a clean breast of everything that had happened from the first night of our meeting to the night when we had quarrelled and parted. I did not hide a single detail.

"What a marvellous bond of love has tied you together," said the ex-Emperor. "And he was so infatuated with you that he enlisted Takaaki's aid in forwarding his suit. And then you refused him. He must be very bitter against you for the heartless way in which you have treated him. He will make you suffer for it. There have been many instances of this all through the ages. Love is blind. That is true not only of laymen but also of priests. Shinsai, the High Priest of the Kakinomoto temple, who fell in love with the Empress Somedono, was because of this turned into a fiend, and in spite of all her devotion to the saints, she fell a victim to his lusts. On the other hand, when the Chief Priest of the Shiga temple declared his love for the Empress Kyogoku, she calmed his passions by the poem she composed,

> Guide me to Paradise,
> For there pure lovers will meet
> On one lotus leaf,
> And then to you I shall feel
> An eternal gratitude.

"My brother seems to be utterly deranged. Deal warily with him. So long as I keep silent, no one will learn anything about this matter. When he has to come here to hold a service of intercession, try to make him forget his resentment against you. You may think it is wicked to use such an occasion for this purpose, but I have a deeper plan in mind. Do not then worry yourself about what I shall think of what you are doing." His voice took on an even more affectionate tone as he went on, "You have kept nothing secret from me. And I am glad that, in your bewilderment as to what you should do, you have asked for my help. That has cleared away completely from my mind any suspicions that I might have had." It is no wonder that his sympathy made me feel all the more wretched.

"I fell in love with you first," he went on. "Many years have passed since that day, but never, whatever happened, have I treated you with anything but the highest respect, even though something always happened to prevent my realising fully my plans for you. Oh, how I wish I could make you understand the depths of my feelings for you. It was your mother who first initiated me into the pleasures of love in bed when she was in my service.[2] I loved her in secret although I remained shy and reserved with her, feeling that I was not yet old enough to take an active part in beginning such an affair. And then later your mother left my service to receive the love of Fujiwara no Fuyutada, and later still she became your father's wife. All this time I had waited for her to make some approach to me. Even before you were born, I was hoping that the child would prove to be a girl. When you were born, I made up my mind that one day you should enter my service. In this case, everything turned out as I had hoped that it would." He had never before spoken to me of these things, and I was touched to the heart.

Next day the service of intercession was to begin. People crowded round the artificial mound that had

[2] This must have been before Higashi Nijo became his wife when he was fourteen years of age.

been erected for the ceremony. I felt wretched whenever anyone looked at me, wondering whether my secret anxieties showed in my face. The prince's arrival was announced. I sat by the side of the ex-Emperor, apparently unconcerned but wretched at heart at the thought of what the prince was thinking.

As usual, I was sent with a message to the prince. I always had a guilty conscience on these occasions, but this time I felt guiltier than ever, yet there was nothing else that I could do but to go. It was still early in the evening. The message was an enquiry on some doubtful point of doctrine of Shingon Buddhism. There was no one else in the room with the prince, a rather unusual thing. In the dim light of the hazy spring moonlight, leaning on an armrest, he was reciting from one of the sutras.

He interrupted his devotions to talk to me. "I vowed to Buddha," he said, "to put out of my mind forever every remembrance of the sorrowful events of that moonlight night when you rejected my proffered love. But I have not been able to keep my vow. Is there no way in which I can give up my love for you except by sacrificing my life? I have prayed to the gods to transplant me to a land where you are not, but they give no heed to my prayers. What am I to do?" He went on to beg me to stay with him for a little while, and though I feared that this might lead to the spread of malicious rumours about us, I could not but share with him a momentary dream of love, which was cut short by calls outside that the service was about to begin. I escaped by the back door, but not before he had pleaded with me again and again not to leave but to stay in the room and wait for him until after the midnight service. He spoke as urgently as if he feared some barrier might rise up to prevent our meeting ever again if I went away then. I was afraid, however, that I might get involved in trouble if I stayed any longer, and so I returned to my own apartments.

I felt more in love with him that night than I had done on that evening when we had first met and he had given me the poem beginning

> In sorrow gazing
> At the autumn moon at night.

It seemed to me that I could not hope to escape from that affinity which drew us together, those pledges of love we had made to one another in a former life. I lay down to sleep, but no dream came to me. The day dawned, and having nothing else to do, I went to serve the ex-Emperor's breakfast. No one else happened to be there.

"He didn't know that I had sent you to him with a message so that he could talk to you, did he?" the ex-Emperor said. "Don't let him find out that I know all about his secret passion. I should be sorry if he had to conceal his feelings because he learnt that I knew all about this." I felt too ashamed to say a word in reply. I felt also a deep compassion for the prince who was having to officiate at these solemn services while feeling himself impure in mind and body.

On the sixth day of the services, on the eighteenth day of the second month, the ex-Emperor was sitting up late, admiring the crimson plum blossoms in front of the great hall of the palace which were especially beautiful that year both in colour and fragrance.

"Tonight is the last night of the special intercessions," the ex-Emperor said to me when we heard the late night service ending. "It is already very late. Go to him at the first opportunity."

I was surprised at this suggestion, but when the midnight bell tolled the Lady of the East Wing was invited to join the ex-Emperor in the ante-room off the Mandarin Orangery. When the ex-Emperor left to go there, I went to the prince's room, not because it was what the ex-Emperor had suggested that I should do, but rather because I felt something of a longing for him on this last night of his at the palace. He was obviously waiting for me, expecting that I should come. I knew well what remorse might follow if I did not resolve to give up meeting him, and yet I had to come. The voice of the ex-Emperor still remained in my ears, and the perfume of his incense-scented robes still permeated my sleeves. How could I allow another to cover those sleeves with his own? Yet I had come, and if anything went wrong, I had only myself to blame. The prince wept as if this night was to be our last, and our parting at the end of it a parting forever. My mind was in a whirl. How much better it would be, I thought, if we had parted then forever than that we should meet again and have to part with our love for each other unsatisfied. But for the moment such thoughts had no relevance. The short night passed quickly, and I was left in the morning to

wonder whether the evening would ever come. I
waited all the day for his coming after parting from
him at dawn with still unsatisfied longings. Alas, that
day had little chance of coming, I thought, as I composed this poem to express my thoughts,

> Your face, quite unchanged
> Since the night when we parted
>   In bitter discord,
> Is reflected in the tears
> I shed when we met tonight.

Next morning the little princess seemed rather
better, and the prince went away from the palace
after the early evening service, leaving me feeling
rather lost without him.

A strange thing had occurred that morning. I was
lying down in my room after having come from the
prince's room just before dawn, when the ex-Emperor
sent Lord Kiyonaga to call me to him at once. I knew
that the Lady of the East Wing had spent the night
with him and wondered why he had sent for me so
early. Somewhat uneasy, I hurried to his room.

"It was very late when I let you go to his room as
I thought he would be waiting anxiously for you,"
he said to me. "If it hadn't been something out of the
ordinary, I would not have sent for you so early in
the morning, when your face still shows the emotions
he has aroused. Forgive me for doing so. It is all due
to my being so anxious about your well-being. Last
night I had a very strange dream about you. In my

dream the prince gave you a five-pointed mace which you put in the bosom of your robes to hide from me. I caught hold of you by the sleeve and asked why you had hidden it from me when I knew everything about you. Weeping, you showed me the mace. I saw that it was a silver one that had belonged to my father. I said that I would take it, and just as I took hold of it, I awoke to find it was a dream. I am sure that the mace is a symbol of something you have received tonight. If that is so, it seems to me to indicate that I shall have to take charge of Iwane no Matsu[3] myself." I did not know how far I could trust him to do that. For the next month, however, he never called on me to spend the night with him. It was all my fault, I thought, and I could not hold it against him; I did not then realise the real reason for his doing this. By that time, all the signs showed that I was once more pregnant. How would things go now with me and the prince, I wondered.

At the beginning of the third month, one evening when there were few people about and I had noticed that the ex-Emperor had eaten hardly anything for his supper, he called me into his own little private room. I wondered why he was doing this, and was overjoyed to hear him pledge his unchanging affection for me.

---

[3] "Pine tree growing on a rock." In *The Tale of Genji,* in an incident omitted in Waley's translation, the hero on seeing the child his wife has had by someone else expresses his feelings in the poem: Should any ask you, / Pine on the rock, who it was / That planted you there, / What would then be your answer / To the one who questioned you?

"I have not called you to me since I had that strange dream," he said. "I was waiting for one month to pass. I have been very sad and lonely waiting for the time to go." I was surprised to hear that this was the reason why he had not sent for me. There was now no doubt at all about my being pregnant again; that short dream of love had brought a new source of trouble on me.

That one whom I had always regarded as my first real lover,[4] and who on his part had always regarded me as his nearest and dearest, had seemed more distant with me since those dream-like nights at Fushimi. It was only natural that he should have disliked seeing me wooed and won by that other lord, but it saddened me that we should have been estranged so long. At the beginning of the fifth month when I returned home to take part in the memorial services on the anniversary of my mother's death, however, he sent me this poem,

> With longing for you,
> Missing you always so much
> Since I saw you last,
> Till now unceasingly still
> I weep in bitter sorrow.

The letter accompanying the poem was very touching and ended, "If no barrier has been erected to bar

---

[4] Lord Sanekane, Snowy Dawn, who might have been expected to feel disgruntled about Lady Nijo's relations with Lord Konoe at Fushimi.

my approach, I should like to visit you at your home, if only to stand and look."

I replied with a poem expressing my sorrow that circumstances had prevented our meeting,

> Against my own will,
> Changes have befallen me,
> To my great sorrow;
> So that through all these changes
> I weep unceasingly still.

To this I added, "I am sure that our love for one another will endure for ever."

I was afraid that our former intimate relations would never be resumed, but he did come late that night. We began to talk over the unhappy incidents that had happened, but before very long, there was a noise of shouting and we heard that fire had broken out on the corner of Sanjo and Kyogoku streets at Tominokoji. He thought he ought to go to the palace in haste.

The nights are short at that season of the year. It was soon daylight and then it was too late for him to come back to me. As soon as it was broad daylight, I received a letter from him. "Last night's unexpected incident," he wrote, "appears like a warning that our attachment for each other is likely to grow weaker and weaker. I fear that the future course of our love will be like that of a boat pushing its slow way through the reeds that impede its progress." With the letter was the poem,

> Has this long absence
> Caused the current of our love
>   Not to end in one,
> Like two converging streams, but
> Disappear into the sand?

It was indeed unfortunate that, when after a long interval I had seen him again the night before, we had been prevented from spending a happy night together. In answer to his letter, I sent a letter,

> Although it may seem
> That our love for each other
>   Has come to an end,
> Still will my eyes be always
> Filled with sad tears of longing.

If I had been allowed to stay at home a little longer, we might have found another opportunity of meeting, but that evening the ex-Emperor sent a carriage with a message that he wanted me back at the palace at once, and so I returned.

At the beginning of autumn, I was getting over my morning sickness. "You are getting to the stage now," the ex-Emperor said to me jocularly one day about this time, "when you should have a sacred rope hung round you to warn people that you are taboo. Have you told the prince anything about it yet?"

"No, I haven't. When have I had an opportunity of telling him?" I answered.

"You do not need to hesitate about doing anything

because of what I might say. He may try to conceal from me his relationship with you, but I shall tell him that it is useless for him to try to hide things from me and that he cannot escape from what is so obviously his destiny."

There was nothing I could say in answer to that, but I could imagine what the prince's feelings would be if the ex-Emperor spoke to him in such a way. If I had suggested to him, however, that he should not do this, it might have led him to accuse me of taking the prince's side against him. I could therefore only say, "You must do as you think best," and say no more.

Soon afterwards a course of instruction on the doctrines of Shingon Buddhism was organised at the palace, the ex-Emperor drawing up a list of questions to be answered. The prince attended and stayed four or five days. When the course of lectures was over, a drinking party was held. I waited on the prince and the ex-Emperor.

"I have made enquiries far and wide," the ex-Emperor said to the prince, "and I am deeply convinced that sexual relations are not sinful in themselves. Force is powerless against the love one man is predestined to feel for a certain woman. History provides many notable examples of this. The ascetic Jozo, convinced that he was fated to enter into a love relationship with a woman from the northern province of Michinoku, tried to kill her. He failed, and eventually he became her lover. The Empress Somedono tried to persuade the High Priest of the Shiga temple to give up his love for her. She failed, and he became a deep blue demon. A woman whose husband had died was changed by her love for him into a rock which was later called Bofuseki, Yearning-for-Husband Rock. People may even be forced, as a result of the deeds of a former life, to fall in love with an animal, wild or domestic. These things are impossible for us fully to comprehend."

I had a feeling that he was referring to me and the prince in all this. Tears were in my eyes, and I was in a cold sweat with fear. People were going out quietly, and Wan Morning Moon was about to leave also, when the ex-Emperor prevented him going.

"Stay a little longer," he said. "Let us talk further about religion in these quiet midnight hours." I do not know what was said, for, thinking their conversation would involve me, I left and went back to my room.

It was well after midnight when the ex-Emperor summoned me to his room. "I took the opportunity," he said, "to tell him everything I had been thinking about you. Parents are blinded by their love for their children, and no parent could dote on his child as I do on you." I could not say a word in answer. I could only weep. He was speaking even more affectionately than usual. "You heard what I said to everyone about how impossible it is for anyone to avoid the person he is fated to love. After you had left, I told my brother that I had by accident overheard what he had said to you. I quite understood, I told him, how afraid he might be of what I might say to him, but that he should even at the cost of his life continue to pledge his love for you. He and I should have no secrets from one another. I pointed out to him that it would be most unfortunate if people discovered his secret. No doubt it was due to his actions in a former life that he could not repress his love. I told him that I did not blame him in the slightest for the way in which he had acted. I informed him that you had been in a delicate condition since the spring. At that time I had had a dream in which you had tried to hide from me a silver mace. This dream appeared to me to have a meaning and I had patiently refrained from approaching you until I was absolutely certain that I had understood the meaning of the dream correctly. I told him that I had done this so that I could assure myself of the sincerity of his feelings for you and of his concern for your future. I warned him not to hide anything from me, or he would lose the divine assistance of the protectors of the country, the gods who are worshipped at the Ise, Iwashimizu, Kamo, and Kasuga shrines. If he did this, then my attitude towards him would never change. He remained silent for a time, and then brushing away his tears, he told me that after what I had said he wished to hide nothing from me. It was sad, he told me, that his deeds in a former life had led to his present unhappy situation. He would never cease to be grateful to me for my advice and help not only for the rest of his life but also in the world to come. His remorse for having formed such a strong attachment to you had been utterly unendurable, and he had for three years struggled to free himself. He had prayed to the gods

and Buddha for no other thing than this, and he had
written out for you a solemn oath. Even then he had
not been able to free himself, and now at the end
found himself just where he had been at the beginning, like a wheel that had turned full circle. Now
that the lady was pregnant, he would retire from his
post at the temple in favour of my son who has already taken his vows and go into the mountains to
live as a black-clad hermit. He thanked me for my
kindness all through the years, but especially for the
great consideration I had shown on this occasion. He
would be indebted to me through many worlds to
come. Then still weeping bitterly, he left me. I
felt very sorry for him, for I realised how deeply
he loves you."

For myself, my feelings as I listened to the ex-
Emperor's story were mixed; my tears were tears
of gratitude as well as of resentment. I realised again
the feelings so well expressed in the poem in *The
Tale of Genji*,

> Both my sleeves were drenched
> Equally with bitter tears,
>   But the one with tears
> Of bitterest resentment,
> The other tears of longing.

As I felt I would like to hear from the prince himself what his feelings were, since he was leaving the
palace the next day, I went to his apartment late that
night under the pretext that I was taking a message

to him from the ex-Emperor. There was no one there with him except a young page who was sleeping in the same room. He took me into the room where we usually met.

"I had hoped," he said, "that the bitterness of our parting that dreadful morning would have led to a happier and more pious life for me. That it has not proved to be so must be because I still long for your love. I am sorry for myself at finding myself still in this quandary."

Reminded by this of the look on his face on the morning we parted with so much bitterness, I felt impelled to run away from him at once. Realising at the same time, however, that we should be parting when he left the palace at the conclusion of the study sessions, as is usual at such times, I came to feel more and more drawn to him and finally spent the night with him. His tears fell on my sleeves the whole night through, and I had no thought to spare for what would become of me afterwards. I listened to his story and heard all over again what the ex-Emperor had told him.

"It shows how much I love you," he said, "that now that His Majesty knows all about our relationship with one another, my only worry is whether we shall have an opportunity of meeting each other in the future. Now that you are bearing my child, it does not seem as improbable as it did formerly for me to hope that we can marry and I can bring up the child as my son and not have to leave him to the care of others." On hearing this, my joy and my love were unbounded. "The coming baby," he went on, "is

already the cause of a great deal of concern to me."
So we talked, weeping and laughing in turn, till dawn
broke. Choked with tears, he asked when we could
meet again and I expressed my hope for such a meeting in the poem,

> Would that the image
> Now of the wan morning moon
> Mirrored on my sleeves
> Could show a face as loving
> Tomorrow as it does now.

His tender love for me had roused in me a love for
him as tender as his.

I was still lying down in my room, continuing to
ponder over the manner in which I had been caught
fast in the foreordained chains of love, when the ex-
Emperor summoned me. He was still in his bedroom.

"I was expecting you last night," he said abruptly.
"I lay awake waiting for you all the night." I made
no answer. "You must be missing him and bewailing
the fact that the night has passed so soon," he went
on. I still had no answer to make. I wondered why
I should have to be so torn between two men when
so many women in the world could devote themselves
solely to one man. I could not help bursting into
tears. What kind of tears did he think them to be,
I wondered. "Were you lying in bed living over at
your leisure the events of last night's happy meeting?"
he enquired. How wrong he was! Listening to him
thus cruelly criticising me, saying things which hurt
me more than anything he had ever said before, I

realised that things were turning out just as I feared
they would. The future seemed very black. I tried in
vain to hold back my tears. He took them for tears
of yearning perhaps. "You are still missing the one
from whom you have only just now parted. You are
offended because I sent for you." He broke off what
he was saying, looking very angry, and I left him to
go back to my room.

Feeling very wretched and miserable, I kept away
from him all the day, but fearing that he might be
even more angry with me if I continued to do so, I
went to him in the evening, wishing with all my heart
that I could get away from life at court which had
brought so much sadness to me and hasten to the
peaceful life on the other side of the mountains. The
old poem says,

> I wish I could find,
> Beyond Yoshino mountains
> Clad now with blossom,
> A lodging and a refuge
> From the world's annoyances.

After the study session had finished, the prince
had stayed on and was still there with his brother.
They were chatting more pleasantly together than
usual, but I did not feel comfortable sitting there
talking with them, and I soon left. Coming out through
the kettle-room, I met him.[5]

[5] This refers, as the reader has no doubt realised, to the third
man, Snowy Dawn, Saionji no Sanekane.

"I have come to the palace today as I am on duty from tomorrow," he said to me. "I'm sorry I've not had a chance lately even to hear the sound of your voice." I was listening to him with the feeling that there seemed to be no place where I could feel at ease, when the ex-Emperor called me back.

I went in, wondering what I was wanted for this time, and found that he was going to have a drinking party in the quiet, matted room. There were one or two ladies-in-waiting there, but he obviously thought this was not enough. Hearing the voices of Lord Morochika and Lord Sanekane in the main hall outside, he called them in too. There was a great deal of noisy merrymaking, but it was all over before I was ready for it to end, and when the prince left for the early evening prayers in the room of the little princess, I missed him very much. This evening I had put on the maternity belt which had been given to me without any ceremony by the ex-Emperor, but I could not help feeling forlorn as I wondered what attitude he was going to take about me and the child. I was on duty that night and he talked to me all through the night in a most affectionate manner. That made me feel all the more wretched.

The ex-Emperor had requested that the annual ceremony of offering flowers to Buddha should be carried out in an even more solemn manner than usual. Everyone was busy with the preparations, but I asked for leave of absence as I felt in my condition it would be better for me not to be there. The ex-Emperor, however, refused his permission; among the crowd present no one would notice, he said. I was attending on him in a pale purple robe, a green over-robe, a scarlet mantle and an under-robe of reddish-brown lined with yellow, when I heard that Wan Morning Moon had arrived. My heart fluttered agitatedly when at the end of the ceremony he came into the hall to make the offering, but I do not think he knew I was there.

At this moment a court lady came to me. "His Majesty has noticed a fan left behind in the hall. He wishes you to take it to him." I felt that there was something rather suspicious about this request. Nevertheless, I opened the middle door and looked into the hall. There was no fan to be seen. I closed the door and turned to the lady. "There's no fan there," I said. The lady then went back to report to the ex-Emperor.

Inside the hall, the prince had seen me when I opened the door. Knowing now where I was, he opened the door a little way.

"It is amazing how much I have missed you," he said. "I've been more wretched than ever since I left you. Don't be cruel to me. Go to your home, and we'll get someone who can keep a secret to arrange for me to meet you there."

I had not the heart to refuse him, although I was frightened that our secret should leak out and the prince's reputation be ruined. "If we can be certain that our secret will not be discovered, I agree," I said, and closed the door.

When the ceremony was over and the prince had

left the palace, I went in to the ex-Emperor. "What did you do about the fan?" he said to me with a laugh. Then for the first time I understood that he had had his usual kind purpose in sending me the message.

 A drinking party at Saga. The ex-Emperor Kameyama declares his affection for Lady Nijo

CHAPTER II In the tenth month, with the gloomy overcast sky and the frequent showers making me sadder than ever before, I left for my step-mother's house at Saga and went into retreat at the Horinji temple. At Arashiyama, the winds were blowing as if they would blow away all my sorrows; the autumn-tinted leaves were falling into the waters of the river Oi until it seemed a wonderful brocade. The sight reminded me of many episodes of the past, private as well as public. I remembered especially the ceremony when the late Emperor Go Saga had recited the Lotus Flower sutra from the copy he had written out with his own hand. How splendidly all the lords and ladies were dressed! What extravagant offerings they had made! Now all these people had gone, never to return; only to my envy the river Oi flowed on just as it had done that day. I wondered sadly with whose lament the belling of the deer now harmonised. The poem I wrote as I listened to them expresses something of my feelings,

> It is I alone
> Who sorrow-laden must weep.
>   What then ails the deer
> Who continue ceaselessly
> Their melancholy wailing?

It was on an evening even more melancholy than usual that a visitor of high rank was announced. It was the Yamamomo Chujo, Fujiwara no Kaneyuki. He was ushered into my room, and I went to meet him. I found something rather strange in his attitude towards me.

"The Empress Dowager Omiya has suddenly fallen ill," he said. "His Majesty came to the Saga palace this morning to visit his mother and is staying at the Oi mansion there. Before his departure he enquired where you were and when he learnt that you were here, he asked that you should join him at Oi. He asked me to inform you that as he had undertaken this visit at such short notice he had brought no lady with him. If you were in retreat as, he knew, you had intended, he would like you to interrupt it in order to join him."

It was the fifth day of my retreat and my conscience was rather disturbed at the prospect of not being able to complete the last two days. I could not, however, easily refuse and so I went to join him in the carriage which had been sent for me. At the Oi mansion I found, as Lord Kaneyuki had said, that there were no ladies in attendance; most of them had been sent home on leave, the ex-Emperor relying on my being available. The two ex-Emperors had come in the same carriage, no one accompanying them except Lord Sanekane who rode in the rear seat. Just as I arrived, dinner was being brought over from the palace.

The Empress Dowager, they had found, had been suffering merely from a slight attack of beri-beri, and the ex-Emperors, relieved to find that their mother's illness was not very serious, decided to hold a party in celebration, the ex-Emperor to act as host and Lord Sanekane to make the arrangements. Ten lunch boxes decorated with paintings and filled with rice and fish and relishes were placed in front of each guest. Wine cups were exchanged three times, the boxes exchanged for fresh ones, and the wine cups exchanged nine times.

The Empress Dowager was presented with a model harp and a model lute of red and purple cloth with a plectrum of silver. The new ex-Emperor was presented with a miniature shrine covered in purple with curtains of various colours on the four sides and a piece of crystal set in a wooden stand in a bowl to represent the ashes of Buddha. The ladies of the house received a hundred quires of letter paper and dress-lengths. The lords were presented with saddle-cruppers and dyed leather harness. Everything was done without consideration of the expense, and the merry-making went on all through the night.

I served the wine as usual. The ex-Emperor played the lute, the new ex-Emperor the flute, Lord Kimmori and the princess who was being brought up by the Empress Dowager the harp, Lord Sanekane the lute, Lord Kinhira the pan-pipes, and Lord Kaneyuki the flageolet. As the night wore on, the wind among the pines of Arashiyama sounded louder and louder and the bell at the Jokongo-in temple could be heard. The ex-Emperor recited part of the poem by the tenth-century scholar, Sugawara no Michizane, "Looking out at the tiled roofs of the Capital." Everyone admitted his performance surpassed all the rest.

"Who has the wine cup now?" said the Empress Dowager.

"It's in front of me," said the new ex-Emperor.

She expressed the wish to drink to the accompaniment of the new ex-Emperor's singing. He agreed. The ex-Emperor took the cup and the wine bottle, went in to her behind her bamboo screen and offered her one cup of wine. He then began to recite an old Chinese poem, and his brother joined in to make it a duet.

"Listen to what an old woman has to say to you both," their mother said to them. "It must always be a source of sorrow to me that I was born in such an age of decadence and corruption as this is. Yet I have been fortunate enough to attain to the dignity of an empress. As the mother of you two ex-Emperors, through your two reigns I was Empress-Mother. I have now reached the age of three score years and can look back on my life with no regrets and can look forward to a rebirth in Paradise in as exalted a rank. My pleasure this evening is a foretaste of the pleasure of that dawn on the exalted Lotus Flower, your voices as beautiful as those of the immortal birds of Paradise itself. Sing to me a ballad, and I will take another cup of wine.''

The new ex-Emperor was invited inside her screen, Lord Sanekane being asked to put up a small screen behind her while the bamboo blind was wound half up. The two ex-Emperors then sang charmingly,

> I recall those evenings
> When I waited patiently
> For her at the trysting place.
> With what emotion
> I remember those pledges
> And those sweetly sad partings
> Under the morning moon.

The singing of this ballad brought all those present to maudlin tears and tipsy talk of old times. Finally, not so full of spirits now perhaps, the Empress Dowager left the hall, and the two ex-Emperors went to the Oi mansion, two or three courtiers accompanying them. Lord Sanekane, saying that he had caught cold, did not go with them.

''As no one else is here,'' the ex-Emperor said to me, ''you will have to stay on duty with us.'' The two brothers went to bed. I was told to massage their legs, but I was a long time about this as I was alone and had no one to help me.

''Lie down by our side,'' the younger brother said to me repeatedly.

"No," said the elder, "she is in a delicate condition. She has been on leave of absence until I asked her to come here as there was no lady on duty with us here. She is already finding it difficult to move about easily. It would be different if she were not like that."

The younger brother persisted. "There is no reason for worry as long as you keep her close to your side. In *The Tale of Genji* the Emperor Suzaku gives even his daughter to his younger brother, Genji. Why should just this lady be forbidden me? I have told you that any lady in my service is at your disposal."

Just then it was time for the new ex-Emperor to go out to welcome the former Vestal Virgin who had come on a visit to Lady Azechi and had been invited to stay at the Oi mansion. While his younger brother was absent, the ex-Emperor, who was really very drunk, went to sleep without calling me to him.

On his return the new ex-Emperor, seeing that no one was in the room with his brother, brought a screen behind him over to me. To my misery, his brother knew nothing of what was going on.

When it was nearly dawn, the new ex-Emperor went over to his sleeping brother and shook him until at last he woke up.

"I was so sound asleep that the Lady got up and left me," said the elder brother.

"She was here till just this minute," the younger one said.

What had happened was not my fault, I thought, as

I waited for the ex-Emperor to call me to him. But there was no call.

That evening the new ex-Emperor was the host at the entertainment, and Kagefusa, Lord Sanekane's father's retainer, was in charge of the arrangements.

"Yesterday Lord Sanekane made the arrangements. Today his father's retainer does it. There's no balance," a carping critic might have said about this, but in reality everything was quite up to the standard of the evening before. The Empress Dowager was presented with a sleeve ornament of rocks made of cloth on a background of waves on which was a wooden boat containing cakes of clove powder. The ex-Emperor was given an agilawood pillow in a silver basket-work case. Each of the ladies was presented with an embroidered miniature landscape with hills and waterfalls. The lords each received a persimmon of dyed leather. Probably because the new ex-Emperor had suggested to his elder brother that I should be the only one of his ladies invited to accompany him, I was given a special present of a book of ten pages of figured satin and ten of purple silk with the titles of the fifty-four chapters of *The Tale of Genji* written on them. The party was quite uneventful; perhaps that of the previous night had exhausted all the merriment. Lord Sanekane was not present. He had a cold, he said; but some thought that this was just an excuse.

That night, too, the two ex-Emperors stayed at the Oi mansion. They had a meal after the party, and I waited on them. They slept in the same room and I found it very distasteful to have to sleep with them, but there was nothing I could do about it. This was one of the reasons why I wished so heartily to be completely finished with life at court.

The two ex-Emperors left for the Capital together. I excused myself from accompanying them because I had interrupted my retreat at the Horinji temple and also because of my condition. I would like, I said, to stay on at the Oi house and then return home. Lord Sanekane accompanied the ex-Emperor, and Lord Kimmori the younger brother.

It was very lonely when they left with a great deal of noise and laughter. I stayed on for the day at the invitation of the Empress Dowager. During the day a letter arrived for her from the ex-Empress Higashi Nijo. I wondered what this could be about. I was soon to learn.

"What's all this?" the Empress Dowager muttered to herself as she read the letter. "She must be crazy."

"What do you mean?" I asked.

"She says I favour you too much, that at some party or other I spoke of you as the ex-Emperor's greatest favourite. She's jealous of you because you were brought to my party. She says that although she is no longer young, having been married to him for twenty-five years, she is sure that he still thinks more of her than any other woman." The Empress Dowager wanted me to read the letter, but I was unwilling to do this and left the palace to go to the home of my old nurse at the corner of Shijo and Omiya streets.

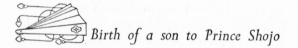 *Birth of a son to Prince Shojo*

CHAPTER III Soon afterwards I had a letter from Wan Morning Moon. He was staying in the neighbourhood at the home of his much-loved page boy. I was much afraid that my frequent visits to him there would cause malicious rumours about him to spread and wished he would cease coming into the neighbourhood. It was not that I feared any misfortune which might come to me. He did not mind either; as he said to me, "If the worst comes to the worst, I can always go and live in a hut in the mountains."

Towards the end of the tenth month, I felt very sick, much worse than the last time, as well as feeling helpless and lonely. The ex-Emperor had asked my grandfather, the War Minister, to see to everything for me, but I felt as if no one really cared what happened to me.

One night, very late, I heard a carriage draw up stealthily. There was a knock on the door. "The Lady Kyogoku has come with a message from the Tominokoji palace," a voice called out.

With some misgivings I opened the door to find to my amazement that it was the ex-Emperor himself, heavily disguised, in an ordinary, simple basket-work carriage. His visit was quite unexpected. He had something particular to discuss, he told me, speaking in a most affectionate manner.

"Everyone seems to know about your relations with Wan Morning Moon," he said to me when he had come in to my room. "Some people are falsely accusing me of being responsible for it all. I shall have to resign myself to that. Now I happen to know that a lady with whom I have been intimate for some time gave birth to a still-born child this evening. I have told the family to keep this secret and to pretend that the birth has not yet taken place. I want you to let her have the child and pretend that your own child was still-born. In this way, I hope, people's criticism of you both will be scotched. I have been extremely worried about the scandal that might ensue if it became known that you had had a child by him and I thought out this plan to avoid it."

Surprised by the songs of the birds at dawn to find it so late, he hurried away. I was grateful to him for his thoughtfulness, but it all reminded me too much of the old tales of such exchanges of babies at birth. I was sad to think that for the third time I was to lose my baby to someone else.

While I was still sunk in such dismal thoughts, a letter arrived from the ex-Emperor. "This night's visit had an uncommon purpose," he wrote, "and will remain memorable for long." He added the poem,

> Now for the first time
> Have I stayed in such a house,
> Rustic and shabby;

> Yet because it is your home,
> It will remain dear to me.

How long would his affection for me endure, I wondered, and felt uneasy at the thought. My poem in answer read,

> Sadly I wonder,
> As I sit in this garden
> Overgrown with weeds,
> How long you will continue
> To come here to visit me.

Towards evening I heard that Wan Morning Moon was in the neighbourhood, but feeling unwell, no doubt because I was getting near to my time, I did not feel like going to see him. After midnight, however, I was surprised to have an unexpected visit from him. There were only two or three people of the house there, all of them trustworthy, and so I let him into my room. I told him what the ex-Emperor had arranged on his visit the night before.

"I realise how impossible it is for me to keep the child," he said sorrowfully. "It must be a great blow to you not to be able to do so when so many people in the same situation can do so. Still, now that His Majesty has kindly arranged all this, we can but fall in with it."

And as he was saying this, with the dawn bell beginning to toll, a baby boy was born. I could not say which of us he took after, but he was certainly very lovely.

The prince took the baby on his lap and talked to him. "You were so devout in your previous life," he said to him, weeping bitterly and speaking to him as if he were a grown-up person, "that you have had a safe and easy birth." Then as dawn was breaking, he left the house reluctantly.

I gave away the child as the ex-Emperor had arranged and heard no more of him. People may well have believed my story that the child was still-born; in any case no unpleasant rumours spread about the prince. This was all due to the ex-Emperor's forethought, and I felt under a deep obligation to him, both from a private and a public point of view. Yet for a long time I dreaded that someone who had helped in the exchange and knew of the secret from the ex-Emperor might reveal the truth about the prince and me.

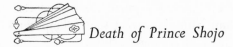 *Death of Prince Shojo*

CHAPTER The child was born on the sixth day of
IV the eleventh month and the prince continued to visit me every night. This was causing me a good deal of uneasiness, but he took no notice of my complaints and late on the night of the eleventh he came as usual.

"The whole nation is in a state of turmoil," he said. "Rumour has it that the sacred tree of the

Kasuga shrine which was brought up to the Capital by armed monks the year before last is to be taken back to Nara.[1] In addition, an epidemic is raging. People get a pain in the side of the chest and die in a few days. It is very depressing to hear of so many deaths. Feeling that I might die too, I had to come to see you." Our conversation that night was even more dismal than usual. "I would not fear death," he said, "if it meant that in whatever form we may be reborn, I should be able to be with you. As a disciple of Buddha I must so live that I may be reborn on the most exalted seat in Paradise, yet the highest happiness for me would be to live with you even though it was in the humblest thatched cottage."

We spent the whole night talking together in this strain with no sleep at all, and when he got up to go, it was already broad daylight. The house in which I lived being inside the same fence as the main house, anyone who left my house could not avoid being noticed. He therefore stayed with me all the day so that his visit could be kept secret. I was much afraid that he might be seen and recognised, although no

[1]The armed monks were at this time demonstrating in favour of firmer action by the Military Government in face of the continued threat of invasion by the Mongols. The defeat of the attempted invasions in 1274 and 1281 did not put an end to these fears. In all times of crisis the armed monks were in the habit of coming in to the Capital to demonstrate violently in support of the cause they were supporting at the moment, carrying a branch of the sacred *sakaki* tree with a mirror hung on it. Altogether there were thousands of these monks at the various important temples, the most active being the Enryakuji temple at Otsu and the Kofukuji temple at Nara.

one in the neighbourhood knew his identity except his page. He was therefore quite at his ease sitting with me, undisturbed by any fear of discovery. As for me, I could not understand how he could be so unperturbed; my heart was in a flutter all the day.

We talked on and on all through the day. He told me what he had done when we parted in bitterness under that morning moon. We spoke of my disappearance. "It was a great shock," he said, "when I heard that you had run away from court and that your whereabouts were unknown. There was no one to whom I could talk about it. So I set myself the task of copying out the Five Great Mahayana sutras. Copying characters from your letters I fixed one to each volume of the sutras in token that I had undertaken the task of copying these sutras to further my ardent desire while still in this world to spend one more night with you in exchanging pledges of love. That shows the measure of my improper love for you. I finished copying the sutras, but I held no ceremony of dedication to celebrate the completion of the work, for I wished to celebrate that together with you when we were reunited after our rebirth. For if I give these volumes of the sutras which I have copied, over two hundred of them, into the safe-keeping of the Dragon King in his palace under the sea, they will surely help us to be reborn into this world together, and then we will hold the ceremony of dedication together. So if I die, use these sutras with the wood on my funeral pyre."

The utter depravity of his ideas terrified me. "Let's

content ourselves with the prayer that we may be reborn together in Paradise on the same lotus leaf," I said.

But he went on with his wild ideas. "No, I cannot give up thoughts of treading the way of love with you in this world," he said with the utmost sincerity. "I am determined to be reborn as a man in this world. The smoke that rises from my funeral pyre will turn to you and will not depart from you to disappear into the sky." He dozed for a little while and then he awoke with a startled look and broke into a perspiration.

"What is the matter?" I asked.

"I have just had a dream," he answered, "in which I was a mandarin duck[2] which entered into your body. Perhaps it is because my soul has entered into your body that I find myself suddenly running with perspiration."

Just before dawn he prepared to leave as I did not think it proper for him to stay another day. The morning moon was about to set behind the mountains, and a bank of cloud on the western hills was whitening as those in the east were disclosing themselves. He went away as the dawn bells rang out, and I missed him much more than ever before. Soon the page who lived in the neighbourhood brought me this poem,

> Now that I have left
> My heart behind with you,

[2] *Oshi,* a bird proverbial for its conjugal fidelity.

> No part left in me,
> Yet why is it I am still
> Pensively longing for you?

I felt a greater sorrow at parting from him and a greater love for him than ever before, greater than I could bear. With this filling my mind, I wrote a poem in answer,

> Set my sleeves with yours
> And see which is drenched the more
>   With tears of sorrow,
> Then tell me which one of us
> Misses the other the more.

Later in the same day I heard that he had gone to stay at the Tominokoji palace, and on about the eighteenth day I learnt that the doctors had been called to him as he was suffering from the epidemic which was sweeping through the country. Then to my great distress I heard that he was dangerously ill.

On the twenty-first I received a letter from him. "I did not think," he wrote, "when we met the other night that this was to be the last time we should meet in this world. It seems to me now that the strength of the ties which bind me to the things of this world is more sinful than the impure life I have lived. What can be the meaning of that dream I had that night?" At the end of his letter he added the poem,

> My body may die
> But my longing heart is left

Behind with you here,
My last prayer that my smoke may
Turn towards the place where you are.

How could I possibly describe my feelings on reading this letter? My grief was unbearable when I realised that our parting the other morning was in all probability for ever. I wrote a poem in answer to his,

If I live till then,
I hope I shall see the smoke
Rise and turn towards me
But the question still remains,
'Can I bear to live so long?'

In the circumstances I thought it best not to write all I felt, for I was still not without hope that this was not the end of everything, but on the twenty-fifth day of the eleventh month I learnt that he had passed away. Everything now seemed to me as ephemeral as a dream within a dream. I could not tell whether it was reality or whether everything was a dream. I did not know what to do, because perhaps my whole life had been such a life of sin.

I pondered over all the details of our relations from the time when he had complained that his love for me had found no answering love. I recalled our meeting when he had left me with such bitter feelings. If only I had never met him again after that sad parting, I should not have grieved in the way I was doing now. The sky was overcast that evening with fast-moving clouds and occasional showers. There was a deep gloom everywhere. The last letter he had written me hoping that the smoke of his funeral pyre would turn towards me lay as a forlorn reminder of him in my writing case. His perfume still lingered on my sleeve which he had used as a pillow. I longed for him and missed him more than ever. I wished even more than before to renounce the world to enter the True Way, but to do that at this present moment might revive the rumours and injure his reputation. I felt thwarted and frustrated.

At daybreak next morning I was told that the page boy had come. More or less in a trance I hurried out myself to see him. His robe of yellow lined with blue with a design of pheasants embroidered on it was creased and crumpled, his sleeves wet with the tears he had shed through the night. It would be impossible to set down on paper the story he told me with tears that day. That night, when he had parted from me, leaving me the poem beginning, "In sorrow gazing at the autumn moon at night," we had exchanged gowns. Mine he had always kept neatly folded small beside him on his prayer desk while he was at his devotions. Now on the evening of the twenty-fourth, he put it on.

"Have my body cremated with this gown on," he said to the grieving page boy. At the same time he handed him a letter for me with a present.

The page then handed me a large letter case, gold-lacquered with a design of a sacred *sakaki* tree. In it was a letter, if it could be called that. The handwriting resembled nothing so much as the footprints of a bird, the meaning impossible to decipher. It began with the words "For one night more" and I could hazard a guess that the next words might be "in this present world" but the rest of it was completely indecipherable. My tears fell uncontrollably at this evidence of the writer's extremity, and that made the characters even more impossible to read. I felt that I was being washed away by the same swift current as he, and my thoughts expressed themselves in the poem,

> If to the next world
> I could go to meet him there
>   At the Three-Way Stream,
> Then would I willingly go,
> Sacrificing my own life.

It seems that even at such a time and stricken with grief, my mind was still capable of composing poems. Inside the letter case too with the poem was a bag of gold dust.

After telling me how the prince's body had been cremated with my gown still on it and how his copy of the five sutras had been placed on his funeral pyre, the page left the house, still weeping bitterly. Looking after him as he went away, I felt that I should go crazy with grief.

The prince's death must have grieved the ex-Emperor very much, for the two brothers had been very close to each other. "How are you taking the news of his death?" he asked in a letter to me. It was obviously difficult to give a simple plain answer to such a question as that. The poem accompanying his letter read,

> Now that from your sight
> He has faded completely,
>   Still to the mind's eye
> The face of Wan Morning Moon
> Must still remain clear to you.

To the poem he added the words, "The world is truly a world of sorrows. Great was his love for you, and deep must be your grief at his passing. From my heart I feel for you."

There was nothing, I felt, that I could say in answer to that. I sent only the poem,

> Immeasurable
> Indeed my grief at his death;
>   In my mind's eye though
> Not alone seen clearly is
> The face of Wan Morning Moon.

Finding both my heart and my words incapable of expressing my feelings of grief, of love and longing, my days were passed in tears from morning till night.

The ex-Emperor continued to send me a messenger from time to time. Formerly he had urged me to come back to the palace as soon as possible, but now he only asked me why I was staying away from him. I gathered from his words that his love for me had grown weak, though he did not say so in so many words. It seemed natural that he should have become indifferent to me, because my misconduct had been repeated more than once, though not quite of my own will. I was not willing, however, to return to the court, and at last the time came when it was only a day or two to the end of the year. I was sorry both for the departing year and for my own self. I was engaged in copying the Lotus Flower sutra on the back of Wan Morning Moon's letters to me, recalling that he had copied the Five Great Mahayana sutras on the back of my letters to him, but that he would not dedicate the copied sutras to the campaign of people's enlightenment on Buddhism. It was a thousand pities that his endeavour was all for his own life of pleasure in this world. The New Year came to my grieving anxiety.

 Lady Nijo enters her twenty-fifth year on New Years' Day, 1282. She gives birth to Prince Shojo's second child

CHAPTER V   I passed New Year's Day immersed still in grief. The fifteenth day was the forty-ninth day after the prince's death. On that day I went into retreat at the temple at Higashiyama, whose High Priest I respected greatly. I attended a special service and conference and made an offering to the temple of some of the gold dust from the bag which the prince had left me. On the outside of the wrapper, I wrote the poem,

> Though we are parted,
> Be thou my guide on the way
>   To the world to come,
> That we may meet on that dawn
> When the Buddha greets the saved.

The High Priest was a preacher of some renown, and I wept as I listened to his sermon, for it seemed it was the prince's voice I could hear preaching.

I stayed in retreat until the fifteenth day of the second month, the anniversary of the death of S'akya Buddha. My mourning on this sad commemoration was increased by my own recent sorrowful bereavement. Afterwards in the private apartments of the High Priest there was held a series of lectures for fourteen days to follow the week of special services for the spring equinox. It was a happy occasion for me, spending the days reciting the sutras. At the same time it was sad, for I had to keep secret the name of the person for whose intention I was reciting them and could write down each time only the words, "Unforgotten pledge of love." On the last day of these devotions I wrote this poem on the last page of the prayer book,

> The setting of the sun
> Has renewed my sorrow;

> I must wait so long
> For the rising of the moon
> Heralding that glorious dawn.

I had no letter from the ex-Emperor while I was staying at Higashiyama. It was just as I had feared that it would be. I was so depressed that I decided I would return to the Capital on the day following the end of the devotions. On the last night, services continued throughout the night, none of the priests going to sleep. I lay down in the lecture theatre and just as dawn was about to break, I dozed off and dreamed. In my dream the prince appeared to me, looking just as he did when he was alive.

"Life in this sad world is one long, dark road," he said, clutching me tightly.

I awoke to find myself feeling really ill. I was near to fainting.

"It would be better for you to stay here today and continue your devotions," the High Priest said, seeing how ill I looked.

I had, however, already ordered a carriage and it would have been inconvenient to cancel it. I therefore set out for the Capital. When I came to the western end of the Kiyomizu bridge, I felt that the prince's spirit was with me in the carriage just as I had seen him in my dream. I was so upset that I fainted away. The maid who was with me took care of me and brought me safely to my old nurse's home. I was seriously ill, not even being able to drink water, remaining in this condition until after the middle of

the third month, by which time it was obvious to me
that I was again pregnant. Since my last meeting with
the prince, I had kept myself absolutely pure, re-
fraining even from the exchange of meaningful
glances with anyone. There could be no doubt about
the prince being the father of my child. Our relationship had left me with many sad memories, but now
I had a precious and lovely memory because it was one
unknown to anyone else. Now I began to be anxious,
perhaps immoderately so, about the future of my
child, now my dearest memory of the prince.

About the tenth day of the fourth month, the ex-
Emperor sent for me, saying he had some special
business he wished to discuss with me. I was reluctant
to go as I did not wish to be seen by people in my
delicate condition. I excused myself, saying I was too
ill. He replied with the poem,

> Why is it that still
> You so occupy yourself
> With his memory
> Who has now cut himself free
> From all the ties of this world?

To this he added the note, "Believing that you
had no time for anything but mourning your loss, I
have refrained from intruding on your grief now that
I have no other claim on you but that of an old, old
friend." He was obviously offended with me. At
the time I believed it was because he thought I was
still obsessed with my longings for Wan Morning

Moon. I learnt later, however, that while Kameyama was still the reigning emperor, my old nurse's son, Nakayori, one of the most trusted of the emperor's officers, had told the ex-Emperor that Kameyama and I had, by his help, become lovers and that I was contemplating leaving the ex-Emperor for Kameyama. The ex-Emperor suspected that the liaison was still continuing, although at the time I knew nothing of his suspicions.

I gradually recovered from my illness and at the beginning of the fifth month, I decided to return to my duties at the court. I considered it was better not to leave it till later or my condition would be too obvious. The ex-Emperor appeared to avoid talking to me, though when he did, his attitude did not appear to be unusually cold. I continued to feel depressed day and night, but I stayed on at the palace until I was able to leave on the excuse of going into mourning for a relative who had just died.

From this time I particularly wished to hide the fact that I was going to have a child, and so I secluded myself at the house of a relative near Higashiyama. There were very few visitors to the house, and I felt I was living in a totally different world.

About the twentieth of the eighth month my labour pains began. On the previous occasions, however much I had had to hide myself from people, there were always a few visitors who came to see me. Now there was no one; I had no friend save the sad belling of the deer on the hills night and day. Still there were no complications and the boy was born. How can one help loving the child one has borne? Especially when the child is a son, just as his father's dream of a mandarin drake had foretold. It was a strong tie that united the three of us. I had always felt it sad that, as I lost my mother when I was two years of age, I could not remember her face. This child would grieve too that his father had died before he was born. With this thought in my mind, I always kept him at my side. As there was no one in the neighbourhood who could act as his nurse, I fed him myself, fondling him tenderly as I did so. When his bed next to mine was wet under him, I would take him into my own where I kept him in my arms and for the first time in my life experienced the joys of motherhood. For more than forty days I looked after him on my own because I could not bear his leaving my side. Even when I had a suitable nurse come from Yamazaki, he still had his little bed next to mine. I could not bring myself to leave him to go back to my duties at the court, but it would soon be winter and the ex-Emperor urged me not to remain away any longer. I therefore went back at the beginning of the tenth month and so the end of the old year came.

Lady Nijo enters her twenty-sixth year on New Year's Day, 1283. She is forced to leave the court

CHAPTER At the New Year I felt extremely miser-

VI able for several reasons. For one thing, I was not happy about having no suitable clothes to wear for the celebrations. Also, although the ex-Emperor said nothing to me that I could reasonably object to, yet he seemed rather distant with me. Only the one who was my friend of bygone days came to see me.[1] Love is strong and will always prevail over feelings of jealousy and rancour.

In the second month there was a series of sermons at the equinox at the Saga palace with the two ex-Emperors present. While I was there, I could not forget the image of the one who had attended the sermons one year before. In my misery, I prayed for help to Buddha, "In accordance with your pledge to save all souls, graciously lead into Paradise the soul of my dear one who may still be wandering in the nether world." My thoughts found expression in the poem,

> The tears shed for you
> Flow onward like a torrent,
> As this Oi river;

[1] Snowy Dawn, Lord Sanekane, no doubt.

I would I could drown in it
So might I see you again.

Whatever I thought of made me unhappy. Ties of
love made me disgruntled. What I wanted to do was
exactly what I had suggested in my poem, to drown
myself. I set about destroying old letters and keepsakes. But then I thought of my child. If I abandoned
him, he would have no one to look after him with
loving care. My resolution weakened. One's ties with
one's child, I realised, are the most formidable ob-
stacles to one's renouncing the world. I expressed
my thoughts in the poem,

Why was it his fate
Thus to be born fatherless
And left to stand
Like a solitary pine
On a long-deserted shore?

When the ex-Emperors returned to the Capital,
I got leave to go to see my child. He had grown quite
a lot. He prattled, smiled, and crowed. It moved me
to tears to watch him, and I felt I ought really not to
have come.

Then, at the beginning of autumn, I received a
letter from my grandfather, Lord Takachika, the
Minister of War. "Vacate your room immediately,"
he wrote, "and come here prepared to stay per-
manently. I will send to fetch you this evening."

I could not grasp the full import of this letter and

went to see the ex-Emperor. "What does he mean by this suggestion?" I asked. He made no answer.

I could think of no cause for this. I went to Lady Genkimon, who was perhaps called Lady Third Grade then, the Lady of the East Wing. "What has caused my grandfather to make this suggestion?" I said. "I have already asked the ex-Emperor about it, but I could get no answer from him."

"I don't know either," she said.

It seemed impossible for me, however, to persist in remaining at the palace.

As I got things ready that day for my departure, I could not help recalling bygone days. It was in the ninth month, when I was only in my fourth year, that I had come there for the first time. Since then it had been my home, and I had thought of it in that way even when I was away from it on home leave. Now that I was seeing it for the last time, I was moved to tears by the sight of every familiar plant and tree.

While I was packing, it happened that the lord who had most cause for being distant with me[2] came by. "You are in your room then," he said. I was so moved by his friendliness that I went out to him.

"What is the matter?" he asked, for he could see by my tears that something was wrong. I could not say a word for my sobs and showed him my grandfather's letter of that morning.

"That is why I am weeping," I said.

I invited him into my room, and we talked about

[2] Again, no doubt, Lord Sanekane.

the letter, but he had no idea what was the matter. Those ladies whom I had known for a long time also tried to comfort me, but they had no idea of the reason for the letter either. I could do nothing but weep.

Although I was now convinced that the ex-Emperor did not wish me to remain any longer in his service, that evening I ventured to go in to see him, in spite of the fact that he might resent my intrusion. It might be for the last time, I thought.

It was a great mistake to have gone. I found him chatting with two or three lords. I was dressed in a thin glossy silk robe embroidered in blue with a design of arrowroot and pampas grass with a red mantle.

"Well, you're leaving us tonight, aren't you?" he said, glancing at me. I remained silent, not knowing what to say. "People say that the meaning of 'arrowroot' is 'come.' By wearing a robe with that design, I hope you're not implying that you are coming back." Then he went off, perhaps to the apartments of the ex-Empress, humming the tune, "How hateful to me is this arrowroot!"

How could I feel anything but bitter hatred for him? We had pledged everlasting love for each other many, many times over the years, vowing that nothing should ever separate us from one another. How could he be so unfeeling now? I wished I could die on the spot. What had caused him to be so callous? Still, there was nothing I could do. I thought of hiding myself somewhere, but I wished to know for certain what the real reason was. The carriage was waiting, and I went off to the Minister's house on Nijo street.

My grandfather came out to welcome me himself. "It's just old age that's the matter with me," he said. "I don't know when I shall get over it. I've got so weak and tired lately that I wanted you to come here. I felt anxious about you as you have no father and Takaaki is no longer alive. Also I have had a letter from the ex-Empress which made me consider that it would not be wise in the circumstances for you to continue in the service of the ex-Emperor." He took out the letter and I read it. "I disapprove of your granddaughter's behaviour in continually belittling me," the ex-Empress had written. "Recall her from the ex-Emperor's service at once and look after her. As her mother is dead, that is your responsibility." She had written the letter in her own handwriting. After reading it, I could not but conclude that the wisest course for me was to leave the palace when the ex-Empress showed such hostility.

All through the long autumn nights the cloth-beaters' mallets brought to my sleepless pillow from every direction their melancholy thuds while the wild geese flying high in the sky dropped tears of dew on the bush clover shrubs in the garden. So the days passed, and the year was coming to an end.

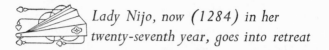

CHAPTER As I was not looking forward with any
   anticipation of pleasure to the New Year,
VII I decided to go into a thousand-day retreat
at the Yasaka shrine, thus fulfilling a vow I had been
prevented from performing by this circumstance or
that for a number of years.

On the second day of the eleventh month, it being
the first day of the Hare, there was to be a performance
of Sacred Dance and Music at the Hachiman shrine at
Iwashimizu. I went there to worship, remembering
the words of the old poet who wrote,

> To the worship of the gods
> Have I devoted my soul.

I wrote at the time this poem,

> Ceaselessly I pray
> For the favour of the gods,
>   Yet must I bewail
> My fate that my prayers always
> Remain still unrewarded.

After seven days of retreat at the Yasaka shrine, I
went back to Iwashimizu where I offered up this
prayer to the god, "Having no wish to continue my

life in this world, I pray you deliver me from the raging fire of this world that I may enter the gate of salvation.''

On the anniversary of the death of Wan Morning Moon, I had the Lotus Flower sutra recited for seven days at the temple at Higashiyama. I attended the service every day, returning each evening to the Yasaka shrine. The recitation came to an end on the anniversary of his death on the twenty-fifth day of the eleventh month. The ringing of the bells moving me to tears, I wrote,

> Why am I afraid
> Of leaving this present world
>   So full of sorrow
> Where I weep to the ringing
> Of the peals of mourning bells?

I now took over the care of my child whom I had kept hidden away in the hope that he might prove to be a comfort to me. I was touched to see him full of vigour, walking about or running, and talking, free from all anxiety and worry.

My grandfather had passed away during the year before with the dews of autumn in a year full of saddening incidents. I ought to have described his death in more detail perhaps, but my mind had been too preoccupied with my having left the court. Now that I had nothing else to occupy me during the long days and nights, I had more leisure to see him as being the only relative I had had on my mother's side on whom I could rely after my mother's death. It must have been because I was at heart deeply conscious of this that I now mourned his death with such grief.

Gradually the different varieties of cherry trees came into blossom in the garden of the shrine, recalling to my mind the divine oracle ascribed to the shrine's god which foretells prosperity to those who plant a tree when at last a thousand trees are planted,

> When the time comes that
> In the garden of the shrine
> A thousand trees bloom,
> Then those who have planted them
> Will enjoy prosperity.

I thought, therefore, that I ought to present at least a branch to the shrine in the belief that, whether it was a root or just a branch, it would bring prosperity to me. Through the favour of a cousin of mine, the High Priest Shingen, I was able to present a cherry branch in front of the Amida-in temple which is a chapel of the Danna-in temple on Mt. Hiei in charge of the High Priest Kin-yo.

This I did on the first day of the Horse in the second month, the ceremony being conducted by the High Priest En-yo, administrator of the temple, to whom I made a present of a thin silk robe and a white one lined with red. To the branch I attached a pale blue label with the poem,

> Come into full bloom,

> Even though no root you have,
>   For the god knows well
> How sincere the petitions
> I have entrusted to you.

The branch did take root and bloom, and I was certain my piety would be rewarded. I then began the recitation of one thousand volumes of the sutras, but feeling it rather a presumption to occupy a room at the temple any longer, I moved into the eastern one of the two hermitages at the rear of the Hoto-in temple. So I continued with my retreat until the old year came to an end.

 On New Year's Days 1285, Lady Nijo enters her twenty-eighth year. The Titular Empress of Kitayama celebrates her ninetieth birthday[1]

CHAPTER In the first month of the new year, I
VIII received a letter from the Empress Dowager Omiya, the mother of the two ex-Emperors. "The titular ex-Empress of Kitayama has attained the ripe old age of ninety," she wrote. "I have been busy since the beginning of the year with preparations for the celebration. I am not concerned at all with the reasons why you have been away from the

[1] She died in 1302 at the age of 107.

court for a long time and would like you to join the
other ladies-in-waiting on this occasion. Please come
to the ex-Empress's residence."

"I thank you for your kind invitation," I wrote in
answer. "I have been away from court because the
ex-Emperor appears to think ill of me. Although I
should have been pleased to accept your kind invitation, I am afraid that in these circumstances it would
not be advisable for me to join the other ladies."

"You need not worry about these difficulties,"
the Empress Dowager wrote in a letter in her own
handwriting. "You must bear in mind that from the
time of your childhood you and your mother stood
high in the favour of the ex-Empress of Kitayama.
You are in a different position from any of the other
ladies. In the circumstances you cannot absent yourself
from the celebration."

So, fearing that any further refusal on my part
might seem to be unaccommodating, I accepted the
invitation. As I intended to return to complete my
retreat, I had a substitute there to represent me for the
period of my absence. A carriage was provided for
me and all the arrangements made by Lord Sanekane.
As I already thought of myself as a countrywoman,
I was afraid that I should mar the brilliant atmosphere,
but I went to the palace in a set of three white robes
lined with dark red and a cloak of yellowish green
lined with pink. As I had expected, preparations had
been made for the celebration to be carried out on a
lavish scale.

The two ex-Emperors, the ex-Empress Higashi

Nijo, and her daughter Princess Yugimon, who later became consort of the Emperor Go Uda, had already arrived. The new ex-Emperor's consort, Shin-yomeimon, was present, though incognito. On the twenty-ninth day of the second month the Emperor and the Crown Prince arrived for the celebration which was to begin the next day. The Emperor came in a procession of three palanquins, his own palanquin being halted outside the main entrance where to the sound of court music he was greeted with divine honours by the appointed official. Lord Kinhira, Commander of the Gate Guards of the Left and Steward of the Household of the Empress Dowager Omiya, having reported the Emperor's arrival to her, had the Emperor's palanquin brought round to the middle gate where the Chujo Nijo no Kanemoto took charge of the Imperial regalia, the Sacred Sword, and the Sacred Jewels. The Crown Prince arriving then, straw mats were laid up to the gate for him to walk to the main entrance. At the temporary pavilion erected for the reception of the Emperor were Fujiwara no Akiie, who was in charge of the arrangements; the Imperial Adviser, Takatsukasa no Kanehira; the General of the Left, Takatsukasa no Kanetada; and Chujo Nijo no Kanemoto. The Minister of the Left, Nijo no Morotada, had accompanied the Crown Prince as his tutor.

On the day of the celebration a dais was erected in the middle room on the south side of the main hall with a picture of Buddha hung above the dais and a bamboo blind behind it. In front of the dais was a stand for a censer and flowers with candlesticks on either side. Before the stand was a rostrum for the priest with a stand in front of it with holders for the two sutras, the Longevity sutra and the Lotus Flower sutra. The prayer to Buddha was composed, I heard, by Fujiwara no Mochinori, the Emperor's tutor, and written out by the Imperial Adviser. Each of the pillars of the room was decorated with a streamer of various colours and an ornamental tablet.

In the room on the west behind a bamboo screen was a cushion of Chinese brocade for the Emperor's seat on two mats bordered with red figured brocade.

On the north of the room two mats bordered with Korean brocade were placed for the ex-Emperor and in the next room two mats of the same kind for the new ex-Emperor. In the room on the east was the Empress Dowager Omiya's seat with its screen. It gave me real pain to see the silk robes of the ladies in the service of the ex-Emperor, as I now saw them from the outside. In the same western room there was a seat for the ex-Empress of Kitayama on two mats of red and white brocade.

The Titular ex-Empress of Kitayama was the wife of Saionji no Sadauji, Chief Minister, and was the mother of the Empress Dowager of Omiya and of the ex-Empress Higashi Nijo. As the grandmother of the two ex-Emperors and the great-grandmother of the reigning Emperor Go Uda and of the Crown Prince, it was natural that she was held in the highest respect and that everyone should wish to make this a happy occasion for her. She herself was the granddaughter of the Washi-no-o Dainagon, Shijo no Takafusa, and a daughter of the Dainagon Shijo no Takahira. She was therefore a close relative of mine on my mother's side. My mother had been brought up by her as a child and I had myself often stayed with her.

I had asked if I might attend the celebration in ordinary dress but had been advised by the Empress Dowager to wear purple robes shaded from dark to light. Upon further consideration, however, she had ask me to come over to her residence first to consult about the matter. Her ladies were all wearing red robes shaded from dark to light with a scarlet mantle. Finally, at Lord Sanekane's suggestion, I wore a set of eight red robes lined with dark red with a dark red under-robe, a yellow cloak lined with pale green, and a blue mantle, all in most brilliant colours. It made me feel rather wretched, however, that I was not dressed in the accustomed garb of a lady-in-waiting.

The ceremony began; the two ex-Emperors, the Crown Prince, the Empress Dowager Omiya, the two ex-Empresses, and the young princess of Imadegawa entered in procession to the sound of chants and bells. To the east of the rostrum sat the Imperial Adviser, the Ministers of the Left and Right, with many other high officials and officers of the guards, all the officers of the guards wearing on their backs their bows and arrows. The Emperor, the two ex-Emperors, and the Crown Prince, all simply robed, sat within the bamboo screens.

The musicians and dancers began to perform classical music led by the hand drums, halberds swinging in time with the music. Then, to the music, the musicians, dancers, and priests entered in two files and passed to their seats, entering the middle hall, moving on either side of the rostrum, and climbing the steps. The preacher, the High Priest Kenjichi; the reader, the High Priest Shujo, brother of the Empress Dowager; and the leader of the prayers, his elder brother, the High Priest Doyo, took their seats, and the stone gong was struck. The temple pages were waiting in two groups, and when a hymn had been sung by the choir of priests, they scattered flower petals while the music played. At the conclusion, the musicians made their reverence to the Emperor and their chief received their fee from the official in charge.

The priests' rostrum was then removed and a dance performed. A steady drizzle was falling, but the people standing round in front of the hall took no notice of this. For myself, however, I soon got bored with the whole expensive but rather tasteless performance and wondered how long I was going to have to endure it. The right group of musicians played, and then the left group of musicians played. Ono no Hisatada danced "The Emperor's Reward," and the Minister of the Right left his seat, summoned the dancer Chikayasu of the left group, and gave him honours and rewards for his group. Chikayasu then retired; he should have made another reverence to the Emperor as he did so, but as the dancer Hisasuke and the musician Masaaki of the right group were called up then to receive their honours and rewards, this was

not necessary. When Masaaki, flute in hand, made his
reverence, Their Majesties praised his skill. When the
High Priest Kenjichi left his seat, music was played
while the priests received their rewards. The guards
officers, Fujiwara no Kin-atsu, Kyogoku no Tamekane,
and Lord Yasunaka, wore military dress with their
quivers, but most of the attendants wore wadded
formal robes and carried service swords, though
mainly of the lightweight pattern. The priests left the
hall, and more music followed. Then the musicians
and the dancers left. Dinner was then served to the
Empress Dowager and the ex-Empresses, Shijo no
Takayasu serving them while the Commander of the
Left brought in the trays.

The next day was the first day of the third month.
Breakfast was served to the Imperial party. The dais
for the dancing had been removed and curtains hung
round the hall with a screen to the west. In the centre
hall there were large Chinese brocade cushions for
the Emperor and the ex-Emperors on two mats with
edgings of various shades. In the room to the east
there was a cushion of Togyo brocade on a similar mat
for the Crown Prince. The Imperial Adviser raised
the bamboo blind for the Imperial party to come out,
and Lord Sanekane raised the blind for the Crown
Prince, Lord Morotada being late in arriving. Breakfast was served to the Emperor and the ex-Emperors,
who wore red wadded silk robes, and the Crown
Prince, who wore an unwadded robe, each served by
a high official and an officer of the guards. My uncle
Takayoshi bore the dishes for the Crown Prince,

238 • Lady Nijo's Story

wearing a white formal cloak lined with red, a pale purple robe, trousers of the same colour, and a scarlet under-robe, with a quiver and a head dress with ear flaps, a dress eminently suiting the occasion.

Afterwards there was a concert of wind and string instruments. For the use of the Emperor, the famous flute Katei was brought in its case by Taira no Tadayo. The Imperial Adviser received it and placed it before the Emperor. The famous flute Genjo was brought in by Minamoto no Chikasada for the Crown Prince. His Lord Steward Sanekane received it and placed it before him. Flutes for the other players were brought in another box. A concert then began with various lords playing the flute, the harp, and the lute, the Dainagon Tokudaiji no Kintaka beating time with the wooden clappers and Lord Munefuyu singing.

Next a poetry competition was held. Officials set out a desk and round straw seats. Poems already written were collected in order of rank beginning with those of the lower ranks. First, Nijo no Tamemichi, Lieutenant Commander of the Bodyguard of the Left, dressed in formal garb wearing a leather-thonged battle sword and quiver, went up to the desk with his poem and his bow together in his hands and placed the poem on the desk. The poems of the other officials were then collected. Earlier, Fujiwara no Akiie had placed the Crown Prince's seat to the east of the desk where he stayed throughout the contest. People commented on how much it reminded them of contests in former days. It was announced that poems had been handed in by all the high officers of state from the

Imperial Adviser and the Ministers of the Left and the Right down. All these officials were in court dress and wearing a sword except my cousin, Koga no Michimoto, General of the Right, who wore the full dress of a general, reddish-brown lined with yellow. He presented his poem holding it in his hands with his mace. The other lords all wore bows and arrows on their backs.

The Kazan-in Dainagon summoned those who were to recite their poems, and the judges, the Vice-Director of the Imperial Archives, the Ministers of the Left and the Right, the War Minister, and the Chunagon Fujiwara no Kinyasu, went to the desk.

Lady Gon Chunagon, in the service of the Empress Dowager, handed out her poem written on thin scarlet paper from behind the screen. She had some reputation as a poet.

"Why hasn't Lord Masatada's daughter[2] handed in her poem?" the new ex-Emperor said.

"She is not feeling well and doesn't feel like composing a poem today," was the answer he received from the ex-Emperor.

"Why haven't you handed in a poem?" Lord Sanekane said to me.

"I was told that the ex-Empress Higashi Nijo had asked the Empress Dowager not to accept a poem from me," I answered. I had, however, composed a poem and, as I could not enter it in the contest, I kept on repeating it to myself,

[2] Lady Nijo; but, as we have learnt earlier, she did not like the name. Kameyama was nice about things like this.

> When I have been told
> That today I do not rank
> Among the poets,
> How then can I bring myself
> To hand in a poem now?

The Imperial Adviser, Takatsukasa no Kanehira, recited the poems of the Emperor and the ex-Emperors, while the Crown Prince's poem was recited in the ordinary course of the readings. These were repeatedly commended as the best by the judges. When the contest was over, the Imperial party left, the Crown Prince first, and the prizes were awarded.

The Emperor's poem written out by the Imperial Adviser read,

> The poem composed by the Emperor at the celebration of the ninetieth birthday of Fujiwara no Teishi, a noble vassal of the Junior First Court Rank. (This Emperor is now living in religious retreat at the Daikakuji temple, his name in religion being Zenjosen-in.)[3]

> With the lengthening
> Of the day as spring goes on,
> We see the promise
> Of a further lengthening
> Of your days in this our world.

[3] This note would appear to have been written in A.D. 1313, when Lady Nijo was fifty-six years old.

The new ex-Emperor's poem was written out by the Minister of the Centre, Fujiwara no Iemoto. The introductory remarks were exactly the same except for the reference to "Teishi" which was omitted.

> Now that you have seen
> Of your life these ninety springs
>   In this present world,
> The nightingale is singing
> To welcome your hundredth year.

The Crown Prince's poem was written out by the General of the Left, Fujiwara no Kanetada, the Imperial Adviser's son,

> Following the Emperor's example, this poem was composed by the Crown Prince during his stay at the Mansion of Kitayama in spring on the occasion of the celebration of the ninetieth birthday of Lady Fujiwara of the Junior First Court Rank. (The words "Respectfully presented" were added to the introductory remarks in accordance with ancient precedents.)

> Having now passed this stage
> Of ninety long years of life,
>   We may boldly say,
> You will now go on to live
> To see a thousand more springs.

All the other poems I will give in some other place,

but I must add here the poem of Lord Sanekane which was praised by all present, both high and low, as being the most interesting of all,

> You now take your place
> Among those famed for long life;
>   The reason for this—
> Till today you have lived on
> To welcome His Majesty.

Some years before, Lord Sanekane's grandfather, Saionji no Saneuji, at that time Chief Minister, had invited the Retired Emperor Go Saga and the two ex-Emperors to a recital of the complete collection of sutras. All then present had praised the poem which the Retired Emperor had composed at that time which ends,

> The cherry blossom and I
> Are both in our prime today.

as well as that of the Minister which speaks of,

> The eternal praise
> Of these three generations
> Of the great Imperial House.

But everyone said that Lord Sanekane's poem on this occasion was not surpassed by either of these.

After the poetry contest there was a ball game. It was a sight to remember to see the Emperor, the new ex-Emperor, the Crown Prince, the Imperial Adviser, and the other lords taking part in the game, displaying their many-coloured sleeves. Following the precedent of Emperor Go Toba, the new ex-Emperor kicked off.

After the game, the Emperor left for his palace. He was reluctant to go, but the Spring Appointments list was due to be published, and he could not spare any more time.

The next day, the Emperor having left, things were less formal. About noon, straw mats were laid down along the path from the North Hall to the Saionji temple. The two ex-Emperors in their formal robes and headgear and the Crown Prince in his formal robes with trousers tied at the ankles paid little visits to all the chapels in the grounds of the temple. Finally they reached the Myo-on chapel where they found one cherry tree still in blossom as if it had been waiting for the honour of this royal visit. Looking at these blossoms, with the old poet I wondered who had taught it

> Thus to keep its blossom still
> While all the rest theirs had shed.

A musical entertainment was held in the Myo-on chapel. Many of the common sort had gathered outside to hear the music, the women with their heads covered over with a garment. I stood among them to listen. The royal party was inside the chapel, while in the porch one lord played the flute, another the pan-pipes, another the flageolet, the Crown Prince the lute, Lord

Sanekane the harp, and two other lords the drums. They played several pieces, and Lord Kaneyuki recited part of the Chinese poem "The cherry blossom in the courtyard holds the eye" in perfect time with the music. His recitation was so enjoyed by everyone that he had to repeat it a second time. Then the ex-Emperor recited, with the new ex-Emperor and the Crown Prince accompanying him in chorus, part of Sugawara no Michizane's Chinese poem, "Resenting the weaver's lack of sympathy." The effect was truly marvellous, and everyone was sorry that the concert had to come to an end and the royal party leave.

Seeing that life in the scintillating world of the court was so pleasant only deepened my gloom, and I could not bring myself to go to see that day's ball game which was just beginning. I was sorry that I had come to the celebration at all. The sound of the ex-Emperor's voice as he recited the poem in the Myo-on chapel still rang in my ears and saddened me with memories of former happy days. In such a pensive mood was I when my uncle Takayoshi brought me a letter.

"Haven't you brought this to the wrong person?" I asked him. He assured me that the letter was for me and insisted that I should open and read it. I did so. It contained a poem from the ex-Emperor,

> I had hoped I might
> By keeping away from you
>   Cease to long for you.
> Do you not need to tell me
> Your resentment against me?

To this he added, "I can't forget you. I can't change my feelings for you. Let us meet again tonight and end the wretchedness of the past months."

My poem in answer read,

What bitter feelings
Can I have had about you
For these two long years?
What of those you feel, learning
My vows I have not taken?

I was much surprised that evening about eight o'clock when the ball game was over and I was lying down to rest to receive a visit from the ex-Emperor. "We are just this moment going for a boat trip. Come with us," he said. Wondering if I dared to face all that company again, I just lay there. "Your ordinary clothes will do," he said.

I got up and he helped me to tie the strings of my skirt. I was astonished to find him so affectionate, and wondered when it was that he had begun to feel this way again about me. But, I felt, two years of bitter suffering and resentment were not going to be so easily smoothed over. "Still," I thought, "I must do as he wishes," and wiping away my tears, I went with him. It was getting dark as we boarded the boat at the fishing pavilion.

First, the Crown Prince and the Ladies Dainagon, Uemonnokami, and Kononaishi, all in the ceremonial dress, went aboard. The two ex-Emperors went on board a small boat with me accompanying them in my ordinary clothes. Then I was told to go on board the Crown Prince's boat. The musical instruments were taken on the small boat where the same lords as before played much the same kind of music as they had played in the chapel during the afternoon, and just as enjoyably. Lord Kaneyuki recited the Chinese poem "Mountain on mountain," and the ex-Emperors followed with "The complexity of these ever-changing scenes." It seemed that their lovely voices raised in harmony must astonish the spirits under the water.

When the boat had rowed far out from the pavilion, the sight of the old pine trees with their branches interlaced over the water of the pool was indescribably beautiful. We felt as if we had rowed far, far away over the wide ocean.

The new ex-Emperor began a poem,

> Our boat comes cutting
> Straight through the clouds and the spray
> Of the bounding waves.

"You have stubbornly vowed never again to make music," he said to me. "I hope you won't refuse to finish my poem."

I did not wish to do so, but I capped his lines with,

> To view the wide open sea—
> Which is our Emperor's reign.

Lord Sanekane began,

> Greater tribute now
> Does the Emperor receive
> Than in olden times,

Lord Tomoaki completed the verse by,

> His brighter glory is due
> To the favour of the gods.

The Crown Prince began,

> The journey goes on
> Passing these ninety milestones
> Slowly one by one

The new ex-Emperor capped this with,

> On life's wearisome journey
> Of everyday worries.

I started another poem,

> With all my sorrow
> Pent up in this heart of mine,
> Heart-broken I feel,

"I know exactly what is pent up in that heart of yours," said the ex-Emperor, and capped my verse,

> As blinded with tears, I look
> Up at the Wan Morning Moon.

"Is there anything particular implied in the reference to the wan morning moon?" the new ex-Emperor asked his brother.

It was quite dark by this time, and it was strange and interesting to see the park keepers going about making fires here and there on the bank to guide the boat back to the pavilion. There we reluctantly disembarked, all feeling unsatisfied perhaps. For myself, I wondered why no one could spare a thought of compassion for me, so tossed about on a restless sea, the sport of all the winds of fortune. That lake was certainly in no sense the heavenly beach of Yasu where the gods meet in perfect harmony, for no one spoke a word of kindness to me; in this world men and women are not allowed to become intimate with one another with impunity.

During the day the personal appearance of Kiyo-kage, one of the Crown Prince's guards, attracted a great deal of attention. His carriage and behaviour and dress were all much admired; he was wearing reddish blue silk robes with a pattern of wistaria against pine branches.

A messenger was sent to court while at the same time the Finance Minister, Taira no Tadayo, was coming from the court, but they missed each other on the way.

A lute was presented to the Emperor, and a Japanese harp to the Crown Prince. On the recommendation of the ex-Emperor, the grade of senior fourth rank was conferred on Fujiwara no Toshisada, and on the recommendation of the Crown Prince that of senior fifth rank on Taira no Koresuke. Junior fourth rank was conferred on Fujiwara no Tamemichi in return for the prize that was to have been presented to Lord Sanekane who had played the harp so well. Other ranks were conferred, but I do not need to note them here.

On the departure of the party, I settled down to a cheerless life. The ex-Emperor sent me many messages asking me to accompany him to Lord Sanekane's residence, but I felt no inclination to go; it seemed certain that I should find no happiness wherever I went.

Book Four

Three years have elapsed since the events described in Book Three. The year is 1289. Lady Nijo, now thirty-two years of age, had taken her vows the year before. She now goes on a pilgrimage to the eastern provinces

CHAPTER In the latter part of the second month,
    I   I left the Capital before daybreak, the
           moon being still high in the sky. I had
thought that it would be easy to leave now that there
was nothing to detain me there, but when I considered
that fate might prevent my ever returning, I wept
afresh, and the reflection of the moon on my wet
sleeves showed a tearful face. I had become very faint-
hearted by the time I arrived at the Ausaka barrier.
This reminded me of the old poet and lute player,
Semimaru, who settled near here, and his poem,

> Whether our home is
> In a humble thatched cottage
>   Or in a palace,
> The world appears just the same;
> In both we find life too short.

There was no trace to be found now of his thatched
cottage.

In the water of the spring at the barrier my figure was reflected, that of a nun in a travelling habit. The sight disheartening me, I found myself more and more disinclined to go on with my journey and felt my steps becoming slower and slower.

Here there was only one cherry tree remaining in full bloom. That by itself made it an attractive subject to me for a poem, the more so because there were four or five persons on horseback, country folk but quite respectably dressed, resting under the tree, presumably with much the same feelings as myself. The beauty of the scene expressed itself in my poem,

> At Ausaka
> The beauty of the blossoms
>   Halts the traveller.
> Does it not seem the blossoms
> Are the real barrier keepers?

I went on to the post station at Kagami[1] where I arrived towards evening. It is a sad world, I mused, as with compassion I saw prostitutes busy soliciting custom and offering their company for the night to travellers. I stayed for the night in the village and continued my journey as the bells tolled for dawn with this poem forming in my mind,

> As drawing nearer,
> I gazed at you, O mirror,

[1] *kagami*, a mirror.

> You could not know
> What a lasting impression
> A person left in my mind.

Several days passed before I arrived at the post station of Akasaka in Mino province. Exhausted and depressed after so many days of unaccustomed travel, I stopped for the night at the inn. The landlord's two daughters who worked at the inn, soliciting custom, serving as prostitutes, and playing the lute and harp, seemed to be of a rather romantic turn of mind. Thinking of my own childhood in the service of the court, I decided to have a little drinking party of my own with the sisters serving the wine. The elder sister seemed to be very pensive. She appeared to be trying to cheer herself up by playing the lute, but her eyes often filled up with tears. I was attracted to her, for I felt that she had much the same outlook on life as I had had as a girl. She must have thought it strange that I in a nun's black habit should weep in sympathy with her, for she wrote a poem on a slip of paper and passed it to me on a salver,

> Would I could know
> Where goes the smoke which passes
>   Out from Mt. Fuji—
> As why, renouncing the world,
> You come here on pilgrimage.

She showed in this poem a feeling so akin to my own that I answered,

> Smoke from Mt. Fuji
> Comes from the fierce flames within;
>   So, I must confess,
> My action stems from the flames
> Of passion deep in my heart.

It was then with a feeling of tearing myself away from friends and a place I did not wish to leave that I went on from there to Yatsuhashi, a place I knew from *The Tales of Ise*,[2] but there I found no sign of the eight bridges which gave the place its name or even of any stream at all. To this place had come the traveller in *The Tales of Ise*, but on this journey, he notes, no friend had accompanied him. I had the same feeling, too, of being companionless as I wandered about looking for the eight bridges,

> In perplexity
> I wandered by the river,
>   Nowhere could I find
> Eight bridges said to be there
> Crossing over the eight streams.

I visited the shrine at Atsuta in Owari province. As I stood in front of the sacred fence, my mind was full of memories for my father who had been in charge of this province. Every year at the festival of the shrine in the fifth month, he had always presented a sacred horse to the shrine as an offering for his own intention.

[2] *Ise Monogatari*, written between 980 and 985, uses the poems of Arihara no Narihira in a story of travel.

During his last illness, he had made such an offering of a sacred horse as well as of robes, but at the post station, Kayatsu, the horse had suddenly died. Shocked at this, the local officials had presented another horse in its place. I heard of this at the time and considered it an omen of my father's death. All this coming back to my mind at this time to my great grief, I stayed for one night at the shrine.

It was now the beginning of the third month. I had left home after the twentieth of the second month and ought to have made much better progress. I was, however, not used to travelling; it was my mind alone that was hurrying on. The evening moon was shining brightly in the sky, just as I remembered it shining in the Capital. I felt as if the ex-Emperor were by my side looking up at it as we had so often done together. The cherry trees within the confines of the shrine were then in full bloom. For whom were they showing their beauty? Looking at them, I expressed my impressions thus,

> For how short a time
> Will they retain their beauty,
>   These cherry blossoms,
> Among the cedars under
> The spring sky of Narumi!

I had the board on which I had written this nailed to a cedar tree in front of the shrine. Then, as I had long wished to worship at this shrine, I went into retreat there for seven days.

Afterwards as I left the shrine, walking along the beach at Narumi at ebb tide, I looked back towards the shrine, seeing its vermilion fence indistinctly through the haze. Thinking of former days, my eyes filled with tears as I murmured,

> Have mercy on me,
> God of the Atsuta shrine,
> I beseech you now,
> Though I am now but a nun
> Clad in this sad black habit.

As I passed through the barrier at Kiyomi by the light of the moon, my heart was sad with memories of the past and forebodings of the future, my misgivings about the future as numberless as the grains of sand on the white glittering beach.

When I walked along the beach at Ukishima at the foot of Mt. Fuji, the high peak still seemed deep in snow. That was as it should be, for I remembered how *The Tales of Ise* describes the summit dappled with snow even in the fifth month. How profitless it was, I thought, to pile up anguish on anguish; all this would disappear the moment I died. The priest Saigyo had written,

> Blown on by the wind,
> The smoke trail from Mt. Fuji
> Is dissipated,
> Just as my tender passion
> Disperses I know not where.

But now no smoke rose from the summit.

As I went on, I was on the lookout for the maple and the ivy of Mt. Uzu as described in *The Tales of Ise*, but I went over the pass without noticing it and was much surprised when I learnt that I had already crossed the mountain,

> In what state of mind
> Can I have been that I now
> Have crossed Mt. Uzu
> Without noting the ivy
> So far famed in poetry?

I visited the shrine at Mishima in Izu province. The custom there of offering sacred paper streamers is just the same as at the Kumano shrine. In both shrines, too, models of serpents were much on display. Just as in the story told by the late General of the Bodyguard of the Right, Minamoto no Yoritomo,[3] quite well-dressed women were to be seen walking up to and away from the shrine, thus making ten thousand visits to the shrine to offer some petition. I realised from this that there were innumerable women who felt as miserable as I did.

It was well past the middle of the month and the moon did not rise until after midnight. It was interesting, if not particularly exciting, to watch the strange gestures of the girls dancing before the shrine, going to and fro and passing and repassing each other. I was

[3] Yoritomo established the Military Government at Kamakura and became Shogun (1192).

sufficiently amused, however, to sit up all night watching them. Then, to the sound of the chirping of the birds at dawn I went on my way.

I arrived at Enoshima after the twentieth day of the third month. The scenery here is indescribably beautiful. There are many caves on an island a good distance out to sea, and in one of these cave dwellings, Senju, I stayed with an old hermit who lived there all alone, practising asceticism and cultivating holiness. His fence might be the sea fog and his gate a humble bamboo trellis, yet he lived a gracious life. He was most hospitable to his guests, serving them with shell-fish from the sea round the island. I made him a present of a fan from the Capital which my travelling companion had carried in a basket.

"As I live in this kind of house," he said to me when he thanked me for it, "I have no contact with life in the Capital and in fact this is the first time I have ever seen such a thing as this. Meeting you tonight makes me feel as if I am meeting an old friend." At the time it seemed to me to be quite natural that he should feel about me in this way.

Nothing particular happened during the evening. At night everyone seemed to be drowsing peacefully, but I could not get to sleep in that strange cave and lay awake, thinking over incidents on my pilgrimage. After trying for some time to stifle my sobs, I got up and went outside. The clouds merged with the spray of the waves, and all was blurred with the haze. Then the sky cleared gradually and the moon appeared, standing almost still in the cloudless sky, which seemed to widen as I looked up at it until at last I felt as if I had journeyed five thousand miles away from this world. From the hills at my back monkeys chattered. Still, my sadness remained: I was heartbroken, my grief seemingly as fresh as when I had felt it for the first time. I had left the Capital on this long pilgrimage so that I might meditate alone and might dry my tears in solitude. My efforts were in vain, for misery had accompanied me even here. I expressed my thoughts in a poem,

> Would that I could dwell
> In a hut thatched with cedar,
> And with bamboo blinds
> Between corner posts of pine,
> And forget this world's sadness!

Lady Nijo's stay in Kamakura

CHAPTER
II

Next morning I went on to Kamakura and visited the Gokurakuji temple. The priests were going about their duties just as they did in the Capital. This made me realise how much I was missing the life there. When I had looked towards Kamakura as I crossed Kehaizaka hill, it had all seemed so different from the view of the Capital from Higashiyama. Here the people lived in houses built on the hills in terraces which went up like steps one after another, the houses standing in scattered clusters that seemed to be separate from one another like little parcels each in its own little bag. They looked so wretched that I felt I should never be able to settle contentedly in Kamakura.

I went to the beach at Yui where there is a large *torii*. In the distance I could see the new shrine dedicated to the Emperor Ojin. The god of the Hachiman shrine is said to have promised to be the special guardian of the prosperity of the Genji clan. Although it was my destiny to be born in this clan, still for some reason or other this divine protection had certainly not saved me from misfortune. When I prayed at my father's family shrine, the Hachiman shrine at Iwashimizu, that he might receive his just reward by being reborn in this world in an honoured family, the oracle revealed that this would be at the cost of my own happiness in this world. I could have no reason for complaint against this decree of divine providence, for my written petition had expressly stated that I would not complain even though this would entail my being reduced to beggary, just as it is told of the famous poetess of ancient times, Ono no Komachi, that though she was a descendant of Princess Sotori, she was in old age reduced to begging, wearing a straw cloak and carrying a bamboo basket to receive food given as alms. I doubt whether even then her grief was as great as mine. Thinking of these things I went to pay my visit to the shrine. The site is far superior to that of the chief shrine of Iwashimizu Hachiman at Otokoyama in the Capital, for here the shrine looked out over beautiful views of the sea. It was startling, though, to see feudal lords paying visits to the shrine dressed in robes of all sorts of colours instead of being dressed all in white.

I also visited the Egara Tenjin shrine, the Eifukuji temple at Nikaido, and the Shochoju-in temple. Lady Komachi, a relative of my cousin, the Chief Minister, Tsuchimikado no Sadazane, had come to Kamakura in the train of the Generalissimo, Prince Koreyasu, and was living at Okuranoyatsu. When I informed her of my arrival in Kamakura, she wrote that the news of my coming was a pleasant surprise and invited me to stay with her. I replied that I did not wish to inconvenience her and would rather stay at the inn nearby. She wrote again, sending me various things I might need and expressing her concern about my not being comfortable at the inn, but hoping I would be able to rest awhile to recover from the hardships of the journey.

Then about the middle of the fourth month, the one who was to be my guide on the journey to the Zenkoji temple in Shinano province fell seriously ill, sometimes becoming completely unconscious. I was at my wit's end with anxiety. Then when she was a little better, I had to take to my bed. With two patients seriously ill, the people of the house were much alarmed.

"Don't worry," said the physician whom they had called in. "It's just the exhaustion of a long journey causing a chronic constitutional weakness to become more pronounced." The illness, however, caused me to be very depressed. Formerly, if I had a cold in the head or a runny nose or some other trivial ailment, within two or three days all the resources of medical science and fortune-telling would be tapped for me. Some treasured heirloom or a nationally famous horse would be offered to an especially sacred shrine or temple with a petition for my recovery, while oranges and pears from far-off countries would be sought for me. Now, though I lay on a bed of sickness day after day, no prayers were made at any shrine, no petition at any temple; no one was anxious about what I could manage to eat or what medical treatment I ought to have. I just lay there night and day, feeling as if I had been reborn in this present world in a lower station of life. Still, life or death is a matter of predestination. I was destined to live longer, and by the sixth month I was feeling much better but still not well enough to consider going on another long pilgrimage for some time. I killed time by taking pleasant walks in the neighbourhood until the eighth month.

On the morning of the fifteenth of that month, I received a letter from Lady Komachi. "Today is the day when in the Capital they hold the ceremony at which they set free birds and fishes at the Iwashimizu shrine," she wrote. "Wouldn't you like to see how the ceremony is carried out here in Kamakura?"

I replied with the poem,

> To me this custom
> Now seems profitless to see,
> For am I not now

In a quite different stream
From that which flows from that source?

Lady Komachi's poem in reply was,

> Be not faint of heart,
> But with single-minded faith,
>   Look up to the god
> And rely on his mercy
> To preserve you in safety.

Curious to see how this ceremony was carried out at Kamakura, I went to the Tsurugaoka shrine, a daughter shrine of the Hachiman shrine at Iwashimizu. In this remote spot I saw the Generalissimo making a great display of his dignity. The feudal lords all wore their official robes and the rest of the officers theirs. It was a rare sight to see them all in their varied dress. When the Generalissimo alighted from his carriage at the red bridge, only a few court nobles were with him, all looking rather mean and shabby. Taira no Suke-mune, heir to the Nyudo Taira no Yoritsuna, the Governor-general, attended on the Generalissimo as Vice-Minister of the Samurai-dokoro and behaved in much the same manner as the Imperial Adviser did in the Capital, having a magnificent warlike appearance. I did not wait to see the exhibition of archery on horse-back and the other shows, thinking I should be rather bored watching them, but went back early to my lodgings.

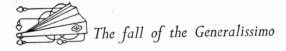 *The fall of the Generalissimo*

CHAPTER

III

Not very long after this there were whispered rumours that events were moving towards a crisis in Kamakura. Then, while I was still wondering who would be involved in this, I learnt that the Generalissimo was to return to the Capital. Next, I heard that the Generalissimo was just about to leave. I hurried off to his palace to see him go. A shabby-looking palanquin with rush mats hanging at the sides was standing by the entrance. A lieutenant named Nikaido no Yukisada was in charge of the affair. Taira no Sukemune came along with orders from the Regent, Hojo no Sadatoki, that the palanquin should be reversed so that the occupant would face Kamakura as he left. This, he said, was according to precedent.[1] Even before the prince set off, vulgar-looking fellows from the General Affairs Department had entered his mansion without taking off their straw boots, and had already set about tearing down the bamboo blinds and taking away the furniture, a truly horrifying sight.

As the prince's palanquin was carried away, his ladies-in-waiting came out in twos and threes with no veil to screen their faces from the public gaze. There was no means of transport for them. ''Where has His Excellency gone?'' they said, weeping. Those who had

[1] The dead and criminals rode in this way.

formed ties with feudal lords had an escort to take them back to the Capital, but the rest had to make their own way back, individually, as best they could. No words could describe their grief.

The Generalissimo went first to Sasukenoyatsu where he stayed five days before going on to the Capital. As I wished to see the prince's final departure from the eastern provinces, I went to the temple near this place where the miracle-working image of Shoten Buddha is enshrined. There I was told that the time fixed for his departure was two o'clock in the morning. It had been raining steadily since the previous evening, and about the time of his departure there was a violent storm. It seemed as though it was the work of devils. In spite of this the palanquin was got ready so that his departure might not be delayed, and was covered over with matting. The prince was already in the palanquin, it seemed, but for some reason or other they did not start on their journey but put it down again in the courtyard where it was left for some time. I heard the prince blow his nose several times, and I could imagine that he was weeping bitterly.

Prince Koreyasu was not a member of a warrior family who had come to power by quelling the barbarians. His father was Prince Munetaka,[2] second

[2]Shogun, Generalissimo, from 1252 to 1266, the first of a succession of four imperial princes to have this title as figurehead chiefs of the Military Government. After the forced resignation of Munetaka's son, Prince Koreyasu, in 1289, Hisaakira, sixth son of the ex-Emperor Go Fukakusa, was appointed and held the title from 1289 to 1308 and was succeeded by his son Morikuni, 1308 to 1332.

son of the Emperor Go Saga. Prince Munetaka was older than his brother, Go Fukakusa, and would have ascended the throne except that his mother was not of sufficiently high rank. He did not, however, descend to the rank of a commoner but continued to rank as a prince, being chief of the Intermediary Department before going to Kamakura as Generalissimo. He was indeed a very worthy prince, his mother being a daughter of the Imperial Adviser, Konoe no Kanetsune. Tears came to my eyes as I put my thoughts of him, of his high descent and his fall from power, into the poem,

> Ise's great goddess
> Will surely have compassion
> On the fallen prince,
> For he belongs to a branch
> Of the stream that flows from there.

He doubtless shed many tears on his journey back to the Capital, though there is no record of any poem he wrote on this sad experience; his father, his predecessor in the office, had in a similar situation written,

> Looking forward now
> To receiving special grace
> At Kitano shrine,
> On this bright sunny morning
> Virgin snow still blocks my way.

It is a thousand pities that his son did not so express his thoughts for us.

Soon we heard that Prince Hisaakira, sixth son of the ex-Emperor Go Fukakusa, was to come to Kama-kura as Generalissimo. The palace of the Generalissimo was splendidly redecorated, and seven feudal lords were to leave to meet him and escort him to the city. Among these was the lord of Iinuma, Taira no Suke-mune, second son of the Governor-general of the Military Government, Taira no Yoritsuna. This feudal lord, who had adopted the title of Lieutenant of the Gate Guards of the Left without being formally raised to the rank by Imperial order, is said to have refused on this occasion to go by the ordinary route through the Hakone barrier as he did not wish to follow in the tracks of one who had been exiled. Instead he was to cross over Mt. Ashigara. Everyone considered his action in doing this pompous and quite uncalled for.

As the date of the Generalissimo's arrival drew near, everyone was busy making elaborate preparations for his reception. Early in the morning two or three days before his arrival, I had a message from Lady Komachi. I could not think what this could be about and found it was a most unexpected request. The ex-Empress Higashi Nijo had sent to the household of the Gover-nor-general's wife a present of a set of five robes which had been cut out but not sewn up. I was asked to help them to do this properly. I replied that I was not in a position to do so.

Lady Komachi would not listen to any excuses.

"Now that you have taken your vows," she wrote, "you are free to do as you wish. Besides, I have told no one who you are. I have said only that you are 'someone from the Capital.' " I still continued to beg to be excused, but she insisted. She even enclosed a letter from the Regent, Hojo no Sadatoki, supporting her plea. Finally I consented and went to the Governor-general's residence, thinking that it would not be difficult to limit myself to just making suggestions and that to do otherwise would be to incur their displeasure and make my stay in Kamakura unpleasant.

While the Generalissimo's house was very ordinary-looking, the residence of the Governor-general was lavishly decorated. Everything was costly, inlaid with gold and silver and studded with jewels. Everything glittered, the rings and fringes worn by the ladies, their dresses of silk and brocade, the screens and furnishings.

The Governor-general's wife came in. She was tall and stately with a proud bearing, a truly magnificent figure in a set of two robes of pale blue Chinese material with a raised design of maple trees in violet, dark and light, with a white skirt. Then the Governor-general, Taira no Yoritsuna, came tripping in, dressed in a white formal robe, the sleeves of which looked too short for him, and stood beside his dignified-looking wife. I was most disappointed to note the contrast.

The robes sent by the ex-Empress consisted of one dlue under-robe and a set of five of purplish red deepening inwards in colour, piece by piece. They had been tacked up, but I was surprised to see that the pieces were all reversed.

"Why have you put them together in this way?" I asked, for it looked very strange to me to have the darkest part put next to the lightest part.

"The people in the dressmaking department told us that they hadn't the time to do it and so we have had them tacked together by people who have very little experience."

I suggested which pieces should be reversed, though I had really begun to think that it would have made the dresses look very attractive to have them sewn up as they were.

Then she had a message from the Regent. "The authorities will make themselves responsible for the outside decoration of the Generalissimo's residence with the help of the records. The person from the Capital will inspect and report on the progress of the work of interior decoration," it said.

I was afraid that my further cooperation with the Kamakura authorities might lead to trouble in the future, but I had already gone so far that I could not very well refuse to continue to help them without offending them. I therefore went to the mansion, which I found had been furnished fairly well. I made no criticism, however, and confined myself to a suggestion as to where the miniature Buddhist shrine should be placed and how the robes should be hung on the dress hangers and went back to my lodgings.

The day of the new Generalissimo's arrival came. The Wakamiya road was crowded with spectators. The vanguard of his party came in sight, accompanied by the seven feudal lords who had gone as far as the barrier at Ashigara to welcome him. Twenty or thirty horsemen passed in an imposing procession, and then forty or fifty servants and retainers in variously coloured robes ran past in groups of twenty. Then came the procession of the feudal lords, crowding together, all splendidly dressed, stretching half a mile in length. At last the Generalissimo passed by in his palanquin, the train of his under-robe of blue and yellow silk lined with blue showing below the half raised bamboo blinds. The new Lieutenant of the Gate Guards of the Left rode just behind the palanquin dressed in an ordinary court robe of pale green lined with white. Everything looked most solemn. At the Generalissimo's mansion, all the high officials present, including the Regent and Ashikaga no Sadauji,[3] wore robes with no crests. The parade of war horses followed.

On the third day after his arrival, the Generalissimo visited the Regent's villa at Yamanouchi where, I learnt later, a great banquet was held. This touched me, for it reminded me of my old life at court.

[3] Sadauji's son, Takauji, was later to put an end to the rule of the Kamakura Bakufu and found the Ashikaga regime at Kyoto, which lasted 237 years.

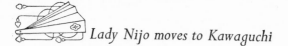 *Lady Nijo moves to Kawaguchi*

CHAPTER
IV

The year drew to a close, and to my sorrow I had still not yet had an opportunity of visiting the Zenkoji temple in Shinano province. Lady Komachi. . . .[1]

This deeply mortified me as the days passed by.

The lord of Iinuma, Taira no Sukemune, the son of the Governor-general, often sent Wakabayashi no Jirozaemon to me inviting me to be present at verse-capping and other entertainments, having heard possibly that I had some reputation as a poet and a person of cultivated tastes, and at last I accepted one of his invitations. Surprisingly enough, I found him to be a man of culture and wide sympathies, and from this time I often went to his house for contests in poetical composition.

In the last month of the year, I moved to Kawaguchi in the province of Musashi, where the widow of a man named Kawagoe was living in religious retirement. Her message inviting me to visit her had delighted me, as it had held out the hope that early in the new year we might make the pilgrimage to Zenkoji together. Snow was falling as I went there, and it was difficult to find the way over the moors

[1] A note by the seventeenth-century copyist of *Towazu-gatari* says here, "The next section of this chapter has been cut away with a knife for some reason or another. How I wish I knew what followed!"

273

deep in snow, but I eventually got to the house after two days of travel from Kamakura. It was a remote spot on the bank of the river Iruma, with the post station of Iwabuchi and the usual prostitute quarter on the other side of the river.

There are no mountains to be seen in the province of Musashi. The plain is a wilderness overgrown with miscanthus grass, a sad wintry sight at this time with stems and leaves bent down with the weight of hoar frost. Through this wilderness I had pushed my way, my sadness at the passing of yet another year, so natural to all of us, heightened by the fact that I was ever removing myself to secluded spots more and more remote from the brilliant life of the Capital.

Whenever I look back over my past life, it is always of my mother that I think first. I was parted from her at the age of two, so early that I do not know what she looked like. I had grown a little and was in my fourth year when on the twentieth day of the ninth month I was taken into his service by the ex-Emperor. From that time on, I enjoyed his special favour. I learnt to hold my own among people and after some years I came to hold a position of considerable influence at the court. I had hopes of attaining the highest position of all there and of becoming the pride and glory of my family, but I realised at last that it was my destiny to renounce this gracious way of life to enter religion, heeding the warnings of Buddha that no one can take with one the treasures in this life, one's spouse, one's wealth, one's rank. In spite of this, however, I could not but feel regret sometimes that I had left the life at court to which I was so accustomed. Thoughts of the ex-Emperor's love and affection often came to me, and I had nothing to allay my grief but the tears that dampened my sleeves.

Snow fell heavily from the dark wintry sky and deeply covered the moors and roads. I felt that I should never be able to find my way back, and, when my hostess asked me how I felt on being snowbound, I replied with the poem,

> Take pity on one
> Whose griefs piling up on her
> Like high drifts of snow
> Prevent any of her friends
> From making a call on her.

Words of sympathy unlock the floodgates of tears, but I controlled my feelings lest people should think my outbursts of sorrow very strange. Thus came another year.

 Lady Nijo enters her thirty-third year on New Year's Day, 1290. She visits the Zenkoji temp e in Shinano province

CHAPTER V   The New Year came, and the nightingales sang their spring songs among the branches of the plum trees under the eaves, but sad memories of the happy days gone beyond recall continued to fill my eyes with tears.

About the tenth day of the second month, I started out on my pilgrimage to the Zenkoji temple. The steep slopes of the Usui pass are well known as being as dangerous to cross as the hanging bridge over the Kiso gorge.[1] I would have liked to have had more time on the journey for rest and sightseeing, but I was with a large party, and so I could not stop as often as I wished to do. I therefore came to prefer travelling alone, and, after venerating the image of Buddha there, I told the rest of the party that I would not be returning with them as I was proposing to go into retreat at the temple for several months.

"Who can accompany one on the path through the dark shadows of death?" I said when members of the party expressed anxiety about leaving me on my own. "One comes into the world all alone. One leaves it alone. All meetings end with a parting. All births end with death. However beautiful the peach blossom, it returns at last to the earth. The autumn foliage, beautiful as it is, is scattered when the winds blow. The emotion we feel when reluctantly we part from one another is only a temporary one."

So I remained there all alone. But there is nothing much worth seeing at Zenkoji except the image of Buddha which is believed to be a real incarnation of Amida Buddha. With a firm belief in this, I devoted

[1] As Kiso is on the route from the Capital to Zenkoji, Lady Nijo cannot have passed through it on her way there from Musashi province but seems to have crossed the Usui pass.

my mornings and evenings to reciting a million times daily the invocation of the sacred name.

Near the town, there was living a former provincial governor, Takaoka no Iwami, who had a great reputation as a man of wide sympathies, well read in poetry and fond of music. Introduced to him in the first place by someone in the party, I often went to his residence which I found furnished very tastefully, much more so than one usually finds in country districts. Feeling the place soothing and attractive, I stayed at Zenkoji till autumn.

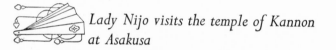 *Lady Nijo visits the temple of Kannon at Asakusa*

CHAPTER
VI
At the beginning of the eighth month, I started back on my journey to Musashi province, with the feeling that it was to enjoy the scenery of the moors of that province in autumn that I had delayed my return until then.

At the temple at Asakusa there is a much venerated image of Kannon, the goddess of mercy, portrayed with eleven faces, which I felt I ought to visit.

The way there was across moors where nothing grew but bushclover, yellow scabious, rushes, and pampas grass, tall enough to hide a man on horseback. From this you can imagine the wildness of the scenery. I pushed my way through this wilderness for three days to reach Asakusa. If I had gone along the main roads, I could have found post stations, but the way I went, there was nothing in front of me or behind me but this wilderness.

The Kannon temple stands high above the plain on an open, treeless moor. As I arrived there, the moon was rising over the plain, reminding me of the old poem,

> Where the earth at last
> Merges into distant sky,
> Lo, the moon rises
> Out of the waving grasses
> Of the plain of Musashi.

It was full moon, and the sight reminded me of that party at the palace when we had gone out to enjoy the sight of the harvest moon. I no longer had the ex-Emperor's robe which he had given me on that occasion as a souvenir, for I had presented it to the Hachiman shrine at Iwashimizu when I had copied out the Lotus Flower sutra. If I had kept it till now, no doubt the smell lingering on it would have reminded me of the ex-Emperor just as the robe given him by his emperor had brought back memories to Sugawara no Michizane.[1] Even now the emotion I felt was no less than his.

The moon shining over the wilderness was growing brighter and brighter with the passage of the night, the dew on the leaves of the bushes glittering like jewels.

[1] The famous scholar and statesman, 845–903.

> Hard to forget is
> The glory of that bright moon
> I viewed at the court;
> Brightest in my memory
> Tonight's moon will ever be.

I felt as if the moon and I were both floating in the flood of my tears,

> Through a cloudless sky
> The moon rides in majesty,
> The sight reminds me
> Of his as gracious image,
> His presence I miss so much.

At last dawn broke and I started on my way back to Kawaguchi, for there was no place to stay at in that barren plain.

As I was crossing a long bridge—which could be compared with the Kiyomizu and Gion bridges in the Capital—over the grassy bed of a river which I thought might well be the river Sumida, I met two fairly well-dressed men.

"I was told that I should have to cross the river Sumida. Is this it?" I said to them.

"This is the river Sumida," one of them said. "And this is the Suda bridge. Before the bridge was built, people crossed over here by ferry boat, but as that was not very convenient, a bridge was built. The local people, thinking the name 'Sumida' rather too high-flown a name, call it the Suda bridge. The

village on the other side of the river was formerly
called Miyoshino, Beautiful Wilderness, but the farm-
ers so often found the ears of their rice plants empty
that the governor of the province, hearing of this and
thinking it quite natural that it should be so when the
village had such a name, changed the name to Yoshida,
Happy Field. Since then they have had good harvests.''

Hearing that this was the river Sumida I recalled
the poem of Arihara no Narihira in *The Tales of Ise*
when he saw *miyako-dori* flying about here,

> Miyako-dori,
> If Birds of the Capital
> You really are,
> Tell me how does she fare now
> Far away in the Capital.

I looked round but could see no birds there.
Certainly there were no *miyako-dori* about.

> Vain it was, I found,
> For me to come to this place,
> The river Sumida,
> In search of Capital Birds
> Reputed to haunt this spot.

As I murmured this poem to myself, the river mist,
as well as my tears, prevented me from seeing clearly
the way I was going. Then I heard, seeming to be in
sympathy with my feelings, the call of the wild geese
flying high in the sky above the clouds,

How sorrowful now
Seems to my ears the loud cry
    Of the wild geese
As they seek to console me,
Tearful and solitary.

At Horikane there was no trace of the well, famed in poetry, and no ruins, only one dead tree.

I had wished to continue my journey north to Mutsu province, but I abandoned the project, being afraid that the keepers of every barrier which I came to would try to obstruct my wandering any further, and so I returned to Kamakura on my way back to the Capital.

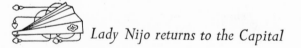 *Lady Nijo returns to the Capital*

CHAPTER VII   The time soon passed, and on the tenth day of the ninth month I started on my way back to the Capital. The friends whom I had made during my previous stay in Kamakura were all reluctant to see me leave. During the evening of the day before my departure, Taira no Sukemune, the lord of Iinuma, the Governor-general's second son, brought me several presents and invited me to join him in one last verse-capping party. On some previous occasion, I had asked him where Namida-

gawa, the river of tears, was. He had told me then
that he had no idea.

"Are you bent on leaving tomorrow?" he said.

"We cannot stop halfway on our journey through
life," I answered.

Just before he went away, he wrote on the salver
on which our wine cups had been served this poem,

> You asked me where
> Flows the river of tears;
> Now I know it flows
> Down my sleeves because I have
> No right to ask you to stay.

I was just about to write a poem in answer to this,
when he returned with a present of travelling robes
and a poem,

> Short-lived our friendship,
> But I hope that you will wear
> These robes on your way
> To bring me back to your mind
> Who am sad to see you go.

I had often suspected that our frequent meetings
for poetical composition had led malicious rumour-
mongers to insinuate that our friendship for one
another went deeper, and my answering poem read,

> Once my eyes were filled
> With tears of indignation;

> From their evil speech
> I did not defend myself;
> Now I weep with tears of yearning.

There was little reason for me to hurry on to the Capital, but there was just as little reason to remain any longer where I was, and so at sunrise I left Kamakura for the last time. By the kindness of the people at the various post stations on the way, I was carried all the way by palanquin. At last I reached Sayanonakayama, a place which reminded me of Saigyo's poem,

> How could I have known,
> When in youth I crossed this pass,
>   That in my old age
> I should cross it once again?
> So is our life ruled by fate.

My own poem written at this spot was,

> My heart beats sadly
> And my endless tears flow down
>   As I cross this pass,
> For I know that I shall never
> Pass along this way again.

I arrived at the Atsuta shrine, where I kept vigil for the night. There were some itinerant priests there who told me that they were from the Grand Shrine at Ise. When I asked them about the way to the shrine, they informed me that it was easy to cross over to Ise by boat from the port of Tsushima. I was happy to learn this and decided to make the trip.

Before I went to Ise, however, I wished first to copy the remaining thirty volumes of the Kegon sutra and present them to the Atsuta shrine. I therefore collected together the few remaining travel robes I had been presented with in Kamakura, intending to sell them to pay the expenses of copying the sutra, but the Chief Priest of the shrine raised objections to my staying there. In these circumstances it was obvious that I should have to give up the idea. Just then also I had another attack of illness, and so, there being no hope of my being able to continue my devotions at the shrine, I went on my way to the Capital.

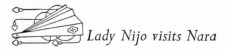 *Lady Nijo visits Nara*

CHAPTER VIII Back once again in the Capital at the end of the tenth month, I could not seem to settle down to life there and I therefore decided to go to Nara, a place I had very seldom visited, not being a member of the Fujiwara family.[1] It is such a short distance from the Capital that I thought it would be a good place to stay for a while after my long journey. I went alone as I knew no one there. I first went to

[1] The Kasuga shrine at Nara was the Fujiwara family shrine and the Kofukuji their family temple.

worship at the Kasuga shrine. The two-storeyed gate and the buildings of the four sanctuaries are most impressive and awe-inspiring. The roar of the stormy wind blowing from the surrounding peaks seemed as if it would rid one of all earthly passions and cares, while the babble of the stream at the foot of the hillock seemed to promise to wash away all earthly pollution. Strengthened with these thoughts, I went to the Lesser shrine, where I found the maidens in the service of the shrine looking very graceful. I enjoyed watching the beautiful dancing of two of them dancing together while the afternoon sun lighted up the roofs of the buildings and the tops of the ancient trees.

That night I kept a vigil in a room off the corridor at the Lesser shrine. All night I could hear people who were keeping their vigil by singing songs all the night through. Humorous recitations are, I knew, one method by which the great masses of the ordinary people are brought to spiritual enlightenment, but it was not until this occasion, I believe, that I fully realised what a potent force for good they are in the work of divine providence for the salvation of souls, and I found my faith much deepened and strengthened.

There was, I have heard, a High Priest named Shinki, a disciple of the High Priest Rinkai,[2] head of the Kita chapel at Kofukuji, who had been so indignant at the interruption of his prayers and meditations by the noise of drums and bells that he vowed, that if he were ever appointed to the Kofukuji temple

[2] Lady Nijo is mistaken. The story is told of Rinkai, Shinki's disciple, who was in charge of this temple from 983.

in charge of the six Buddhist sects, he would prohibit
the use of bells and drums. When at last he realised
this ambition, he forbade all sacred music and
dancing in Buddhist worship. The ban was in force
for a long time; the precincts of the temple became
deserted and the musicians and dancers were in
desperate straits. They had no one to complain to;
they could only trust in providence.

The High Priest later went into retreat at the Kasuga
shrine. "I have no further aim in this life," he said,
in explaining his reasons for this step. "I will so devote
my service to Buddha that I may attain happiness in
the next world. In this retreat I will make an offering
to the god of all that I have learnt of the mysteries of
Buddhism."

The god appeared to him in a dream. "I have left
high heaven," he said to the priest, "to descend to the
world of mortals so that I may bring happiness to all
in the next world. Your officiousness in prohibiting
to pious people the enjoyment of the music of drums
and bells has angered me, for this stupid action has
deprived them of a means of salvation. I refuse to
accept your offering to me of what you consider to
be the soul of Buddhism."

Since that time, music and dancing have been
permitted at all the temples of the district, and no
petition to the god to prohibit these popular amuse-
ments has been allowed. When I heard of this episode,
I realised how gracious divine providence is.

Next morning I went to the Hokkeji temple where
there was living in Number One quarters the nun

Jakuembo, a daughter of the Minister Fujiwara no Fuyutada, and we spoke together for a long time on the stern Buddhist doctrine of the frailty of human life. How calm and peaceful it would be, I thought, to live in such a temple as this. Still, I was not endowed by nature, I concluded, to live a serene life of Buddhist scholarship. So, lured on by my blind search for spiritual enlightenment elsewhere, I found myself on my way back to the temples of Nara.

On my way there I happened to stop at the house of Nakatomi no Sukeie, the priest in charge of the Kasuga shrine. Passing by a house and not knowing whose it was, but supposing from its splendid ridge-roofed gate that it was a part of a temple, I went into the garden. At once I saw that I had made a mistake; it was not a temple but the house of a well-to-do family. Beautiful chrysanthemums were growing along a rough woven fence. They were perhaps a little past their best, but they quite held their own with any growing in the palace gardens.

One or two young men came out of the house. "Where are you from?" one of them said to me.

"From the Capital," I said.

"I am ashamed," he said to me in a rather formal manner, "that you should see the chrysanthemums when they are really past their best." The young men were, I learnt later, the sons of Sukeie: Sukenaga, his father's deputy at the shrine; and his younger brother, Suketoshi, deputy-governor of Mino province.

As I left the garden, I wrote a poem on a card and fixed it to the chrysanthemum fence,

> Wandering about
> Far from the city, I find
> My perfect delight
> In things soon passing, the dew
> On flowers in your garden.

Then I went on my way, but soon a man came running to call me back. They had no doubt found my poem on the card. I had to go back to the house and they were most hospitable, urging me to stay with them for some time. And, as usual, I did so.

The Chuguji temple was founded by the great prince Shotoku,[3] and hearing that some of the treasures there had been presented by his consort, I went there to worship. I had known Shinnyobo, the abbess, when I was in service at the court, but now, no doubt on account of her great age, she did not recognise me. I did not tell her who I was, but she was most hospitable, and I stayed with her for some time.

I went on from the Horyuji temple to the Taimadera temple. There is a tradition here which tells that when the abbess, Lady Chujo, a daughter of the Minister Fujiwara no Toyonari, prayed that she might have a vision of Buddha, a nun appeared to her.

"I will weave a cloth," the apparition said, "which will show you all the peace and splendour of Paradise,

---

[3] Prince Shotoku (574–622), son of the Emperor Yomei and regent during the reign of his aunt, the Empress Suiko, a wise and able statesman who promulgated the first Japanese constitution and promoted the spread of Buddhism.

if you will provide for me a hundred horse-loads of lotus stalks.''

As she wished, the fibre was extracted from a hundred loads of stalks and dyed in five colours in specially dug dye pits. When this was prepared, the nun appeared again and asked for oil for a lamp. She then began to weave a picture of Paradise, working from ten o'clock at night till four o'clock next morning, until, having finished the picture, she prepared to leave.

"How can I see you again?" the abbess asked. In answer, the apparition, as it flew away to the west in the form of a Buddha, recited the verse,

In ancient times when the Buddha preached,
His disciple Kasho was transformed into a Buddha;
In Japan En no Ozuno did the same.
At your petition I have come to explain
That, if you believe in what the picture represents,
You will be free from mortal agony.

Prince Shotoku's tomb at the Eifukuji temple is worthy of him, with an impressive stone wall round it. I had the good fortune to be present at the ceremony of copying the Lotus Flower sutra at this temple when I presented a tight-sleeved gown.

So the New Year came round.

Lady Nijo, now (1291) in her thirty-fourth year, meets the ex-Emperor Go Fukakusa at the Hachiman shrine at Iwashimizu

CHAPTER On my way back to the Capital in the second month, I visited the shrine of IX Hachiman at Iwashimizu. It is a long distance from Nara to Yawata where the shrine stands, and it was already sunset before I climbed up the Inobana slope and arrived at the forecourt of the main shrine.

I had made the journey with a woman of Iwami province, a hunchbacked dwarf, and we had talked together on the way about such things as the cause of her deformity and her fate in being so afflicted.

When we got to the Riding Pavilion, we saw that the main door of the pavilion was open. I took no particular notice of this at the time and went on walking towards the two-storeyed gate, for no one had told me when I had been in retreat here earlier that the opening of this door showed that an Imperial visit was taking place. Then a man who seemed to be a porter approached me.

"Please go to the Riding Pavilion," he said to me.

"Who asked you to call me back?" I said. "Has he mistaken me for someone else? Is the message for the short lady over there?"

"No, I haven't made any mistake. The message is

for you. The ex-Emperor of Tominokoji has been
in retreat here since the day before yesterday.[1] He
sent for you."

The news struck me dumb. His image had always
filled my mind and would not be banished from it,
but I had thought I had seen him for the last time two
years before when I had paid my farewell visit to him
from the apartment of Lady Kyogoku on the occasion
of my taking my final vows. Now I wore a nun's habit,
moss-grown, travel-stained, weather-beaten, thread-
bare. I had been certain that no one would recognise
me. I wondered who it could have been that had
done so, for I never dreamt that it was the ex-
Emperor himself who had seen me; I decided that
perhaps one of the ladies-in-waiting had thought it
was possibly me that she had seen and had asked me
to come to her so that she could make certain that I
was really the person she thought I was. I therefore
continued to walk on quite undisturbed, when a
warrior came along and urged me to go with him at
once. There was no way to escape. I went with him
to the side door on the north side of the hall.

"Come in. You'll attract people's attention standing out there." I recognised the ex-Emperor's voice,
sounding to my ears just as it had always done. This
was something I had not expected at all, and his voice
came as such a shock to me that I could not move a
limb. "Hurry up," he went on, and without much
hesitation I went in.

"It was pretty sharp-eyed of me to pick you out in

[1] The ex-Emperor had already entered the religious life.

such a crowd, wasn't it?'' he said. "It shows how much I still love you even though such a long time has passed since we met last." From this we went on to talk of former days and of the happy chance that had brought about our present meeting. "Love affairs have not the charm nowadays that they used to have," he said. So we passed the whole of the short night talking together without going to bed, not leaving each other till dawn came.

"I shall spend the period of my retreat in purity and with a religious frame of mind. Then, when my retreat is over, we can meet with peaceful happy hearts." As he was leaving, he took off three of the tight-sleeved gowns he was wearing and gave them to me. "This is my secret keepsake to you. Wear them always," he said. My heart was ready to break with love and sorrow. I thought no more of what had happened to me in the past or what would happen in the future or even of what would be my lot in the next world. All such thoughts passed from my mind.

Inexorably, day came. The ex-Emperor said goodbye, and I left. Only the scent of him on the gowns he had given me remained to remind me of him. I was afraid that the perfume of incense still lingering on my black habit would betray me, for everyone would be able to recognise it, and this made me even more reluctant to wear the gowns under my habit.

> Many years have passed
> Since with throbbing hearts we laid
> Our sleeves together;

> Meeting again once more now,
> His sleeves are wet with my tears.

So I expressed my thoughts as I left the hall as if in a trance, with his beloved features reflected in my tear-drenched sleeves. I longed to see him again, even if only once more in the course of that day, just to talk quietly together. Yet I could not put the thought from me that he might already be regretting that he had brought about our meeting together now that we had both taken our vows. It would be most imprudent, I thought, for me to stay on in the hope of meeting him again. My feelings can easily be imagined as, stifling the desires of my heart, I made ready to leave at once for the Capital. Even then, however, I could not resist waiting around the shrine in the hope that I might catch another accidental glimpse of him as he was making his tour of the sanctuaries within the precincts of the shrine; in order not to attract his attention by my black habit, I put on one of his tight-sleeved gowns over it and stood among the court ladies as he came past. His appearance now that he wore a monastic habit was quite different from what it had been in the old days, and my heart was filled with sorrow at the sight of him being helped up the steps of the shrine by Lord Fujiwara no Suketaka, who was at that time perhaps a chamberlain. I recalled how he had said to me the night before, "I am delighted that we are both wearing these habits." I remembered how he had spoken of this and that innocent episode of our early days together.

So, with the sound of his voice still making music in my ears and his beloved features still reflected in my tear-drenched sleeves, I left the shrine and went northwards to the Capital with the feeling that I had left my soul behind me.

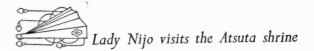 *Lady Nijo visits the Atsuta shrine*

CHAPTER Thinking that I ought not to make a long stay in the Capital, I decided to do what
X
I had planned to do the year before and visit the Atsuta shrine. On the very night I kept vigil there, a fire broke out. Naturally there was a great deal of noise and shouting as the people of the shrine tried to extinguish the flames. It was the will of the gods, however, that they could not control the conflagration. Soon clouds of smoke were rising to the sky, and by morning the buildings of the shrine were reduced to ashes.

As soon as it was daylight, the builders and the carpenters were busy with plans for rebuilding. The chief priests and the soothsayers of the shrine then found among the still smouldering offerings a box one foot wide and four feet long lying beside the undamaged foundation-stones of the Never-opened Hall, the door of which, tradition says, Prince Yamato Takeru himself walled up in ancient times. Everyone was amazed at this strange find. As he lived in closest contact with the god, the chief of the soothsayers ventured to pick up the box and make a small opening in its side. They looked through this crack and found that the box contained a scarlet brocade bag which they guessed held a sacred sword. They opened the Hakken shrine and offered the sword there.

The strange point about this story is that Prince Yamato Takeru, who was born in the tenth year of the reign of the Emperor Keiko to whom the shrine is dedicated, was sent to the eastern provinces by the Emperor's orders to quell the barbarians. On his way he worshipped at the Ise shrine, where he received a red brocade bag with this divine oracle: "In a previous existence you were born as Prince Susano-o who took a sword out of the tail of the Serpent with Eight Heads and Tails and gave it to me. Now in return for all you did for me then, I give you this brocade bag. When you are attacked by the enemy and are in gravest danger, open it."

Later on, when he was surrounded on all sides by a fire started by the enemy on the hunting moor in Suruga province, his sword unsheathed itself and cut the grass round him. He opened the brocade bag, and with the flint and steel that he found inside he started a fire which spread in the direction of the enemy, blinded them, and finally destroyed them. For this reason the district was named Yakitsuno, Burnt Moor, and this sword Kusanagi, Grass Cutter.

I listened with reverence to the reading of this episode from the part of the records that had escaped burning and was once more deeply impressed by the mystery of the divine power of the gods as revealed in dreams.

 *Lady Nijo visits Ise*

CHAPTER   The noise and commotion consequent on
            the rebuilding of the shrine at Atsuta
     XI   made me disinclined to stay there to
continue with my task of copying the sutras. I there-fore decided to go to the Grand Shrine of Ise, crossing over from the port of Tsushima. It was the beginning of the fourth month and the leaves of the trees were beginning to show a greenish tinge, giving a delightful impression of the stirring of new life.

I went first to the outer shrine. Just as Saigyo had done there, I would have liked to have stayed at the cedar grove of Yamada to wait there for the first song of the cuckoo. At the shrine office I found two or three ritualists and other shrine officials. Knowing that the wearing of Buddhist monastic garb was frowned on, I asked them how and where I should worship.

"You may go as far as the third courtyard to the second *torii*," they said.

This courtyard is certainly a most awe-inspiring spot. I was standing there when two or three men, probably shrine officials, came along.

"Where are you from?" one of them said.

"From the Capital," I said. "I have come here to learn more about religion."

"Your black habit is not welcome here," he said, "but you look so tired and exhausted that the gods will look on you with compassion and forgive you."

They invited me inside and were most hospitable. "I will be your guide," one of them said, "and show you where you may worship, for you are not allowed to enter the main shrine." He took me past the thousand-branched cedar tree to the sacred pool where I could worship. I bowed my head as he wafted the staff with paper streamers over me in purification and blessing. What purification, I wondered with sad doubtings, could ever cleanse my soul from its impurities?

Returning from the shrine, I found lodging nearby. I enquired there about the kind official who had been my guide and found that his name was Watarai no Yukitada, a ritualist of the third grade and chief of the office where I had called. Another of the officials who had been so kind to me was Watarai no Tsuneyoshi, son of the first-grade ritualist. I expressed my gratitude to them for their kindness in this poem, attaching it to a sprig of the sacred *sakaki* tree,

> Gods and the Buddha
> Both mingle with men to bring
>   Happiness to them;
> Most kind were you who serve here
> To me though in black habit.

The answer came back in this poem,

> We humble servants
> Of the great shrine of Ise
> In the cedar grove
> Are taught thus to show kindness
> To all without distinction.

I had thought of going into retreat for seven days at the outer shrine to pray for spiritual enlightenment, but various priests sent me poems and sometimes joined me in poetical contests so that for the moment my time was fully taken up.

Unlike ordinary shrines, this one forbids recitation of the Buddhist sutras there except at the Horakusha temple half a mile away. I therefore spent my days there in devotions. On the first evening I went to the Kannon temple nearby and asked the nuns for lodging for the night. I met with a flat refusal: "It is impossible," I was told abruptly. I therefore wrote this poem and sent it to the abbess attached to a branch of the *nandina* tree,

> My robe is surely
> Of the same colour as yours,
> Of what colour then
> Did you think it to be when
> You turned me away just now?

She did not send me any poem in reply but invited me to stay with them, and we became good friends.

My seven days of retreat were over and I was preparing to visit the inner shrine when my earliest friend here, Tsuneyoshi, sent me a poem,

> How much I wish now
> That I had not made friends with
> One on her travels;
> I would not feel this sorrow
> When a fellow poet leaves.

I replied with the poem,

> There is no meeting
> Without a parting follows,
> Even for those who
> Do not travel. In this world
> One's friends stay not forever.

Quite a few persons with artistic interests seem to have been waiting eagerly for me to go to the inner shrine, having heard that a nun with some skill in poetry was in retreat at the outer shrine and would be coming there later. It was therefore with a certain reluctance that I went on there.

I stayed at a place called Okada next to a house where a lady of some elegance lived. She was the widow of a second-grade ritualist, Arakida no Nobunari. She sent a young girl to me with a letter. "Hearing that you are from the Capital," she wrote, "I long to meet you. I do so wish to have a friendly talk with you."

My reply was the poem,

> You would wish to hear
> From me of the Capital,
> But this reminds me
> Of things I cannot forget
> But too sad to tell in words.

The moon rose late in the night on which I went to visit the inner shrine. I was wearing my black habit, and so I had to look at the shrine from the other side of the river Mimosuso. The sanctuary looked as if it stood a great distance beyond the sacred fence, evergreen trees with dense foliage clustered round it. The ends of the ornamental cross-beams on the gables are cut horizontally as a symbol, it is said, of prayer for the glory and prosperity of the Imperial throne. The sight recalled the ex-Emperor to my mind, and I uttered aloud a prayer for his health and safety, my heart softening with a feeling of pure devotion. This I expressed in the poem,

> Whatever changes,
> Love and devotion for you
> Remain unaltered;
> I offer a fervent prayer
> That you live a thousand years.

The wind blew gently, the river Mimosuso flowed calmly, the moon rose up from behind the hills shining with a brighter light over the sanctuary and from

it spreading out, it seemed to me, far beyond the
confines of our own country.

My act of worship over, as I was passing the shrine
office on my way back, I thought the house of the
first-grade ritualist, Arakida no Hisayoshi, looked
most desolate in the bright moonlight, for all its
doors and windows were firmly shut. I wrote a poem,
attached it to a small branch of *sakaki*, and left it on
the verandah of the house,

> Even though it is
> The Great Goddess of the Sun
>   That all of you serve,
> How can you so shut out thus
> The clear bright light of the moon?

My poem must soon have been found and read,
for a reply came at once to my lodging, also attached
to a sprig of the sacred tree,

> How could I shut tight
> The doors of my lowly house
>   Against the moonlight
> Except for this one reason—
> Profound is an old man's sleep?

"In which direction is Futami[1] Bay?" I asked as
I was leaving the inner shrine at the end of my seven
days of retreat there. "I am interested in the legend
that the scenery of the beach so attracted Princess

[1] *Futami*, looking twice.

Yamato who was searching for a suitable place for
a shrine to the Sun Goddess that she looked twice
at this spot. I should like to go to see this bay." The
priests agreed to provide me with a guide, and one
of them, Arakida no Munenobu, was asked to go with
me. We visited the Beach of Purification, the Gold-
lacquered Pine, and the stone which the God of
Thunder split in two when he kicked it, and then
we went to the Sabinomyojin shrine on the beach.
From there we took a boat and went past the Toshi
Islands, Divine Food Island, and Toru Island. On the
Island of Divine Food the seaweed known as sea-
pine grows and is collected by priests from the Great
Shrine of Ise, who offer it at the altar of the goddess.
The Island of Toru[2] is so called because there is an
arch of rock there under which boats can pass. There
is a lot of good sightseeing to enjoy here on the
boundless expanse of the sea.

The god to whom the shrine of Ko Asakuma is
dedicated is, if I remember rightly, the patron of
bronze mirror casters, the object of worship being
the sacred mirror in which the Sun Goddess looked
at her own reflection. Though the mirror was stolen
and thrown into the sea, it restored itself to the altar
here. As a result the oracle declared, "It is my desire to save from suffering the denizens of the scaly
kingdom," the mirror moving itself from the altar
to appear on the top of a nearby rock. Near the rock
there was a cherry tree where the mirror lodged on a
branch at high tide, returning to the rock at low tide.

[2] *Toru,* to pass.

As this story interested me much, I decided to remain a day or two at Shioai, staying at the house of the chief priest of the shrine, who treated me with great hospitality and made me extremely comfortable.

After two or three days, hearing that it was most enjoyable to see Futami Bay by moonlight, I went there with a party of women. Words fail me to describe how impressive, how beautiful, how touching the scene was. We spent the whole night on the beach, and as we left at daybreak I composed the poem,

> I cannot forget
> The clear beauty of the moon
> Standing in the sky
> Which has shone the whole night through
> On the white sands of the bay.

While I was at this place, a relative of the chief priest of the Ise shrine named Terutsuki who served in the kitchen at the Tominokoji palace heard that I was there and sent me a letter supposedly from one of the ladies-in-waiting whom I knew. Feeling that it was rather strange to receive a letter from her, I opened it. It was from the ex-Emperor.

"Are you so much in love with the moon at Futamigaura," he wrote, "that you have forgotten the court and me? I hope that soon we may have another friendly talk together like the one we had when we met accidentally at Yawata." The letter was so affectionate in every way that I was quite un-

decided as to how I should answer it, but eventually
I sent this poem in reply,

> How could I ever
> Forget the splendid beauty
>   Of the midnight moon
> We loved to watch together
> When I was still there with you?

I felt it was time I was leaving and decided to go
back first to the outer shrine at Ise and then, as the
commotion after the fire seemed to be over, return
to the Atsuta shrine where I could finish copying the
rest of the sutra. At the outer shrine I felt so sad
at having to leave that I recorded my feelings in the
poem,

> O God of the shrine,
> Guide me, I beseech you, as
>   I go on my way
> For the rest of my journey
> Through this world of suffering.

The following morning as I was leaving, I received
a letter from the chief of the priests of the shrine,
Arakida no Hisayoshi. "Thank you for all your good
wishes," he wrote. "Do not fail to come back here
for the annual festival in the ninth month."

I thought that it was most kind of him to give me
this invitation and replied with the poem,

> For the festival.
> I will certainly return
>   To offer up prayers
> That this benevolent reign
> Will continue for ever.

No one could know, however, with what great sincerity I should make my prayer for the continued well-being of the ex-Emperor.

Hisayoshi wrote in answer thanking me for my prayers for himself and his family and sending me two rolls of silk made, as he emphasised, in Ise province and including the poem,

> A long, long time
> It will appear unto me
>   Until you fulfil
> Your promise of returning
> In the ninth month to Ise.

That evening I spent at Ominato in a fisherman's hut near the salt-pans so that I might catch the ferry at high tide next morning, as I thought of the old song,

> Happy I could be
> Even among rocky cliffs,
>   Resorts of cormorants,
> Or on a whale-haunted beach,
> If he I love were but there.

I could not help wondering what would become of me in the future. It was no comfort to look forward to seeing the ex-Emperor again some day. Happy should I be if I were now on my way to join him beyond the mountains!

Just as I was leaving well before dawn, a letter arrived from the priest of the outer shrine, Tsune-yoshi. "This is the poem I intended to send to you before you left here," he wrote,

> As you go away
> Across the stormy billows,
>   I weep as I think
> That you have become again
> A stranger and lost friend.

I replied with the poem,

> Fated to become
> A stranger to you again,
>   As I leave I weep
> When I think that this means that
> We shall never meet again.

At the Atsuta shrine they were still busy on the work of rebuilding, but not wishing to delay any longer the fulfilling of my vow, I had a scriptorium prepared, copied the remaining thirty volumes of the Kegon sutra, and presented them to the shrine.

The priest who presided at the dedication ceremony was only an ignorant country priest who had no idea what kind of sermon to preach, but still the service I had planned no doubt gave pleasure to the ten guardian demons who protect the sutra, and that was the best I could do in the circumstances. Then I went on my way up to the Capital.

Lady Nijo, now (1292) in her thirty-fifth year, meets the ex-Emperor Go Fukakusa at the palace of Fushimi

CHAPTER XII   Not even after my death, I thought, should I ever be able to forget my unexpected meeting with the ex-Emperor at the Hachiman shrine at Iwashimizu. Since that meeting he had often sent messages to me by a relative of mine asking me to meet him. I had thought it better, however, to continue not to consent to do this, and so the days and the months passed by uneventfully until the ninth month of the following year.

Especially whenever he was at the Fushimi palace, the ex-Emperor would write to me telling me how quiet and peaceful Fushimi was and how nothing could ever leak out about anything which happened there. Obviously my love for him must have been stronger than my devotion to the life of piety which I had adopted. I saw nothing unreasonable or sinful in what he suggested, and finally I went in secret to the vicinity of the palace. My relative came out to meet me and took me in. It was quite amusing to be thus shown in to a place which I had known so well of old. While I leaned on the balustrade of the Kyutaido sanctuary waiting for the ex-Emperor, the babbling of the waters of the river Uji seemed compassionate and soothing, for I was reminded of the words of the ancient poem,

> Nothing seemed to be friendly
> Save the rippling of the stream.

A little after eight o'clock in the evening, the ex-Emperor came in. His appearance now in monastic garb in the bright moonlight was so different from the image I had treasured in my memory that tears came to my eyes and blurred my vision of him. We talked of various incidents of our old life together from the time when I had sat on his knee as a small child of four years of age until the time when I took my vows. They now seemed to me to be events of an infinitely remote past, but still it filled me with grief to hear him speak of them. "I am sure," he said finally, "You have continued to have many troubles while you have gone on living in this sorrowful world. Why have you let such a long time elapse without telling me of them?"

Actually there was very little I had to complain about except that, having had to leave his service, I had had to live the life of a nun on constant pilgrimage. He himself was the only person against whom I had the slightest cause for complaint, but, I thought, it would be extremely impertinent of me to tell him so now. I listened and remained silent. The call of the deer on the Otowa hills urged me to tears, and the bell from the Sokujo-in temple told of the coming of dawn. I whispered to myself,

> All night I listen
> To the sad call of the deer
> On the distant hills;
> Then the bell tolling at dawn
> Comes to soothe away my tears.

Too soon it was broad daylight; my sleeves still wet with tears, I left the palace, treasuring in my mind's eye the memory of his form.

"I should like to meet you again," he had said in the course of our conversation the previous evening. "I hope it will be on a bright moonlight night like this. But you, whenever you talk of our next meeting, never speak of our meeting again in this life but only of our reunion in the world to come, when in 5670 million years' time Miroku Buddha comes down to save those who have been left out of Gautama Buddha's scheme of redemption. Why did you renounce the world? What do you expect to happen to us in this world? Men are free to go on pilgrimage to any place they wish, to the eastern provinces and even as far away as China, and to practise all the austerities they want in search of salvation. But many difficulties face women who attempt to do the same. They need a man's support and help. Whose loving care have you depended on during your pilgrimages? I do not suppose for one moment that you went everywhere alone. You tell me of a man at Kamakura through whose sleeves a river of tears flowed because you were leaving him, of another man to whose house at the foot of Mikasa at Nara you were led by a fence of chrysanthemums, of a man you have promised to meet in autumn on the bank of the river Mimosuso in Ise. Were these all casual encounters with no deeper bond between you than that of a common interest in poetry? And besides these you must have travelled often on your pilgrimages in the company of a man."

I believe that in asking these questions he was sincerely anxious to learn the truth about my experiences. "Since the moment when I left the court," I said, "and took my vows and began my wanderings through the provinces, I have had no place to call my own. I have found it true that, as the Lotus Flower sutra says, 'There is no rest in the burning house of this world.' To this fate I am fully resigned, regarding it as the inevitable consequence of my sins in a former life. I realised too that when the bonds of love between a man and a woman are broken, there is no way of restoring them to what they were before. Though I come of the line of the Genji clan which is under the special protection of Hachiman Bosatsu, I do not believe that I should rely solely on his protection. Yet it was to his shrine that I went to worship before I started out for the east, praying that my pilgrimage might in the first place assist in my spiritual development and also incidentally serve in expiation of my sins in this life. The old proverb says that an honest person's conscience is the sole divine arbiter of good and evil. If that is true, then my conscience is clear. I have no doubts about this, for if during my travels as far to the east as the river Sumida in Musashi province, I had had relations with a man even for one night, then I should consider that by doing so I had consigned myself to the darkest depths of hell from which I could not hope to escape, notwithstanding the pledge of the three Buddhas who are reincarnations of Hachiman Bosatsu that they will save all souls from eternal destruction. I went to the pure waters of the river Mimosuso, but if I had relations with a man at Ise and left my heart there with him, Dainichi Buddha who rules over the Worlds of Wisdom and Mercy would deal sternly with me for my sins. The autumn chrysanthemums at the house at the foot of Mikasa hill did nothing for me but free my mind for the writing of poetry. If I had had relations with a man there at that time and gone on from there down the southern slope of Nara to worship at the Kasuga shrine, I should rightly have forfeited the favour of the gods of the shrine and rightly suffered the eight agonies of remorse.

"I lost my mother when I was in my second year," I went on. "I have always grieved that I could not remember her at all. My father died when I was in my fifteenth year. I have always tried to do what he would have wished me to do and even now weep when I recall his great love for me. Your love and compassion for me when I was a little girl assuaged my grief at the loss of my parents. When I grew up, you favoured me above everyone else. How can I cease being eternally grateful to you for that? Animals who have no power of reasoning can feel gratitude and try to show it to those who are good to them. How can I as a human being help being grateful to you who have done so much for me? In the old days when I was a little child, your love for me seemed to me to be as natural a thing as the light of the sun and the moon, and when I grew up, I was just as grateful to you for your love and care as I was to my parents.

"Then," I went on, "I had the unexpected misfortune to lose your favour and be sent away from the court. Months and years passed, but whenever I happened to see you go by in procession, I wept as I recalled the former happy days. When, at the New Year investitures, I heard of honours and court ranks conferred on former friends and learnt of the success and prosperity of other families, my heart ached with envy.

"It was to free myself," I said, "from such vain tears and sinful envy that I decided to go on pilgrimage to this place and to that in order to gain spiritual enlightenment. Sometimes I stayed in priests' quarters at temples, and sometimes there were men sleeping in the same room. Sometimes I stayed at the same place for many days and nights in succession practising the writing of poems and engaging in other romantic pursuits. It may be that people who never move far away from the Capital may think this kind of conduct extremely eccentric. I know that wandering nuns often do enter unthinkingly into casual guilty relationships with hedge priests and flute-playing mendicants and other undesirables. It was, to say the least, my good fortune not to do so. Instead I lay alone, my own sleeves as my pillow, throughout the whole of my journeyings. If it had been otherwise, then at least I should have been protected against the mountain blasts on frosty nights by four thicknesses of sleeve. Also, unlike Saigyo, I had no friend in the Capital waiting for my return to secular life. So I idled away my days under the cherry blossoms and my nights on the open moor, with the frosts of autumn as my covering and the grass as my pillow, listening to the chirping of the insects growing feebler and feebler as winter approached and comparing their fate with my own."

The ex-Emperor listened intently to my story but continued to press me with questions. "I can quite believe," he said, "that you have remained pure and chaste during your pilgrimages, for all that time you were worshipping at various shrines and temples wherever you went. You have not said anything, however, about your life in the Capital after your return, when you were not going round from one temple to another. This must be because you have allowed someone whom you loved formerly to return to your affections."

"I am not expecting to live a long life," I said. "Still, I am not yet forty years of age, and I can promise nothing about what kind of life I may live in the future. All I can truthfully say is that up to the present moment I have entered into no secret relations of this kind with anyone whether he is an old friend or a new one. If what I have said were a lie, then my two thousand days of skimming[1] through the Lotus Flower sutra and my copying out of so many of the sutras with my own hand would not be a work of piety but instead a barrier to my entry into Paradise, for I should find my hopes of salvation, even by the mercy of Miroku Buddha, rendered vain, and I should find myself consigned to the darkest depths of eternal hell."

He was silent for some time. I could not guess what impression my story had made on him. "I see now," he then said, "how unreasonable it is for me to have worried so much about you. After the death of your parents, I took upon myself complete responsibility for you, but circumstances eventually prevented my continuing to do so. I thought at the time that the break was due to the weakness of the ties of love which bound us together. I realise now, however, that in spite of my coldness and indifference towards you, your affection for me has remained warm and steadfast through all your troubles. It must have been by the special favour of Hachiman

[1] This describes the usual method of reciting the sutras, by reading short extracts at the beginning, middle, and end of each volume and skipping the rest.

Bosatsu that I was fortunate enough to notice you when you visited his shrine."

The moon set behind the western hills and the sun rose in the east and lighted up the landscape as I hurriedly left the palace to avoid being seen there in my nun's habit.

"Let's meet once more without fail as soon as possible," the ex-Emperor said as I left. His voice seemed to me a beacon that would guide me along the dark path of my life thereafter.

When he returned to the Capital from his tour, he sent me presents brought to me by a stranger. I felt grateful to him for his kindness at Fushimi and for the presents he had sent in secrecy. The favours I had received from him during my time in his service, though they seemed to no one either scandalous or over-indulgent, showed his true and undeviating affection for me. The old days were well worth remembering after all, it seemed.

 Lady Nijo, now in her thirty-eighth year, pays another visit to Ise

CHAPTER XIII So the years rolled on, and I decided to make another visit to Futamigaura, so called, I believe, because the goddess of Ise returned there for a second look, though earlier I have explained the derivation of this place name in a different way. I wished to pray at Ise for a happy life and a happy death. On my way there from Nara by the pass over the Iga range of mountains, I passed by the Kasaoki temple. . . .[1]

---

[1] Unfortunately, the rest of the chapter is missing.

Book Five

After a lapse of nine years, Lady Nijo's story (as now extant) describes her visit to Itsukushima during her forty-fifth year (1302)

CHAPTER Having made up my mind to travel the
  I   route of the Emperor Takakura on his
          voyage to the Itsukushima shrine after his
abdication [in 1180], I took the boat at the usual port
of Toba on the river Katsura, changing to a larger boat
at the mouth of the river. I did not find life at sea at
all pleasant.

Passing along the shore of Suma, I recalled Chunagon
Arihara no Yukihira, elder brother of the more
famous poet Narihira, who composed this poem while
he was in exile here,

> Should any person
> Happen to make enquiries,
>   Tell them of the life
> That I lead at the salt-pans
> On the lonely Suma shore.

Where was it, I asked the wind blowing off the
shore, just where was it that the poet lived?

It was the beginning of the ninth month when we landed, and the chirping of the insects in the frost-withered bushes was growing feebler and more intermittent. Lying in my berth on the ship, I listened throughout the long cold night to the melancholy thud of the cloth-beaters' mallets in the village against the background of the sound of the rolling waves. It was a touching sight to see early next morning the fishing boats appearing and disappearing in the morning haze among the islets off the town of Akashi. It was easy to imagine the feelings of Shining Genji as he wrote,

> Gallop on quickly,
> Dappled grey horse of fancy,
> Gallop on with me
> To the court—and I shall see
> My darling in one moment.

So at last we reached the port of Tomo, in Bingo province, seemingly a very prosperous post station. Off the shore, on the tiny solitary island of Taika in a row of cottages, there lived far from the vulgar world a group of nuns who had formerly been prostitutes in the town. Before, it had been their custom to perfume their garments heavily with incense the better to attract the men they accosted. They would smoothe down their hair, wondering the while on whose sleeve it would become dishevelled, and wait in the evening in lively expectation for those from whom in the morning they would part with no regrets. These women belonged to families whose business it was to provide sensual pleasures and whose inescapable destiny it was never to be able to rise in the after-life above this degraded existence. All this they had abandoned to live more honourably in seclusion on this island.

"What about your daily services?" I said to one of these nuns. "What was it that impelled you to make this great change in your lives?"

"I was once the owner of a brothel," she said, "where there were many women. Dependent on travellers, we were glad to see boats arrive at the port and sorry to see them pass without stopping. I had these women paint their faces and pledge eternal love to men whom they had never met before, forcing them to drink heavily under the cherry blossoms in spring and in the dews of autumn. Before I realised it, I was fifty years of age, and it was then that I recognised what I was destined to discover—how illusory are the things of this world. I came here and have never since been back to the town. Every morning I climb this hill to gather flowers for an offering to the Buddhas of the past, present, and future in our daily service."

I envied the woman her peace of mind. Our ship was in port for one or two days. The nuns hated to see me going away and asked me when I expected to return there on my way back to the Capital. I replied,

> On this pilgrimage
> As I wander aimlessly,
>   How can I tell you
> When I shall return this way
> Going to the Capital?

The ship arrived at Itsukushima, or Miyajima as it is also called, where in the open sea stands a large *torii* joined to the land by a causeway that seems to float on the surface of the sea and to which a large number of boats were moored. At the temple, preparations were being made for a Buddhist festival. Maidens in the service of the shrine would dance and sing on a stage erected over the sea that could be reached from the land by a bridge. A rehearsal was held on the twelfth day of the ninth month when eight maidens danced, dressed in tight-sleeved gowns of various colours with white silk skirts. The music was not of a high standard, but I recognised it as being a composition by Lady Yang-kuei, wife of the Emperor Hsuan-tsung[1] of the Tang dynasty. The dance was the Ishang Yui, composed by the same emperor.

On the day of the festival two groups of dancers, one on the left in red brocade and one on the right in blue, represented the Buddhas, and a dancer in a crown and large hair ornament played the role of Lady Yang-kuei. As evening approached, the sound of the music grew louder, especially in the rendering of the classical "Music of Autumn Winds" which touched me deeply.

When it was quite dark, the music and dancing ceased and most of the audience went home, leaving the shrine deserted, for very few people remained to make a vigil. The thirteen-day-old moon rising from behind the mountain at the back of the shrine seemed to be coming up from the middle of the shrine itself.

[1] Sixth Emperor (685–762) of the Tang dynasty (618–906).

The tide had risen to the shrine's steps. The bright moon reflected in the water appeared to be lying at the bottom of the sea. Such miraculously beautiful sights as this are said to be one of the forms in which is manifested the mind of Buddha freed from all the appetites of the flesh, having attained the full wisdom of the universe. Admiring the beauty of the scene, I found myself reciting the words of the sutra, "The wisdom of Buddha radiating from his person will shine through the whole world; and the peoples of the world repeating the sacred name of Buddha will be redeemed." At the same time I was much perturbed by the thought that real happiness could come to me only if my heart were cleansed of all sin.

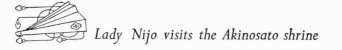 *Lady Nijo visits the Akinosato shrine*

CHAPTER I did not stay long at Itsukushima, but came back towards the Capital by sea

II through the Inland Sea of Seto. On the boat I got into conversation with a rather nicely dressed woman.

"I come from the town of Wachi in Bingo province," she said. "I always wanted to visit the shrine at Itsukushima. Won't you come and see my house?"

"I'm on my way now to Cape Ashizuri in Tosa province," I answered. "I understand it is a place worth visiting. But on my way back, I will call and see you."

On this cape there is a temple dedicated to Kannon, the goddess of mercy. There is no resident priest in charge, and the main building is not divided off into rooms for different classes of visitors, travellers, and pilgrims staying there all together without any distinction of rank.

The reason for this is to be found in the following story: Formerly there was living in this temple a priest who was attended by a page with a very compassionate nature who was in the habit of sharing his meal with another page who came to the temple every day.

The priest warned him against such indiscriminate hospitality. "It's all right to do this once or twice," he said, "but you must not share your meal with him any more."

Next day the unknown page arrived for the meal. "I should like to be able to share my meal with you," the page of the temple said, "but the priest does not approve of my doing so. Please don't come again. This must be the last time."

"I shall never forget your kindness," the other page answered. "Come with me to my own house."

The page accompanied him, followed by the suspicious priest, who saw them take a boat and row away to the south. "Where are you going?" he shouted. "Are you going to leave me?"

"We are going to the island of the goddess of mercy," they replied. Then the amazed priest saw the two pages transfigured, and there stood in the boat, one in the bow and the other in the stern, the figures of the goddess of mercy and the god of wisdom,

The forsaken priest wept and stamped his feet in vexation and disappointment. And so the cape is called Cape Ashizuri, Foot-stamping, from the two footprints which the priest left when he stamped on the rock. Realising that it was his own lack of compassion that had caused him to be thus humiliated, he made the rule that henceforth there should be no discrimination of class or rank at the temple. For myself, I learned from the story that I could rely confidently on the aid of the goddess of mercy, who has revealed that she will manifest herself in thirty-three different ways to redeem the human race.

Like the Yasaka shrine in the Capital, the shrine of Akinosato is dedicated to the ox-headed god who is the keeper of the monastery founded by Gautama Buddha. Feeling a certain amount of devotion to the shrine because of this connection, I stayed for the night there in peaceful meditation and worship.

Lady Nijo visits Shiramine

CHAPTER
III
Our ship stopped near Shiramine at Matsuyama in Sanuki province, the burial place of the Emperor Sutoku and a place I had for this reason longed to visit. Besides, I had friends in the province. I went to the Hokkeji temple in Matsuyama where the devout manner of their services encouraged me to believe that by their prayers

they had freed the Emperor from the punishment he deserved for his evil deeds and would finally bring him to salvation. I recalled Saigyo's poem which he composed here,

> Although formerly
> In exalted splendour you dwelt,
> Now that you have died,
> You must resign yourself that
> The end of your power has come.

I remembered too the poem of the Emperor Tsuchimikado who was also in exile here,

> It is destiny
> Which has forced me to lead here
> Such an unhappy life;
> Unreasonable is it then
> To shed tears of repining.

For my own part, I mused,

> If you remember
> Those sorrowful nights and days
> You spent in weeping,
> Your compassion let me have
> Even from the under-world.

I decided to stay here to copy some of the five Mahayana sutras which to my sorrow still remained to be completed. I went to a small hermitage near

Matsuyama where, finding it a very suitable spot for my devotions, I set to work on my task and to occupy myself with regular acts of penance.

It was the end of the ninth month and the songs of insects had grown feeble, depriving me of even this small comfort in my solitude. Reciting the Lotus Flower sutra morning, noon, and evening with the prayer for absolution from sins committed through the six senses, I yet could not banish from my mind the ex-Emperor's words of love. Though I had vowed never again to play the lute, I still kept on the stand before the image of Buddha his bone plectrum which he had given me as a present when he was teaching me as a child to play the lute. With the thought in my mind I wrote,

> Treasuring this yet
> As my one keepsake of his,
>   Still are my eyes filled
> With bitter tears as I think
> That we are young no longer.

On this occasion I wrote out twenty of the forty volumes of the sutras which I had not yet copied, and presented them to the temple at Matsuyama, being dependent during this time on the help given me by friends who lived in the province. One of the three tight-sleeved gowns which the ex-Emperor had given me the year before at the Iwashimizu shrine I had presented to the Atsuta shrine as a reward for the help given me while I was copying the sutras there. Now I presented one of the others to the temple here in thanksgiving for the dedication service which I had asked them to hold when the completed sutras were presented. With this in mind I wrote,

> When we parted there,
> Why did he not ask me then
> To keep these three gowns
> Until, at that bright dawn, we
> Meet again in Paradise?

Doubtless it was a sinful attachment to his love that caused me now to resolve never to part with that one remaining keepsake, the one tight-sleeved gown that I still had which he had worn next to his own body.

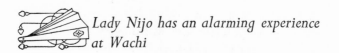 *Lady Nijo has an alarming experience at Wachi*

CHAPTER

IV

Before I realised it, it was the end of the eleventh month. Then I was overjoyed to hear that a ship would be leaving soon for the Capital. I travelled by this ship but unfortunately it ran into a severe snow storm with high wind and waves, and the ship had to put into a port in Bingo province. I landed there and discovered that fortunately it was near the house of the lady I had met on the ship on the outward voyage. With the help of the note she had given me, I was soon able to find the house and had a very happy stay with her for a few days.

I saw, however, that the master of the house had four or five men and women brought to the house every day and had them beaten unmercifully as a punishment for various offences. I was shocked and horrified by his cruelty, for there seemed to be no excuse at all for it. He was also a great hawker and hunter, killing off large numbers of birds and animals. He was a thoroughly wicked man.

A near relative of this man, the Nyudo Hirosawa no Yoso, a man of some influence in the service of the Military Government, was expected on a visit on his way from Kamakura to the Kumano shrine, and not only the household itself but the people of the village and the whole district were in something of a panic preparing for his visit. At the house they had silk-covered sliding doors made, and these had to have pictures painted on them.

"I'll paint them if you like," I said unthinkingly, "if you'll get the paints for me. You'll be able to get them at Tomo." They sent off for them at once, and it was then too late for me to repent of my impulse to help.

The colours arrived, and I decorated the doors. The people of the house were highly delighted with them. "Please stay with us as long as you can," they said to me, to my amusement.

Before long the Nyudo arrived and was very hospitably entertained. "These pictures haven't been painted by any country artist," he said when he had looked at the sliding doors, and admired them. "Where did you get them done?"

"The artist is staying here with us," they said.

"Artists usually have good taste in poetry. I presume he has too. I should like to meet him."

I was puzzled as to what I should do, but knowing that he was on his way to the Kumano shrine, I decided to make this my excuse. "I think it would be better," I said, "if we arrange a meeting when he comes here on his way back." This was agreed to, and the Nyudo left for Kumano. Two or three ladies-in-waiting had come with him from Kamakura.

One of them was a daughter of the elder brother of the master of the house at which I was staying, who lived at a place called Eda nearby. She invited me to go to stay there for a time, as the scenery was quite interesting. I was in fact finding my life at the Wachi house not very pleasant owing to the behaviour of the master of the house. So, as the snow prevented my going back to the Capital for the moment, I went to Eda, not giving the matter very much consideration, but expecting that I should be able to continue my journey back to the Capital from there later on in the year.

The master of the house was, however, very angry when he learned that I had gone to Eda. This was a development I had not anticipated, nor had I expected him to take the line he did. "It was a very lucky thing for me," he said to people when speaking about my departure, "that I was able to find her again at Itsu-kushima. I had had her in my service for a long time before she ran away that time. And now I have had her stolen away from me by my brother. I'll kill her when I get my hands on her."

I could not understand how he could have the audacity to claim that I was a servant of his. "Take no notice of what he says," his brother said soothingly. "That's the sort of senseless thing he's always saying." I was really quite happy at the house at Eda. There were many young girls in the house and the atmosphere was extremely friendly and cheerful. Comfortable as I was, however, I was not sufficiently attracted to the place to want to stay there for good.

When the Nyudo arrived at Wachi on his way back from Kumano, the brother there complained to him that his elder brother had enticed his servant away from him. "What is the matter with you two?" he said to the brother at Wachi, as I learned later. "Your complaint about losing your maidservant is really absurd. You claim she is your servant. She doesn't seem to me to be of the servant class. Her skill in painting shows that. It is quite a usual thing for persons of high social position to go on pilgrimages. I wonder what family in the Capital she belongs to. It is really disgraceful that you should speak about her as you do. I'll see your brother at Eda about it." The news that he was intending to do this naturally put everyone there in a panic of preparation.

"We two brothers are at enmity with each other,"

the elder brother said to his uncle on his arrival at the Eda house, "and all because of some stranger from the Capital on a pilgrimage."

"It is really an absurd quarrel," said the uncle. "Send her away to Bitchu province with someone to be company for her."

I was very grateful to him for the decision which he had made, and when I saw him, I told him my story.

"Talent often makes enemies for one," he commented. "You are so talented an artist that he couldn't bear to part with you!"

The Nyudo was extremely interested in poetical composition, and we began to amuse ourselves together, versifying and verse-capping. As we did so, I watched him closely and realised that he had been one of those present at Kamakura when I had attended such poetry meetings with the lord of Iinuma. We went on to speak of those meetings and of his sad fate and that of his father, Taira no Yoritsuna. After a few days the Nyudo left for Ida. There had been a heavy fall of snow, and the scenery with its snow-laden bamboo fences looked strange to me, but all the more beautiful because,

> When winter snow falls,
> Against the drifts the fences
>   Are our protection,
> Just as against earthly sins
> Our defences are our vows.

Lady Nijo, now (1303) in her forty-sixth year, returns to the Capital

CHAPTER The turn of the year came while I waited
V   in vain, hoping to return to the Capital,
       but it remained very cold, and since the
voyage was still considered very risky, I could not
make up my mind to leave. It was therefore already
the beginning of the second month before I finally
decided to start. The Nyudo came from Ida to say
good-bye to me, and we enjoyed another session of
verse-capping. He gave me a number of presents when
he left. It was perhaps because he was the guardian of
a daughter of the former Generalissimo Prince Munetaka who was being brought up by the Lady Komachi
that he showed such friendship for me.

At Ebara in Bitchu province where I went first,
seeing a cherry tree in full bloom, I broke off a
branch and sent it back to the Nyudo by the man who
was seeing me off from there on his behalf with this
poem,

        The mist now descends
        To hide us from each other;
          But yet these blossoms
        Remind me of you, and take
        You my message on the wind.

333

It was a two-day journey from there to Ida, but the Nyudo sent back the man at once with his poem in answer to mine,

> Not blossoms alone,
> Your poems also give me
> Messages from you,
> And on the wind my heart flies
> Bringing a wordless message.

As the Kibitsu shrine was on my way, I paid a visit there and found the inside of the shrine furnished in an unusual manner, being provided with screens and furniture more suitable for a noble's residence than a shrine. As the days were long and the winds favourable, I was soon back in the Capital.

What an unexpected and perilous adventure I had been through! How should I have been able to escape from this dangerous situation if the Nyudo had not chanced to go down there at that particular moment? Who would have taken my part when I declared that I was not that man's maidservant? What would have happened to me in the end, I wondered. As a result of this incident, I lost all my enthusiasm for going on pilgrimages and did not stir out of the Capital for a very long time.

CHAPTER
VI

At the beginning of the next year, I heard in the course of general conversation that the ex-Empress Higashi Nijo was ill. Although I was most anxious to know about her condition, there was no one to whom I could go for more definite news of her than I could get by hearsay. I did learn in this way that she was critically ill and that she had left the Tominokoji palace. This struck me as being very odd. Death comes to all of us, it is true, but still I could not understand why she should have had to leave the palace where she had lived so long. Seated on the throne to which so few are raised and only through their virtues in a former life, she had helped His Majesty in the affairs of government by day and kept him company at night. It was therefore only just that she should breathe her last in the surroundings to which she had been accustomed for so long. I was still puzzling over the reasons for her having had to leave the palace when I heard she had passed away.

As I was living near the Capital, I went to the palace to find out if it were possible to catch a glimpse of the ex-Emperor. While I stood outside, it was announced that Princess Yugimon would be leaving, and retainers brought her carriage round to the steps. Then it was moved away again, and it was announced that Lord Kinhira, former Minister of the Right, was leaving. Next, the princess was going to leave at once, and her carriage was brought up to the entrance again. Then her departure was once more delayed. So she came out and then went in again several times. It was sad indeed to see how reluctant she was to go away without just one more sight of her mother. Standing near to the carriage among the crowd of onlookers, I heard people commenting on this, "I thought she was going to get into the carriage, but she's gone back in, hasn't she?" Finally, the princess did get into her carriage, looking quite out of her mind with grief. The bystanders wept in sympathy, and, however insensitive they might be, all those who were told about the incident wept too. As she was the only surviving child of the ex-Empress, all the others having died young, there was an unusually strong bond of affection between mother and daughter. My memory of my own grief at my father's death enabled me to understand her feelings at that sad moment. I wondered what would have been my feelings at this time if I had remained at the court and had been there to see the ex-Empress leave the palace for the last time, and expressed my thoughts in the poem,

> A sad world it is
> Where I see the Empress leave
> On her last journey
> The palace where long she lived
> While a bystander am I!

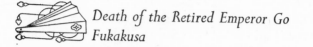 *Death of the Retired Emperor Go Fukakusa*

CHAPTER VII The funeral service for the ex-Empress Higashi Nijo was held at the palace of Fushimi, attended by the Retired Emperor[1] and Princess Yugimon. I sympathised deeply with them in their loss, but I had no relative now through whom I could offer my condolences. I could only spend my days and nights in vain anxiety about them. In the same year in the sixth month, I was distressed to hear that the Retired Emperor was ill, of ague, it was said. In a few days he was reported to be better, and then it was said that he had had another attack. Then I heard that prayers for his recovery were to be offered to Emma, the King of Hades. I went to the palace, but there was no one there from whom I could get any information, and I returned from the palace knowing as little as when I went there, expressing my frustration in the poem,

> How can he learn
> Except maybe in a dream
>   That my eyes are dimmed
> With the tears shed night and day
> In my so sore grief for him?

[1] Go Fukakusa is given the title of Ho-o (Retired), implying that he had now taken final vows.

Then I heard that he was suffering daily attacks, and then several attacks a day. People were all expecting to hear of his death. I was frantic, for I feared that I should never be able to see him again. I went into retreat at the Hachiman shrine at Iwashimizu from the first day of the seventh month and offered up prayers a thousand times for his recovery and for long life at the Takenouchi shrine in the precincts there. While I was there, on the fifth day, I dreamed about an eclipse of the sun. . . .

(Here the rest of the page has been cut away and we cannot conjecture what the rest of the story was and can only continue the story when it is resumed.[2])

. . . Thinking that he might be able to tell me more of the Retired Emperor's condition, I went to the Kitayama residence of Lord Sanekane.[3]

"I once served at the court," I said to the men on duty at the entrance of his house. "I should like to see the Nyudo."

They perhaps did not like the look of my black habit, and no one was in any hurry to take in my message. Anticipating, however, that I might get such a reception, I had brought with me a letter in my own handwriting. I still continued, therefore, to call out for attention asking that this letter might be taken in to the Nyudo, but no one took any notice until late at

[2] Note by the seventeenth-century copyist.

[3] Saionji no Sanekane, Lady Nijo's early lover known as Snowy Dawn, now fifty-six years of age, who had taken vows three years before and so is now referred to by the title of Nyudo.

night when a retainer named Haruo came out to me and took my letter to his master.

The Nyudo sent out an answer. "Perhaps because I am getting old," he said, "I don't remember you very clearly. Be certain to come back the day after tomorrow."

I was overjoyed at getting at last some answer and went back to the Nyudo's residence on the evening of the tenth. There I was told that the Nyudo had gone to the palace as the Retired Emperor was critically ill. The news deepened my distress and I hurried back home. While passing along the side of the Guards' Riding Ground, I worshipped at the Kitano and Hirano shrines. "Take my life for his," I prayed. Yet, if my prayer were granted, I thought, and his life were saved by the sacrifice of my own, he would never know this.

> If his life be saved
> By sacrificing my own,
>   Grant me this, O God,
> That in a dream he may learn
> I offered my life for his.

Every day, all through the day and all through the night till dawn, I grieved for the Retired Emperor in his sufferings. When I went to Kitayama on the fourteenth, the Nyudo himself came out to see me, and we talked affectionately over the old days. He told me that the Retired Emperor was really dangerously ill. I had known this, but yet it came as an added shock when it was confirmed personally by the Nyudo. I had come in the hope that I might be granted permission to see him just once more, but I hesitated now, wondering how I could best phrase my request that the Nyudo should help me in this.

The Nyudo, however, realised what was in my mind. "His Majesty often spoke to me of the affection between you and him," he finally said to me in a very kindly manner. "If you go to the palace and tell them what I have just said, you will be allowed to see him."

I returned home, trying to hide my tears from the eyes of the people on the streets going to and from the Toribeno crematory and burial ground to visit the graves of their relatives, for it was the Festival of the Dead. I was sad as I thought it would not be long before I was buried there too, and I expressed the thought in the poem,

> All these who go now
> To visit the graves and pray
>   For those whom they love—
> How long will it be before
> They are lying there too?

On the evening of the fifteenth I went from my home by way of the Nijo-Kyogoku cross-roads to the palace, and by the kindness of the Nyudo was able to see the Retired Emperor from a distance.

On the sixteenth about noon, I learned that he had died. I was expecting the news, but my grief was the greater as I had no one with whom to share my sorrow.

When I could bear it no longer, I went to the Tomi-nokoji palace. I wept to see that they were already dismantling the altar where prayers for his recovery had been said. There were many people about, going to and fro, but all very quietly. The candles in the main hall had been extinguished. The Crown Prince left before dark to avoid the death-pollution and gradually the whole place was deserted. Towards evening the two High Commissioners resident in the Capital as representatives of the Kamakura Military Government came to present their condolences. A troop of warriors in the service of Hojo no Sadaaki, High Commissioner of the South, stood along Tomi-nokoji street, a torch burning at the door of each house. Another troop of warriors in the service of Hojo no Tokinori, High Commissioner of the North, sat on stools in two lines in front of a bonfire on Kyogoku street, looking most imposing.

It grew late, but I had no thought of going home, and so I remained alone in the courtyard thinking of the past. I pictured to myself his features changing with the mood just as clear to my mind's eye as if I had only that moment looked up at them in the flesh. No words can express the grief I felt. The moon rose in splendour, and I expressed my feelings in the poem,

> The unclouded moon
> Shining in all its splendour
> Saddens me the more;
> How happy now would I be
> To see the moon cloud over!

When Gautama Buddha died, the sun and the moon and even the unfeeling birds and animals were sunk in grief. It gave me unbearable pain to see that this moon at which I vacantly gazed had not clouded over. This thought seemed to indicate to me how deep and strong my love for him still was.

Day broke and I went home, but my mind would not rest. I was told that a relative of the Taira Chunagon was in charge of the funeral arrangements. I therefore went to a lady-in-waiting of my acquaintance who knew him and asked her if she would get permission for me to see the Retired Emperor's coffin even if only from a distance. She replied that this could not be allowed. I did not give up hope, however, and stood beside the entrance all day with my head veiled with a tight-sleeved gown so that I might have a chance of going near his coffin, but I found no opportunity to do this. At last the time came for the lattice windows to be closed. I then went quickly towards the place between two bamboo screens where I believed the coffin had been placed. I peeped in and saw by the light of the candles what I took to be the coffin. At the sight, my eyes were blurred and my mind disturbed. At that moment it was announced that the procession to the funeral pyre would set out. The carriage was drawn up to the steps, and the procession started, the ex-Emperor Fushimi accompanying the carriage as far as the gate and then returning to the hall. It was most pathetic to see him wiping away his tears. I followed the carriage immediately out on to Kyogoku street. I was barefooted, for I had been waiting all the day on the verandah and then, when I stepped down from the verandah, I was so confused that I could not find my sandals.

When the procession turned west at the Gojo-Kyogoku crossing, the carriage collided with a bamboo pole erected in the main street, and one of the bamboo blinds was nearly torn off, one of the servants accompanying the carriage having to climb up to try to mend it. It was while the carriage was standing there that I noticed that one of the lords accompanying the carriage was a relative of mine, the Nyudo Chunagon, Yamashina no Sukeyuki. His obvious grief increased my own sorrow.

Hesitating all the time whether to turn back now or whether to go on, I could not bring myself to stop following the carriage. My feet were hurting me badly and my steps grew slower and slower, until at length I was left a long way behind all alone.

I went on as far as Fujinomori, where I met a man. "Is the funeral procession far ahead?" I asked him.

"It ought not to have passed in front of the Fushimi Inari shrine," he said. "It must have gone some other way. I haven't seen a single person on the road. It is now after one o'clock in the morning. How do you think you're going to catch up with the procession? Where is your home? Be careful about how you go, or you might meet with an accident. Would you like me to see you home?"

Not wanting, however, to return home without having witnessed the cremation, I declined his kind offer and went on alone, helplessly weeping. It was already day when I got to the crematory. There, to my great grief, I saw that it was all over; only a thin whisp of smoke rose up from where the funeral pyre had stood. I had never imagined that I should live long enough to see the day when I should look on that sad sight. When the ex-Empress had died that spring both the ex-Emperor and their daughter Princess Yugimon had mourned her at the Fushimi palace. Now she remained alone. I could well imagine her grief, expressing my thoughts thus,

> Like a drop of dew
> Fleetingly he passed away,
>   Leaving me to weep
> As bitterly as if we
> Were still young and lovers still.

I would have liked to have talked to the princess so that we could have consoled each other in our loss, but the gate of the Fushimi palace was closed for the period of national mourning, and, thinking it silly to wander about aimlessly any longer, that evening I returned home.

Thinking of the princess, now doubtless dressed in deepest mourning as I should have been had I remained in his service, I recalled how, when the late Emperor Go Saga died, my father had insisted that I wear deep mourning, but how the late ex-Emperor had decided that I need not do so, but that I could wear coloured robes if these were not too showy.

In the eighth month of the same year, my father

had died, and then I had had to wear the deepest
mourning for him,

> Garbed always in black
> In the habit of a nun,
>   I wear no mourning,
> Though my grief is just as deep
> As the nearest of his kin.

Thinking to assuage there the grief I could tell no
one of, I went to worship at the Tennoji temple, attracted to it by the general belief that this temple is
Gautama Buddha's chosen vehicle for the salvation of
mankind. There, in peace and quiet, I recited the
sutras, praying for the repose of the soul of the late
ex-Emperor, constantly thinking of him and of the
deep grief which the princess must be suffering, a
feeling I expressed in the poem,

> In deepest mourning
> You are garbed; over that robe
>   You put on in spring,
> You donned yet another robe
> Of deep mourning in autumn.

As the forty-ninth day after the ex-Emperor's
death approached, I went back to the Capital, and
on the day of the celebration at the beginning of the
ninth month I went to the Fushimi palace for the
requiem. No one in the large congregation present
felt such bitter sorrow and grief as I did. After the

346 · *Lady Nijō's Story*

service, all made their offerings, but they did so, it
seemed to me, as if they felt a happy relief that that
day saw the end of their mourning. It grieved me
sorely to think of the princess sitting there behind
her bamboo blinds inconsolable, shedding bitter
tears like dew drops falling on the grass.

Hearing that the ex-Emperor Fushimi was to
move into his father's palace at Tominokoji, I was
reminded of the time when I was at the court and
he, just then appointed Crown Prince, had moved
into the Corner house. Since that time he had suffered
so many misfortunes in his private as well as his public
life that I felt deep sympathy for him, even though
my own lot had been immeasurably more unfortunate
than his had. My greatest misfortune had undoubtedly
been that, in spite of my prayer that the ex-Emperor's
life might be spared at the cost of my own, my prayer
had been rejected and I still remained in this world
of sorrow to keep now the seventh Seventh Day
Memorial of his death.

A tradition of the Joju-in chapel at the Mii temple
tells how, when the High Priest Chiko was at the
point of death, his disciple, the Erudite Priest Shoku,
prayed before the image of Fudo, the god of fire,
enshrined in the temple. He asked that he might die
instead of his teacher in return for the great spiritual
help Chiko had given him. Shoku enlisted the aid of
the soothsayer, Abe no Seimei, in offering this.

The god of fire, however, answered him in an
oracle. "You have prayed," the god said, "that you

should die in your master's stead. I will die in your place.'' So it was that Chiko recovered from his illness and Shoku also continued to live. What then had prevented me from repaying the ex-Emperor's favour with my life when I owed so much more to him than Shoku did to Chiko? The god of the Iwashimizu shrine to whom I had made this vow was given the title Hachiman Bosatsu because his object is the salvation of mankind. My prayer to him ought to have been granted, in spite of my own insignificance and the fact that the ex-Emperor's favour towards me was really only a very small matter. Obviously it was impossible to change what had been predestined in a former life, I thought as I went back home, where, unable to sleep, I mused,

> In the autumn months
> The chirping of the insects
>   Keeps the old awake;
> It sounds as though they too have
> Sad thoughts that keep them from sleep.

Tears shed at memories of bygone days are too much for one person's sleeves to dry away, and I had no one to weep with me. My father had died in autumn, I recalled, and my tears had vied with the autumn dew. Now the smoke of the ex-Emperor's funeral pyre had risen to the sky to merge with the autumn mists and clouds and turn them to rain, while his spirit journeyed on to its unknown goal,

> Why, O why is it
> That no sorcerer can tell me
> Where his spirit goes,
> As it flies on its journey
> Along its path through the clouds?

Lady Nijo sells her mother's keepsake

CHAPTER Twenty volumes of the Great Collection
of Sutras still remained to be copied.
VIII I had wished to finish writing these out
before the hundredth day after the ex-Emperor's
death, but now I had only the clothes I wore and so
had none to sell to cover the cost of the copying. I
could only afford to buy just enough food to live on
and certainly could not save anything in that direction. These things upset and vexed me. Yet I still
had two keepsakes given me by my parents. On her
death bed my mother had asked that I should be given
a flat, gold-lacquered toilet case with a circular design of a couple of mandarin ducks, all the toilet ar-
ticles inside it, including the mirror, having the same
pattern on them. The other keepsake from my father
was a writing case, with a lid of embossed gold lacquer
with a diamond pattern of cranes and an inscription
on the back in gold in my father's own handwriting,
"A day of good fortune and never ending happiness."
I had intended never to part with them until the end of

my life when I hoped they would be cremated with my body. When I had gone on pilgrimage, I had put them into someone's safe keeping with as much care as if they had been my children, and when I returned, it had been my first care to go and see them again as if they had been my parents themselves. I had had the writing case for thirty-three years and the toilet case for forty-six years. I had never thought that I should be able to bear parting with them. Still, nothing is as valuable to a person as his own life, and this priceless gift I had offered to the gods in return for the ex-Emperor's life. In any case, I had no children[1] or anyone else in the world to whom to bequeath these treasures of this mortal world. When I had finished copying the Great Collection of Sutras, I would let these keepsakes I had treasured for so long pass into the possession of some other family. From the proceeds of their sale, I should be able to hold a religious service in honour of Buddha—his faith and its guardians, his priests—for the intention of the repose of the souls of my parents and the ex-Emperor. I took out my treasures again and looked at them fondly. They might not smile at me or talk to me, but they were as dear to me as my babies might have been.

Then I happened to hear of a girl who was going to the eastern provinces to get married and who was looking for a toilet case like mine and did not mind

[1] Her daughter by Lord Sanekane would now be thirty-two years old, and her two sons by Prince Shojo twenty-two and twenty-one. She was, however, not allowed to see these children.

paying much more than I was thinking of asking. I was sad to part with it but I was glad to have my prayer answered, perhaps through the mercy of Buddha, his faith, and its guardians,

> How sad it is now
> I must part with these cases,
>   My parents' keepsakes,
> Which I have cherished so long
> Through fortune and misfortune!

On the fifteenth day of the ninth month, I began to recite the Lotus Flower sutra at the Sorinji temple at Higashiyama as an act of contrition for my sins. When I had been engaged in copying out the first twenty volumes of the Great Collection, my mind had been preoccupied with thoughts of my old happy relations with the ex-Emperor and of my sad separation from him at that moment. No such thoughts distracted my mind now as I concentrated with all my heart and soul, night and day, on my recitation with the prayer, "May all departed souls attain the supreme goal of eternal light." I was grateful that it had been my destiny to come to this life of piety in this place, with the belling of the friendly deer on the hills behind the Seisuiji temple, the sad chirping of the insects in the hedgerows moving me to tears, and the moon, rising in the east or declining in the west, as I sat up late at night after attending the midnight service. Then, when the midnight services in all the nearby temples appeared to have finished, still the solitary voice of the Virtuous Priest of the Sorinji temple on the summit of the hill could be clearly heard invoking the sacred name of Amida. My feelings then I expressed thus,

> May I so traverse
> The steep mountain path which leads
> To the world to come
> That on my way I may seek
> And find some lost soul straying.

I had the Virtuous Priest go with me to the Yokawa chapels on Mount Hiei to obtain paper and ink for my copying work. We went as far as Higashi Sakamoto, and I visited the Hie shrine, much frequented by my grandmother in gratitude for many favours received from the god enshrined there. . . . (The next section has been cut away with a sword. Nothing is known of the contents.[2]). . .

"For whose intention are you offering this service?" the priest asked. The question moved me deeply. As it would seem strange, I was afraid, if I offered the sutras I had copied before the tomb of the ex-Emperor, I was presenting them at the Kasuga shrine for which he had so deep a veneration during his life. At the time I wrote the poem,

> The deer in the hills
> All around me are belling,
> And the insects chirp
> Showing their deep sympathy
> And weeping with me as friends.

[2] The seventeenth-century copyist has to complain again of the mutilation of his copy.

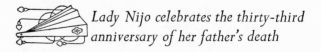

*Lady Nijo celebrates the thirty-third
anniversary of her father's death*

*CHAPTER
IX* Now this year was the thirty-third anniversary of my father's death, and I had
a memorial service held, conducted as
usual by the Virtuous Priest. To the written address
I had asked him to deliver, I added the poem,

> Inexorably
> Time moves onward, on until
>   Ten years of parting
> Are repeated a third time
> And three more years are added.

I went to the crematory at Kaguragaoka, the site
of my father's funeral pyre, where I was grieved to
find that ancient lichens wet with dew and a blanket
of dead leaves half buried the stone tablet which
marked the resting place of his ashes.

As I stood there, I thought with deep sorrow that
none of my father's poems had been included in the
recently published anthology of poems collected by
command of the Emperor Go Uda.[1] Had I still been
in service at the court, I should certainly have pressed
the compiler to include a few, for some had been
included in each anthology since the *Kokinshu, Second*

[1] *Shin Gosen Wakashu,* published 1301.

Series.[2] I myself had taken part in poetry competitions at the court and had carried on the family tradition, but it grieved me that with me would come to an end this tradition of poetical composition which had lasted through eight generations of the Koga family, in fact, ever since the foundation of the family. With the thought in mind of my father's dying wish that I should continue the family tradition, I said to myself,

> A thousand pities
> That now our family fame
> Should thus end with me
> Whose boat drifts so helplessly
> On this sea of poesy.

Having voiced my complaint in this way, I returned home.

In a dream that night I saw my father looking just as he used to look while I felt just as I used to feel in those far-off days. I spoke to him of my anxieties.

"Your grandfather, Koga no Michimitsu," he said to me, "had a poem included in the *Shin Kokinshu* anthology,

> Patience has its limits;
> Mount Shinobu[3] knows its too;
> The dew may hide them,
> But at last the autumn hues
> Of fallen leaves are revealed.

[2] Published 1265 under the Emperor Go Saga.
[3] *Shinobu*, patience.

"I myself," he went on, "had a poem included in the next anthology,

> Why, O you wild geese,
> Do you fly back to the north
>   When spring hazes come?
> Do you not know that even
> To the north the spring will come?

"The poem which your mother's father, the War Minister Shijo no Takachika, wrote in honour of the visit of the ex-Emperor Go Saga to his house at Washino-o was also included in this anthology,

> My humble villa
> Has many times been so honoured
>   By such a visit,
> But never have the blossoms
> So glorified the welcome.

"So," he continued, "whichever of the two families you take after, you are well qualified to carry on the poetical tradition which has never weakened all through the family's long history since its foundation by Prince Tomohira." Gazing at me steadfastly as he was leaving, he recited the poem,

> Be of good courage;
> Guard well the poems you write,

> For the day will come
> When once again good poems
> By low or high are treasured.

I woke up startled as he disappeared, but his image remained only as it was mirrored in my tears, and his voice lingered only on the pillow of my dreams.

From this time I devoted myself more and more to poetical composition and went into retreat at the tomb of the great poet of ancient times, Kakinomoto no Hitomaro. During my vigil on the seventh day of my retreat, I composed this poem,

> Of a family
> So renowned in poetry,
>   Sad is it to find
> I leave to posterity
> No poem worth remembering.

As I voiced in this way my disappointment at the poor results of all my efforts, the figure of an old man stood before me. In accordance with his directions I decided to hold a memorial to him in front of the sketch I had made of him, honouring him as the greatest of poets. By this I hoped that I should be able to further my ambition of creating poems worthy of the poetical tradition of the Koga family.

Actually, however, the sketch I made of the poet and the outline of the memorial service I planned to make remained unheeded for months at the bottom of my letter case until, in the third month of the next year, I did at last make the memorial in front of his picture.

Lady Nijo, now in her forty-eighth year, sells her father's keepsake

CHAPTER In the fifth month I began to prepare for the first anniversary of the death of the ex-Emperor Go Fukakusa. I had thought of celebrating it by completing what I had so long wished to do, the copying of the five Mahayana sutras. I had completed three of them, and I was afraid that at any moment I might die leaving them uncompleted. I had already sold one of my parents' keepsakes to defray the cost of the service of intercession I had arranged. I now began to wonder whether it was worthwhile keeping the other. I should not be able to take it with me when I died. At first I wondered whether it would not be better to let one of my relatives have it. I was afraid, however, that this might cause people who did not know that I wished to use the money for a service of intercession to suppose that I was having difficulties in making ends meet.

Soon after this a high official of the Kamakura Military Government on his way to Tsukushi heard of my intention of selling the writing case and bought it from me. So my mother's keepsake went to the east, and my father's as far away to the west. Sadly thinking of the opposite courses taken by their treasures, I prayed that they themselves might be reunited in Paradise, and murmured this poem as I handed it to the new owner,

> Though from this ink-stone
> The ink may flow down like tears
>   Into a river,
> There in the ocean of bliss
> It will join that other stream.

I planned to copy the remaining sutras by the tenth day of the fifth month, and, finding lodgings near the tomb of Prince Shotoku, I copied the twenty volumes of the Hannya sutra, offered them at the shrine at his tomb, and returned to the Capital at the beginning of the seventh month.

 The anniversary of the death of the ex-Emperor Go Fukakusa

CHAPTER XI On the anniversary of the ex-Emperor's death, I visited his tomb and went to the Fushimi palace to attend the memorial service. When I arrived, I found it had already started, with the High Priest Shakusen presiding. The ex-Emperor Fushimi as chief mourner read a sutra he had copied on the back of his father's letters. No doubt he had set about this task with the same single-hearted purpose as I had, and my heart was filled with sorrow and gratitude. Next Princess Yugimon read a sutra she had copied on the back of her father's letters, the brother of the High Priest Kenki presiding. Her reading touched me more than anything else in the service. The period of national mourning ended with this day's services. As the heat of the day moderated, I stood in the courtyard alone, while around me people bustled about with preparations for ex-Emperor Fushimi's departure at the end of the service. I had no one with whom to share my sorrow,

> Though today now ends
> National mourning for him,
>   I know that not yet
> Will end my mourning for him,
> My tears for him never dry.

Through the bamboo screens I could see the ex-Emperors Fushimi and Go Fushimi sitting in the Sermon Hall. The ex-Emperor Fushimi's robes seemed more sombre in colour than the ordinary mourning dress, and I thought sadly that after this day of mourning all these signs of sorrow would be discarded. The ex-Emperor Go Uda was also present, and seeing there assembled three ex-Emperors—the son, the grandson, and the son-in-law of the ex-Emperor Go Fukakusa—caused me to marvel at the continued prosperity of his line of the succession.

Lady Nijo goes into retreat at the shrine at Kumano

CHAPTER About this time also I heard that the
 XII Retired Emperor Kameyama was ill. I
thought that it was possibly nothing
serious as one does not expect tragedies to follow
so closely on one another and also because it was
not at all uncommon to hear that he was ill. I
did not anticipate that this was going to be the
last in the long series of his illnesses. Soon afterwards, however, I was told that this time it was really
serious and that he was being moved to the Saga palace.
It was sad that he should die only a year after his
brother, but still if it had to be, there was nothing
that could be done about it. I had decided to carry
out this year my plan of copying the remaining twenty
volumes of the Hannya sutra at the Kumano Nachi
shrine before it became cold enough to freeze the ink
on the inkstone, and started for Kumano about the
nineteenth day of the tenth month. The Retired
Emperor was still critically ill, and I now feared that
the next news I received of him would be of his end.
Still, it was with not too heavy a heart that I left the
Capital. Was I so heartless? Or was it because I did
not feel such a sense of impending bereavement as I
had felt at the final parting from his brother, the
Retired Emperor Go Fukakusa, my grief for whom in
his last days had prevented me from sleeping?

For the sake of convenience in making my ritual ablutions in cold water morning and evening while I was copying the sutra, I stayed near the Nachi waterfall. It was the end of the tenth month. Chill winds blew over the summits of the surrounding mountains, and the melancholy sound of the waterfall moved me to tears,

> In such pensive mood
> I weep till my sleeves are drenched
>   With tears of sorrow;
> Ask me the question how often I,
> A stranger, weep bitterly.

It must have been because the god enshrined there was well pleased with the earnestness I had shown in sacrificing my parents' keepsakes and my perseverance in copying the sutras that I had made such good progress in the task and would soon be ready to leave. I was sorry to leave the shrine, and on the night before my departure, I kept vigil there. Then, in a dream at daybreak, I saw my father standing beside me. He told me that the ex-Emperor was arriving. I looked up and saw the ex-Emperor Go Fukakusa in a reddish-brown robe with a pattern of two birds with long tails facing each other come in, his body bending over to the right as he walked. I came out from behind the bamboo blinds on his left to face him. He went into the Shojo Hall at the main shrine, and looking very happy smiled at me from under the half-raised bamboo blind.

"Princess Yugimon is arriving also," my father said. I looked up and saw her in the West Hall, dressed only in a narrow-sleeved gown and a white skirt.

"I was much moved," she said, "by your devotion in parting with your parents' keepsakes, the one to the east and the other to the west, so that you might find the money for these memorial services for your father and my father. Please accept these," and she presented me with two white robes from under her half-raised bamboo blind. I accepted them with thanks and returned to my seat.

"It was doubtless because he refrained from walking in the way of the ten deadly sins in a former life," I said to my father, "that the ex-Emperor was pre-destined to be born of the Imperial line and to ascend the throne. What fate was it then which caused this deformity of his?"[1]

"He had a swelling on the right side which caused him to be lame," said my father. "This was not due to any fault of his but was brought on by his compassion for us, the ignorant masses of the people who are dependent on him."

When I looked at the ex-Emperor again, he smiled happily and appeared to want me to approach him. I got up from my seat and knelt before him. He then gave me two sticks of *nagi* wood, the thicker ends of which were shaved slender and white like chopsticks with two leaves remaining on each.

I woke up from my dream, startled to find that the service of contrition for the sins of the six senses

[1] In infancy Go Fukakusa suffered from a disease of the hip joint.

had begun in the chapel of the goddess of mercy. Unthinkingly, I stretched out my hand and touched a fan with white cypress ribs lying on the matting. It was strange to find a fan there, for it was no longer summer. I picked it up and took it with me to the scriptorium.

"A fan is a symbol of the thousand-handed goddess of mercy," commented a priest of the shrine from Bingo province named Kakudo when I told people of this dream. "It is a great blessing to receive such an omen."

The ex-Emperor's features as I had seen them in my dream remained vividly with me as I went on with my task, and when I had finished the copying, I offered to the shrine the last of the tight-sleeved gowns which he had given me when we met accidentally at the Iwashimizu shrine. I quite realised that sooner or later I should have to do this, but I could not help weeping as I parted with this last link with him, expressing my regret in the poem,

> How sad I find it
> To part with this last keepsake
> Which I have treasured
> All these long years until now,
> Long years of separation!

I returned home from the shrine, having now given up everything I had, saying,

> When I awoke from

Dreaming of His Majesty,
   I shed tears as I
Looked up at the morning moon
And heard the sad waterfall.

I returned to the Capital taking with me the fan I had found. That was now the only reminder of him that I had to comfort me. The first news that I had on reaching home was of the passing of the Retired Emperor Kameyama. This meant national mourning for another year. Though I realised well enough that nothing can escape the perpetual changes and chances of this world, this knowledge did not alleviate the bitter sadness of my heart, and amid this change, I alone remained unmoving, like a column of smoke rising up, never changing, never fading.

And so at last the year came to an end.

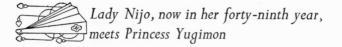 *Lady Nijo, now in her forty-ninth year, meets Princess Yugimon*

CHAPTER
XIII
At the beginning of the third month, I went, as was my custom, to visit the Hachiman shrine at Iwashimizu. I had been at Nara since the New Year and had had no news of what was happening in the Capital, the only sound coming to my ears being the belling of the deer. As I went up the slope of Inohana as usual,

I had no idea that a member of the Imperial family was making a visit until I saw that the doors of the Riding Pavilion were open. I remembered that this was so when I had accidentally met the ex-Emperor there, and I could also see that preparations were under way in front of the shrine for such a visit.

"Who is coming?" I asked.

"Princess Yugimon," I was told.

I felt that this was a strange coincidence. I remembered how she had looked in my dream the year before. I lay awake that night, and early next morning I spoke to a very gentle-looking woman, a servant it seemed, who was engaged in preparing for the visit. I greeted her and asked her name. She replied that her name was Otoranu. She had been specially selected from the maids at the court to go there. It was a great pleasure for me to meet someone from the court, and I casually asked her how things were there.

"Those who used to work there have all left," she said. "There are only young girls there now."

I wondered how I could attract the attention of the princess for her to recognise me. Perhaps, I thought, I could get a glimpse of her as she was making her round of visits to the smaller shrines within the precincts. I waited for a chance to do this without returning to my quarters for breakfast, as it was said that the princess would arrive soon. I hid myself as her stately-looking palanquin halted in front of the shrine. There she was welcomed and blessed with the sacred staff and paper streamers by Lord Kanesue, whose appearance reminded me vividly of his father—the

former Chief Minister, the Nyudo Saionji no Sanekane—when he was young and was Commander of
the Gate Guards of the Left. Many and varied were
the emotions that crowded my heart at the sight of
this man.

It was the eighth day of the third month.

In accordance with established custom, the princess
first visited the Togano-o shrine. As her visit was not
a formal one, her party consisting of two basket-work
palanquins only, I expected that they would not clear
the precincts of ordinary people and that I should be
able to get a view of her at her worship from a distance.
I therefore went forward to the shrine in company
with two or three court ladies who had come on foot.
Standing behind her as she made her act of worship
at the shrine, I could not help weeping, my heart
being so full of deep emotions. I found it impossible
to move away, and when she stood up at the end of
her worship, she spoke to me.

"Where do you come from?" she said.

I would have liked to have told her everything about
myself right from the very beginning up to the present,
but could only answer, "From Nara."

"From the Hokkeji convent?"

"Yes," I answered, very briefly, for I was afraid
that she might suspect something from my tears. I
wanted to move away, but I could not make up my
mind to do so. I remained standing there and felt an
unbearable pain as she turned to leave. I saw her
hesitating before going down the steep steps. I
hurried to her.

"Lean on my shoulder. You will feel safer," I said. She looked rather puzzled. "Long ago, when you were a child," I went on, my tears still flowing, "I was in service at the palace.[1] Don't you remember me?"

She asked me several questions in a very kind manner. "Come and see me often in future," she said finally as she left.

I recalled my dream about her and also reminded myself that it was at this shrine that I had accidentally met her father. I was glad that my faith in the god of the shrine, though unexpressed, had not been in vain even though there was no one but my tears to whom I could tell the story.

I had been accosted by one of the ladies who had come to the shrine on foot. Her name I learned was Hyoenosuke. The princess was to leave next day, I heard, and that evening she was entertained with sacred music and dances. During the evening I broke off a spray of cherry blossom and sent it to Hyoenosuke with the message, "I will call on you at the palace before the cherry blossom is over."

I had intended leaving before the princess was due to start, but thinking that I ought to render grateful thanks to the god for granting me this opportunity of seeing the princess, I went into retreat at the shrine for a further three days before continuing on to the Capital. There I sent a letter to the princess, "What

[1] Princess Yugimon was now thirty-six years old, having been born in 1270 when Lady Nijo was in her thirteenth year. They had therefore both lived at the Tominokoji palace together until the princess was about thirteen.

has become of the cherry blossom I sent you through Lady Hyoenosuke?'' With the letter was the poem,

> I promised to come
> To visit you before this;
> I am late and fear
> By now the cherry flowers
> Have been scattered by the wind.

The princess answered,

> Though you may be late
> In coming to visit us
> As you promised me,
> Do you think I should allow
> Winds to scatter the blossom?

 The third anniversary of the death of the ex-Emperor Go Fukakusa

CHAPTER XIV From this time I often visited Princess Yugimon, not so frequently as to make myself a nuisance to her but often enough to make me feel as if I were back in the old days and once more in service at the palace.

At the beginning of the seventh month the princess spoke of going to Fushimi for the third anniversary of her father's death. I too wished to attend in order to see the impressive manner in which the requiem was to be carried out, or at the very least to go near to the palace and learn by hearsay of what took place. I had no longer any keepsake of the ex-Emperor's to give as an offering, and it would have been impossible to complete in time the task of copying the last remaining sutras. I felt very sad that I had nothing to offer for the repose of his soul.

Early on the morning of the fifteenth day, I went to the Hokkedo chapel where a newly carved image of the ex-Emperor had been placed by the side of the altar. I bowed in prayer before it and then sat gazing at it, my hands still folded in prayer. To him now, I thought, our relations must seem to have been a very trivial thing. Seeing my tears, those who sat in front of the altar, probably priests who were to officiate, thought it strange and invited me to come closer to the image. Joyfully, I went near and gazed at it. My tears again began to flow. I wondered that I still had tears to weep, as I expressed in a poem my feelings on seeing this newly carved image of him.

It was the night of the full moon, and that evening I had a long talk with Lady Hyoenosuke in her room about past days as well as things of the present. At the end, feeling unsatisfied even after all this long conversation, I went out into the courtyard and stood near the Sokujo-in chapel.

"It's arrived at last," I heard people say, and wondered what was happening. I found that what was arriving was the image which I had seen that morning at the convent. It was being carried by litter on the shoulders of four men, probably lower officials, superintended by two men in dark robes whom I took to be Buddhist-image carvers, a clerk, and one or two retainers. In a dream-like state I watched them carry in the image concealed by a paper covering.

I had been too young to understand things when he was the reigning Emperor, served by all kinds of government officials of high rank and of low, but I remembered him as ex-Emperor, surrounded by a crowd of high-ranking court nobles, helped up and down steps, even on a private visit, by a lord. Now I thought of him with love and compassion as I pictured him wandering alone and desolate on his journey through the other world. I grieved for him as bitterly as if he had only just that moment passed away.

Next morning I received a letter from my father's cousin, the Madenokoji Dainagon, Minamoto no Moroshige. "I have just heard that you are here," he said. "What do you think of the memorial service?"

I sent a poem in answer,

> Chirping of insects
> Together with the moonlight
> Made deeper my grief
> As I saw his new image
> Bright and perfect as the moon.

On the sixteenth, a service was held when the Lotus Flower sutra was recited in front of the images of Gautama and Taho Buddhas on the one pedestal. Memorial services then followed one after another. The ex-Emperor Fushimi had already arrived, and strict security measures were enforced. The common people were cleared from the hall and the courtyard.

People in black monastic habit were declared taboo, and to my sorrow we were prevented from approaching the hall. I managed to slip through, however, and get as far as the eaves, from where I heard the service. I wished now with all my heart that I had not renounced the world, that I was living the life still which once I had lived. I wept without ceasing from the moment when the written prayer-petitions were read until the end of the act of contrition for sins committed through the six senses.

A priest was standing near me, obviously a dignitary of some rank. "Who are you?" he asked. "Why do you weep so bitterly?"

I felt that I ought not to reveal the secret of my relations with the ex-Emperor, even now when he had become just an image in a temple. "My father has died," I said, going away from him. "The mourning has just ended. That is why I grieve so much."

The ex-Emperor Fushimi and Princess Yugimon left Fushimi that evening. When they had gone, the palace looked so deserted that I was reluctant to leave, and I continued to stay in the neighbourhood for a few days.

I had kept up a correspondence all this time with a cousin of mine, a former minister, Koga no Michimoto. In answer to one of my letters from Fushimi, he sent a poem,

> Autumn comes and brings
> Melancholy thoughts to all
> Even here in town;

> Sadder, sadder still to you
> Fushimi's wan moon at dawn.

The kindly sympathy of others seems somehow to make one's own grief more intense and harder to bear. I answered him with the poem,

> Three autumns have passed
> Since I suffered that great loss;
> Three days here I stayed
> Made so much more sorrowful
> By hearing his requiem.

He replied with another poem,

> The past must have seemed
> To have returned to the present
> For you at Fushimi,
> Its desolate autumn scene
> Making your grief the deeper.

On the day previous to the requiem I had presented some fans to Princess Yugimon so that she could use them as presents to the priests after the service. With the parcel I sent the poem,

> Did I ever dream
> That on this, the third year's mind
> Of his passing on,
> I should still be alive to shed
> Fresh tears as bitter as these?

I had thought that after the passing away of the ex-Emperor Go Fukakusa I should have no further cause for grief.

On the eighth day of the third month of the last year, I had held a memorial service before the picture of the great poet Kakinomoto no Hitomaro. On the same day of the same month this year, I had met Princess Yugimon. I had seen the ex-Emperor and the princess earlier in a dream at Kumano, but now on this day I had seen his image, and the princess I had seen in person.

I had been anxious too about not being able to complete the task I had long wished to perform, the copying of the sutras, fearing that by not completing this, my piety through so many years should prove to be in vain. It had, however, seemed profitless to me to stay fixed in one place and worry about myself. Besides this, the pilgrimages of the priest Saigyo in search of spiritual enlightenment had attracted me so much as a child that I had tried to follow his example. These are the reasons why I have continued to note down all these trifling details of my life, even though I cannot aspire to having left to posterity anything worth reading.

(The rest seems to have been cut away with a sword.[1])

[1] With this note by the seventeenth-century copyist, Lady Nijo's story ends.

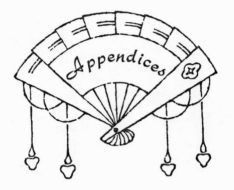

APPENDIX I:

The Historical Background

During the thirteenth century effective political control of Japan moved more and more firmly into the hands of the Bakufu, the Military Government, established at Kamakura in 1192 by Minamoto no Yoritomo (1147–1199), even though sporadic attempts continued to be made at intervals by those connected with the Imperial court at Kyoto to regain some semblance of political power. Exiled to Izu after the fall from power of the Minamoto clan under his father, Yoshitomo, Yoritomo had taken up arms against his rivals, decisively defeated them, and set up the headquarters of the Military Government at Kamakura away from the influence of the Capital. From there, under the Minamoto and Hojo families, it was to govern the country for the next 160 years. Yoritomo had in fact set the pattern for military rule in Japan for 650 years with the gradual erosion of Imperial power, so that by the end of the Kamakura period the Emperor was left with merely ceremonial functions.

By the end of the thirteenth century also, the Bakufu had acquired complete control of the national income. Gradually the receipts from the manorial estates of the Imperial court and from those of the court nobles had been alienated to the Military Government through the constables and stewards whom it appointed over these estates, so that by the second half of the century the Imperial court was in straitened circumstances, dependent in fact on a few families of court nobles to defray much of its day-to-day expenses. By the end of the thirteenth century, the economic power of the Bakufu itself was also showing signs of strain as a result of the rise of powerful local families and the drain on the Exchequer due to the threat of the Mongolian invasions.

All through the thirteenth century the powerful military families, such as the Minamoto and Hojo families, continued their struggle for control of the Military Government, while members of each family strove among themselves to obtain the most influential positions. An incident recorded in *Towazu-gatari* illustrates this struggle. Lady Nijo reports the visit of the two High Commissioners of the Military Government, Hojo no Tokisuke and Hojo no Yoshimune, to the Retired Emperor Go Saga on his deathbed to express the sympathy of the Bakufu. Six days later she mentions that Tokisuke's house in Kyoto had been attacked and he himself had been killed, but gives no further details. What had happened was that, on orders from Kamakura, Hojo no Yoshimune had attacked and killed his fellow Commissioner, who was, it was alleged, planning revolt. The victim was a son of the ex-Regent Hojo no Tokiyori and elder brother of the Regent at the time, Hojo no Tokimune, who saw in his elder brother a formidable rival in the struggle for power.

At the time of Lady Nijo's visit to Kamakura in 1289, the executive power of the Military Government was exercised in the name of the Regent (Shikken), Hojo no Sadatoki, who had succeeded to the post in 1284 at the age of fourteen. Supreme power was, however, actually in the hands of the Governor-general (Kanrei), Taira no Yoritsuna, but he was soon afterwards, in 1293, to fall from power and suffer execution for his usurpation of authority. Increasingly powerful at Kamakura at this time also was Ashikaga no Takauji, who was in the next generation to give the final blow which was to destroy the military power of the Hojo family and establish at Kyoto the Ashikaga Military Government which was to endure for 237 years.

The original basis of the power of the Military Government was in the functions of the Generalissimo (Seii-tai-shogun or Shogun) whose duty it had been in more ancient times to put down revolts in the country, especially among the barbarian aborigines, against the authority of the Emperor. On the establishment of the Kamakura Government, Yoritomo had been granted the title of Shogun in 1192, but after the assassination of Yoriie in 1204 and Sanetomo in 1219, the Hojo family had exercised this authority with the title of Regent, and in 1252 for the first time an Imperial prince, Munetaka, the son of the Retired Emperor Go Saga, was appointed to this post as a figurehead and as a convenient hostage in the hands of the Military Government. On her visit to Kamakura, Lady Nijo saw the return to Kyoto in disgrace of Munetaka's successor, his son Prince Koreyasu, Shogun from 1286 to 1289, and the arrival of a new Shogun (1289 to 1308), Prince Hisaakira, son of the ex-Emperor Go Fukakusa. The prince's mother was Fujiwara no Fusako, one of Go Fukakusa's consorts, who appears in *Towazu-gatari* under the name of Lady Mikushige from her post in charge of the Imperial wardrobe.

During her visit Lady Nijo also met the all-powerful Governor-general, Taira no Yoritsuna, becoming very friendly with his second son, the lord of Iinuma, Taira no Sukemune; they found a common interest in poetry. She describes her meeting with the Governor-general; how unimpressive she thought him as he came tripping in, his official robes too small for him, to stand beside his much more stately-looking wife. Later she records her sorrow on learning that both father and son had suffered death at the hands of the Regent. She also tells about the Regent, Hojo no Sadatoki, and finds little to admire in him; all the orders of the Military Government were issued in his name, but he was too obviously only a figurehead, overshadowed by his more powerful retainers. In general she viewed the Kamakura scene with the detachment of one accustomed to the more cultured way of life of Kyoto, respected by all as "somone from the Capital," while she was most careful not to become too deeply involved in the affairs of the Kamakura administration. She expressed her views on it quite frankly. Indeed, the chronicle of the time, *Masukagami*,[1] which borrows extensively both in matter and form from *Towazu-gatari*, is careful to tone down her adverse criticism of the Kamakura government and of the warrior classes (*buke*) in contrasting them with the court nobles *(kuge)*.

At Kyoto during the whole of the period all the forms of government continued to exist just as they had done in the heyday of the Imperial power in the Heian period three hundred years before. Court nobles still held the titles of the offices prescribed in the Taiho Code of A.D. 702: Chief Minister (Dajodaijin), Ministers of the Left, Right, and Centre (Sadaijin, Udaijin, and Naidaijin). Above them was the more recently created office of Kampaku (Imperial

[1] An historical tale, like its predecessors *Okagami* (Great Mirror) and *Imakagami* (Mirror of the Present), *Masukagami* (Clear Mirror) —written before 1376—is a chronicle of the period between 1184 and 1333, ascribed to Nijo no Yoshimoto (1320–1388), a literary scholar who rose to the position of Imperial Adviser and Regent.

Adviser). The Kampaku at the time of Lady Nijo's story, referred to as the Great Lord Konoe, was Takatsukasa no Kanehira (1227–1294), fourth son of Konoe no Iezane and founder of the Takatsukasa family. His eldest son, Takatsukasa no Mototada (1247–1313), also held the post of Imperial Adviser. Kanehira's elder brother, Konoe no Kanetsune (1210–1259), known as Prince Okanoya, is also mentioned. Kanehira resigned his post in 1287, entered religion in 1290, and died in 1294. Below the Ministers were several Great State Counsellors (Dainagon), their deputies (Gon Dainagon), State Counsellors of Middle Rank (Chunagon), and a host of counsellors and officials of lower rank. Besides these were the officers of the guards, the Bodyguards of the Right and Left (Sakon-e and Ukon-e), the Military Guards (Sahyoe and Uhyoe), and the Gate Guards (Saemon and Uemon). The principal officers were General (Taisho), Lieutenant General (Chujo), and Major General (Shosho).

Control of the Imperial Court by the Military Government was effected by balancing against each other two rival lines of the Imperial succession. In accordance with what was already a long-established custom, a prince was selected to succeed to the throne in infancy and was usually prevailed on to abdicate at adolescence. There were therefore often several ex-Emperors, with the title of Joko, living in Kyoto, each with his own court complete with ministers and officials, some of these ex-Emperors having taken vows of religion and living as religious with the title of Ho-o. The other princes as a general rule entered religion as children and became prelates of important Buddhist temples.

In 1271, at the time Lady Nijo's autobiography opens, the reigning Emperor was Kameyama (1249–1305), whose reign extended from 1260 to 1274. His elder brother, Go

Fukakusa (1243–1304), who had reigned from 1247 to 1259, was still alive, as was their father Go Saga, who had reigned from 1242 to 1246 and still retained his influence as head of the Imperial family throughout the reigns of his two sons, although he had vacated the throne twenty-six years before. During this long period no troublesome difficulties arose in the relations of the Imperial court with the Military Government, for Go Saga showed himself mindful always of the limits set on his authority by the Bakufu, especially as he himself had been raised to the throne through the direct action of the Military Government. To understand the reason for this, we must go back at least to the time of Go Saga's grandfather, the eighty-second Emperor, Go Toba.

In 1221, Go Toba and Juntoku had taken up arms in the Shokyu Incident against the Military Government at Kamakura, but had been defeated by Hojo no Yasutoki, who had the infant Emperor Chukyo replaced by a representative of a new line of the Imperial succession in Go Horikawa and his son Shijo. On Shijo's death in 1242, the Liaison Officers (Kanto Moshitsugi) on behalf of the Imperial Court, Saionji no Kintsune and Kujo no Michiie, recommended that he should be succeeded by a prince in the line of succession of Juntoku, the eighty-forth Emperor, who was still living in exile on the remote island of Sado for his part in the Shokyu Incident. The Military Government hesitated but finally decided to switch back to the line of Tsuchimikado, who had taken no part in this incident. They selected Prince Kunihito (Go Saga) for the throne. (In the latter part of her narrative, Lady Nijo describes her visits to the graves and places of exile of all those emperors who had attempted to regain control of the country since the uprising of Sutoku in the Hogen Incident of 1156. The line of succession throughout the period will be better understood by reference to the list of emperors in Appendix III.)

Go Saga was therefore most careful not to give the Military Government any cause for complaint. He was personally in favour of his younger son Kameyama succeeding to his position and controlling the succession in his own line of descent, but on Go Saga's death in 1272 Go Fukakusa disputed this. For a time the Bakufu sided with Kameyama, but finally Saionji no Sanekane, Lady Nijo's lover, at that time in charge of liaison with Kamakura, prevailed on the Bakufu to nominate Go Fukakusa's son as Crown Prince. So Go Fukakusa was placated. Lady Nijo records the important role she played in the reconciliation of Go Fukakusa with his mother, the Empress Dowager Omiya, consort of Go Saga, who had supported Kameyama, and with his brother Kameyama. In fact, Lady Nijo's favours were the inducement offered to Kameyama, as was also the case in the reconciliation with the Great Lord Konoe, Takatsukasa no Kanehira, the Imperial Adviser who at first had leaned to the side of Kameyama.

Still, although the problem of the succession seemed to be settled amicably and for the moment the two brothers were apparently reconciled, this was, as *Towazu-gatari* explains, only brought about by the warnings of the Military Government, and by 1287 the differences between them again became acute. Takatsukasa no Kanehira resigned as Imperial Adviser. Taira no Munetsuna was dispatched to the Capital as Special Envoy of the Bakufu and arranged with Saionji no Sanekane that Kameyama's son, Go Uda, should abdicate to be succeeded by Go Fukakusa's son Fushimi, thus assuring Go Fukakusa's pre-eminence in control of the "cloister government" in Kyoto.

The rift between the brothers, however, remained and after their deaths deepened with the formation of rival groupings, the supporters of Go Fukakusa's line of succession in the Jimyo-in temple party and those supporting Kameyama's line in the party with its headquarters at the Daikakuji temple. These rival groupings opposed and intrigued against each other, their strife developing eventually into civil war between the Northern Court in Go Fukakusa's line and the Southern Court of Kameyama's line, 1336 to 1392. Both parties found support in the bands of armed monks attached to the various temples who were always ready to invade the capital to demonstrate violently in support of the cause they were upholding at the moment. Carrying a branch of the sacred *sakaki* tree with a mirror hung on it as a symbol of their sacred mission, the most active of these bands were those attached to the Enryakuji temple at Otsu and the Kofukuji temple at Nara. *Towazu-gatari* mentions one such demonstration in support of stronger action in face of the threat of the Mongolian invasions. Their most frequent use was, however, not so much for patriotic demonstrations as to discourage peasant revolts on the temple manors.

APPENDIX II:

Lady Nijo and Her Story

Lady Nijo's story of her life opens in 1271 with the New Year celebrations at the court of the twenty-seven-year-old ex-Emperor Go Fukakusa at his palace in Tominokoji. On this day Lady Nijo (born 1258) entered her fourteenth year; she was therefore, according to Western calculation of ages, between twelve and thirteen years of age. She was of a noble family on both sides, being the daughter of the Dainagon Koga no Masatada (1228–1272), son of the Chief Minister Koga no Michimitsu, and her mother being a daughter of the War Minister, Shijo no Takachika.[1]

Owing to her mother's early death she had been brought

[1] The Koga and Shijo families were both high in the social register of the time. Highest of all were the Sekkanke (the Konoe, Kujo, Nijo, Ichijo, Takatsukasa families), members of which could rise to the posts of Sessho (Regent) and Kampaku (Imperial Adviser). Next came the Seigake (the Koga, Saionji, Temporin-Sanjo, Tokudaiji, Kazan-in, Omikado, Imadegawa, Hirohata, and Daigo families), members of which were eligible for the posts of Dajodaijin (Chief Minister) and Konoe Taisho (General of the Bodyguard).

up first by her grandfather's sister[2] and then, from the age of two or three, at the Tominokoji palace.

Lady Nijo first describes the incidents leading to her seduction by the ex-Emperor Go Fukakusa, her relations with him being one of the main themes of the book throughout.

Meanwhile the story recounts the first secret and tentative but finally successful approaches of a court noble whose identity is concealed under the name "Snowy Dawn" and to whom she refers later as her first real lover. It is made clear that he is really Saionji no Sanekane, grandson of the influential statesman, Saionji no Saneuji. He had throughout his career great influence with the Military Government and as Liaison Officer was instrumental, with the Kamakura envoy, Taira no Munetsuna, in arranging the abdication of Kameyama's son Go Uda and the elevation of Go Fukakusa's son to the throne. He became Minister of the Centre in 1289, Chief Minister in 1291, entered religion in 1299, and died in 1322. His relations with Lady Nijo continued for thirteen years or so, their estrangement being caused partly at any rate by his disapproval of her relations with the ex-Emperor Kameyama.

In 1275, a new lover appeared on the scene, a Buddhist prelate, Prince Shojo, a brother of the two ex-Emperors, who for her sake broke his vow of chastity. At first she was repelled by his too ardent love-making but later fell

[2] Sadako (or, more officially, Teishi), wife of the Chief Minister Saionji no Saneuji (1194–1296) and mother of the Empress Dowager Omiya, consort of Go Saga who was the mother of Go Fukakusa and Kameyama. Kimiko, another of Sadako's daughters, referred to in the story as Higashi Nijo, was Go Fukakusa's consort. In 1285 Lady Nijo joined in the celebrations for the ninetieth birthday of Sadako, referred to in the story as the Titular Empress of Kitayama, who eventually died at the age of 107.

in love with him, their association being actively encouraged by the ex-Emperor Go Fukakusa. To her he was "Wan Morning Moon." Their intimacy continued in spite of all their qualms at entering into such a sinful relationship until his tragic death in 1281, from which date Lady Nijo records a cooling off in Go Fukakusa's affection for her.

During this period the Lady had four children, the first by the ex-Emperor, the second by Sanekane, and the last two by Prince Shojo, all except the last being taken out of her care immediately after birth. She describes her feelings on these bereavements—though she hardly mentions the first afterwards except to record the child's death a year later—and her happiness when she was able to keep and show her love for the last of her children.

The court which is the background of these events was a conscious imitation of that depicted nearly three hundred years before in the pages of *Genji Monogatari,* the great masterpiece of Japanese literature by Lady Murasaki. The court nobles relieved their boredom by poetry contests, concerts, football games, archery competitions, and above all by holding drinking parties, in all of which everything had to conform to the precedents of *The Tale of Genji.* Even the manner of the seduction of Lady Nijo by the ex-Emperor Go Fukakusa had to be seen to have its precedent in the seduction of Murasaki by Shining Genji.

In telling of life at court, Lady Nijo is most interested in describing what she and everyone else were wearing. It is remarkable how regularly, in writing about a ceremony, a funeral, or a drinking party, she singles out for admiration some well-turned-out court noble, and sometimes she comments acidly that a certain lady's style of dress did not become her. When she describes the scene where the page boy brings her the sad news of her lover's tragic death, she can take time out to describe his clothes. No doubt an authoritative essay on thirteenth-century styles could be based on these descriptions. We have not been as meticulous as the importance of the subject deserves in describing the colour and the style, referring to *kosode* as a tight-sleeved gown, *hitoe* as an under-robe, *kinu, uchiki,* or *kouchiki* as a robe, *uwagi* as an over-robe or cloak, and *karaginu* as a mantle.

At the court, Lady Nijo was at the head of the ladies-in-waiting, ranking next below the ex-Empress[3] and the Lady of the East Wing, the Lady Genkimon.[4] Lady Nijo hints at her ambition to rise to the highest position at the court, and in the course of the story Go Fukakusa admits that he had failed in his object of obtaining for her a more honourable name than that of Nijo, which she was ashamed of as being only the name of a street.

This failure was due to the jealousy of the ex-Empress, who at every turn showed her implacable hostility to Lady Nijo, as when she accused her of giving herself the airs of an empress, until at last in 1283 she contrived to have her expelled from the court. The ex-Emperor agreed to this, Lady Nijo hints, because he was jealous of the ex-Emperor Kameyama's too ardent pursuit of her. There may have been good grounds for this jealousy. Lady Nijo seems to agree that there might have been. But the true reason for her expulsion really lay in Lady Nijo's own imperious character.

After leaving the court, Lady Nijo lived for a time with

[3] Kimiko, daughter of Saionji no Saneuji and the Titular Empress of Kitayama, sister of Go Saga's consort Omiya, she was known as Higashi Nijo (1232–1304). She became Go Fukakusa's consort in 1256 when he was fourteen years of age.

[4] Daughter of Saionji no Saneo, Minister of the Left, she entered religion in 1291 and died in 1329. As mother of the Emperor Fushimi, she was given the title of Titular Empress in 1286.

her grandfather, Shijo no Takachika, the very influential Minister of War, but on his death in the next year,[5] after undertaking a thousand-day retreat at the Gion shrine, she made her home for the most part with her old nurse and her family. The ex-Emperor, when he had visited her here earlier, had found it strange; he had never before been in such humble surroundings. The nurse's husband, Fujiwara no Nakatsuna, was, however, of fairly respectable family. He held the title of lord of Owari province and was of Junior Fifth Court Rank; he would have been promoted to Fourth Rank if, Lady Nijo tells us, her father had received the promotion he expected. She tells us how the Imperial Adviser went to considerable lengths to get him to enter his service. His wife, Lady Nijo's old nurse, was the daughter of Lady Iyo in the service of the wealthy Princess Sen-yomon, sixth daughter of the Emperor Go Shirakawa. The family showed great kindness and loyalty to Lady Nijo all through her life, though the son, Nakayori, in the service of the ex-Emperor Kameyama, does appear to have talked too freely of the love felt by his master for the Lady.

In spite of her upbringing at the court, however, Lady Nijo appears to have been just as much at home with people of the poorer sort as she was with ex-Emperors, courtiers, and aristocrats. This is shown very clearly in the record of her pilgrimages in the last two books of her story.

5 *Towazu-gatari* stands up to the test of verification with the facts of history as known from other sources in a remarkable manner, except in one particular. Contemporary official records (*Kugyo Bunin, Official Gazette of Appointments of Higher Officials*) record that the Lady's grandfather, Shijo no Takachika, died in 1279, four years before Lady Nijo's expulsion from court. Perhaps she preferred to be pictured as leaving the court under his protection rather than as having to find shelter in less aristocratic surroundings. She mentions his death as occurring in the autumn of 1283 very briefly and seemingly just as an afterthought.

Lady Nijo has nothing to say—at least nothing is recorded in the autobiography as now extant[6]—of the four years between 1285 and 1289. A few most important events in her life, however, happened during these years. As we learn from *Masukagami,* Saionji no Sanekane's daughter, later known as Lady Eifukumon, entered the court of the Emperor Fushimi, Go Fukakusa's son, in 1288, and Lady Nijo accompanied her to the palace. We may find this significant when we realise that Lady Nijo's daughter by Sanekane had been brought up in his household and would be of about this girl's age.

Later on during this period, Sanekane finally broke with Lady Nijo, presumably because of her decision to take vows of religion. They had drifted apart; his patience had been much tried by her relations with the ex-Emperor Kameyama and above all with Lord Konoe. When they were next to meet fifteen years later, he insisted it was to be as strangers.

In this period, too, Lady Nijo finally took her vows and henceforth wore the black habit of a Buddhist nun as she went on her pilgrimage to the eastern provinces following in the footsteps of the famous poet and priest, Saigyo (1118–1190). She started her life of pilgrimage at the age of thirty-two, travelling intermittently for the next seventeen years through twenty-four provinces, a remarkable feat for a court lady of her time. Ever since she had read Saigyo's book of travels at the age of eight, she had always had the ambition to leave to posterity such a travel book as his, and in the last pages of her autobiography she sums up the result of her efforts in this direction. She has to admit that in

[6] The seventeenth-century copyist of our unique copy of *Towazu-gatari* notes in several places that a portion of the manuscript has been cut away. It is possible also that one whole volume covering this period between volumes three and four has disappeared.

spite of all her efforts and in spite of her reputation as a
skilful versifier, her own poems were but mediocre and
no great credit to the poetic tradition of the Koga family.

It does not appear that Lady Nijo's decision to abandon
the world was due to any strong religious convictions. The
thirteenth century saw the rise of a number of great re-
forming movements in Japanese Buddhism,[7] but no hint
of any awareness of such a development is apparent in the
pages of Lady Nijo's story. She does not mention the be-
ginnings of Zen Buddhism or Nichiren's preaching of a new
gospel which was to be so influential in Japan in the centuries
to come. She does not mention her father's uncle, Dogen,
a son of Koga no Michichika, apparently not realising his
importance as the founder of Soto Zen Buddhism. Her
religion was that of the ordinary man and woman of her
time. She frequented the old established temples of the
Tendai sect founded on the teachings of Saicho (767–822)
and of the esoteric Shingon sect of Kukai (774–835), the
two principal Kyoto sects, seeking salvation for herself
and praying for the souls of those for whom she was
bound to pray. She makes an incidental mention of the six
Nara sects (Kegon, Ritsu, Hosso, Sanron, Jojitsu, and

[7] Prominent among the leaders of such movements were the
following: Genku (1133–1212) studied works of Genshin (942–
1017) and popularised universal salvation through continual
invocation of the Sacred Name of Buddha; Shinran (1173–1262),
Genku's disciple, founded Jodo Shinshu, stressing complete
reliance on Buddha's pledge of universal salvation rather than on
invocation of the Sacred Name; Eisai (1141–1215) founded the
first Zen temple in Japan; Dogen (1200–1253) founded Soto Zen
Buddhism in Japan; Nichiren (1222–1282) made the Lotus
Flower sutra the focus of his teaching and violently opposed the
teaching of the Amida sects; Ippen (1239–1289) founded the Jishu
sect. All these, except Ippen, had been trained at the Enryakuji
temple, centre of Tendai Buddhism.

Kusha) as being under centralised control, in the course of
an interesting comment on the use of popular music and
dancing in the evangelisation of the masses who cannot be
expected to be influenced by prayer and meditation. An
important development during the Kamakura period was
this increased attention paid to preaching salvation to the
masses; in early times the common people had been banned
from the temples and the Shinto shrines.

In the course of her pilgrimage she visits the great
national Shinto shrine at Ise, although her decision to go
there seems to have come about almost accidentally when
she discovered that it was easy to make the journey there.
While there, she finds that on the whole the Shinto ritualists
were more interested than Buddhist priests in cultural
pursuits such as art and poetry. But generally she sees the
Shinto gods as incarnations of the Buddha, as most people
of her time did. Dainichi Buddha, the chief centre of the
esoteric Shingon Buddhist worship, was to be identified
with Amaterasu Omikami worshipped at Ise, while the
god of war of her own family shrine was Hachiman
Bodhisattva, whose care was the salvation of the world.

Thus Lady Nijo's last two volumes are a record of her
pilgrimages, but they are something more than an imitation
of Saigyo's work or a travel book on the lines of the Heian
masterpiece *Ise Monogatari* of the latter half of the tenth
century. She does visit a large number of beauty spots and
sums up her impressions of each in a poem. But she has also
to record her impressions of Kamakura and her meetings
with the personages at the head of the Military Government.
And more important still, she has the story of her own life
to continue. In 1292 she twice meets the ex-Emperor Go
Fukakusa, who had taken final vows in 1290, and friendly
relations between them are resumed. He is interested to
learn of her adventures during the three years that elapsed

since they last met. She tells how she rebuts his insinuation
that she had had lovers. She admits with pride that she made
many friends but only through her skill in poetry. She
denies that there was any deeper attachment, either to
new friends in Kamakura, Nara, or Ise, or with old friends
in the Capital. Her oldest friend in the Capital was Saionji
no Sanekane, but possibly the ex-Emperor Kameyama was
in Go Fukakusa's mind. "But," she says with her usual
candour, "I am still only forty-four and can promise
nothing about the future."

In the same revealing conversation the ex-Emperor
explains why he had always taken such a deep interest in
the Lady's welfare. The first woman with whom he had
had intimate relations had been her mother, and he had lost
her through his youth and inexperience. He had had the
Lady brought up in his palace intending to make her his
lover just as Prince Genji had adopted Lady Murasaki. So,
although we have been given earlier some kind of clue to
the relationship between the ex-Emperor and Lady Nijo's
mother, it is not until the end of the book that we are
given a full account of this intimacy and are thus able to
understand fully the ex-Emperor's motives.

After this interview, Lady Nijo resumes her life of
pilgrimage, relating with detached interest stories and
traditions of the various shrines and temples she visits
but meeting with one alarming experience which, as she
says, puts her off pilgrimages for quite a while. She visits
the tomb of the wise and able statesman Shotoku Taishi
(574–622), son of the Emperor Yomei, regent for his aunt
the Empress Suiko, author of the first Japanese constitution,
and promoter of the spread of Buddhism. She pays a visit
to the tomb of the ancient poet, Kakinomoto no Hitomaro,
and follows Saigyo to the place of exile of the Emperor
Sutoku at Shiramine.

[Immediately after the death of the Emperor Toba, Sutoku (1117–1164), who had ruled from 1123–1141, attempted a revolt in 1156 (the Hogen Incident) because his sons had been excluded from the Imperial succession. He was defeated and exiled. The Emperor Go Shirakawa was confirmed in his position and continued to exercise decisive influence through the next five reigns, disputed only by the Emperor Nijo's abortive revolt in the Heiji Incident of 1159.]

Toward the end of her story, Lady Nijo is obviously living on the borderline of poverty; she has perhaps enough money for food and the necessities of life but nothing to spare to make offerings to shrines and temples or to perform such works of devotion as copying out sutras for the intention of the repose of the souls of her parents. After the meeting with Go Fukakusa in 1292, she is, however, again supported by him. As earlier when circumstances forced her to live in her old nurse's home, so now as a nun she appears to have got on well with common people of various occupations in life. Formerly as a lady-in-waiting she had been present on Imperial visits and state occasions and had noted the common people standing around to watch, the women covering their heads with robes to hide their faces. Now, veiled in the same way, she stands among the common people at temples, shrines, and palaces, and finally at the funeral of the ex-Emperor Go Fukakusa when, in the autumn of 1304, she mourns him as her one true love or perhaps merely as her last link with her former life of splendour at the court.

That scene is virtually the end of her story, though she does go on to tell how she attached herself for a while to Go Fukakusa's daughter, Yugimon, closing her autobiography with the ceremonies attendant on the third anniversary of Go Fukakusa's death. Then Lady Nijo fades from history, for the details of her life after this date are unknown.

Towazu-gatari is then no day-to-day record of trivial events like the earlier diaries of court ladies of the Heian era. It is the story of a life told with masterly skill, each episode carefully selected to carry forward the story. The style too is in sharp contrast to earlier works. Instead of long, involved, halting sentences regularly following each other, Lady Nijo echoes the sense and, when the situation demands it, uses short, breathless sentences to convey the excitement of the narrative. In general the great characteristic of the style is its flexibility, its variation with the subject, whether theological, official, poetic, or narrative. She quotes widely from the anthologies and the classics, and throughout the story phrases reminiscent of the classics are woven into the general phraseology. She was obviously well read, a woman of wide culture, an accomplished player on the lute until in a moment of pique she forswore the instrument. She had some reputation among her contemporaries for her skill in poetry, though her poems are not above the average in an age when creative inspiration was sadly lacking in Japanese poetry.

Throughout her story the Lady is concerned as much with the delineation of character as with a narrative of events. The people of her story are real living people; compared to these, Lady Murasaki's Shining Genji is a cardboard figure. She may follow the path of Arihara no Narihira in *Ise Monogatari*, but the people she meets are flesh and blood, not poetical abstractions, and while she takes this bypath, she keeps alive our interest in her main story and in Go Fukakusa by recounting memories of harvest moon and cherry viewing parties until he comes back into the picture again when they meet at Nara.

Times have changed and Lady Nijo has changed with them. In the first part of the story (Books One, Two, and Three), Lady Nijo had no particular reverence for the Imperial line; she is reprimanded for this by the Empress Dowager. Having been brought up at Court and thoroughly spoiled, she explains, Lady Nijo never seems to have learned the niceties of social distinctions. In the last two books her views have changed; she writes reverently and quite in the character of an aging nun of her constant prayers for the Imperial House, realising how the peace and prosperity of the whole nation depend on the continued wellbeing of the Imperial line.

But the main concern of the story is with the character of the ex-Emperor Go Fukakusa. We see him as he really was, timid of nature, weak of body, with a deformity due to a disease of the hip joint, not nearly so manly and attractive a figure as his younger brother Kameyama, or even as Prince Shojo. She details his numerous amours, one with his half-sister, the Vestal Virgin, showing him as a womaniser but certainly not a great lover. Also, the Vestal Virgin's defenceless, naïve, and colourless character is shown in contrast to the Lady's own independence. She emphasises a psychological abnormality in the perverted interest Go Fukakusa took in furthering her relationships with Kameyama, Konoe, and Shojo. He was not as intellectual as she was, more interested perhaps in popular songs [8] than in classical music, poetry, and literature. She felt superior to him in character and attainments, and there is more than a hint that it was his realisation of this which impelled him to agree finally to the demands of the ex-Em-

[8] The autobiography tells how he initiated Takatsukasa no Kanetada into the mysteries of Imayo singing, the modern popular songs then becoming as popular at the court as with the professional women entertainers among whom they originated.

press for her expulsion from the court. And his final disclosure that his main motivation throughout in his relations with the Lady had been his first adolescent love for her mother seems to explain everything.

This comment on the Lady and her story, while it may have cleared up some doubtful points, yet must leave open many questions to which the reader must find the answer. That is what the Lady intended. She implies this in the title—literally, of course, a *no-questions-having-been-asked* story. In this story the Lady is just talking to herself; she is not making any reply to people who have questioned her way of life. She is not making a "voluntary confession" or an "unsolicited apologia." She is not justifying herself. She is quite satisfied with the life she has lived. She may have felt that there was a moral to her story, but she does not spell out for the reader the lesson to be learned. That is why we have called this translation simply *Lady Nijo's Own Story*.

APPENDIX III: The Line of Succession of Emperors

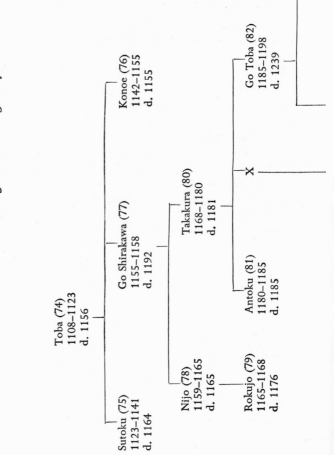

Toba (74)
1108–1123
d. 1156

Sutoku (75)
1123–1141
d. 1164

Go Shirakawa (77)
1155–1158
d. 1192

Konoe (76)
1142–1155
d. 1155

Nijo (78)
1159–1165
d. 1165

Takakura (80)
1168–1180
d. 1181

Rokujo (79)
1165–1168
d. 1176

Antoku (81)
1180–1185
d. 1185

X

Go Toba (82)
1185–1198
d. 1239

Juntoku (84)
1210–1221
d. 1242

Chukyo (85)
1221–1221
d. 1234

Tsuchimikado (83)
1198–1210
d. 1231

Go Horikawa (86)
1222–1232
d. 1234

Shijo (87)
1232–1242
d. 1242

Go Saga (88)
1242–1246
d. 1272

Kameyama (90)
1260–1274
d. 1305

Go Uda (91)
1274–1287
d. 1324

Go Daigo (South) (96)
1313–1339
d. 1339

Go Murakami (South) (97)
1339–1368
d. 1368

Go Nijo (94)
1301–1308
d. 1308

Go Fukakusa (89)
1247–1259
d. 1304

Hanazono (95)
1309–1313
d. 1348

Fushimi (92)
1287–1298
d. 1317

Go Fushimi (93)
1298–1301
d. 1336

Kogon (North)
1331–1332
d. 1364

Komyo (North)
1336–1348
d. 1380